Beyond Rhetoric

ADULT LEARNING
POLICIES AND PRACTICES

OECD

ORGANISATION FOR ECONOMIC CO-OPERATION AND DEVELOPMENT

ORGANISATION FOR ECONOMIC CO-OPERATION AND DEVELOPMENT

Pursuant to Article 1 of the Convention signed in Paris on 14th December 1960, and which came into force on 30th September 1961, the Organisation for Economic Co-operation and Development (OECD) shall promote policies designed:

- to achieve the highest sustainable economic growth and employment and a rising standard of living in Member countries, while maintaining financial stability, and thus to contribute to the development of the world economy;
- to contribute to sound economic expansion in Member as well as non-member countries in the process of economic development; and
- to contribute to the expansion of world trade on a multilateral, non-discriminatory basis in accordance with international obligations.

The original Member countries of the OECD are Austria, Belgium, Canada, Denmark, France, Germany, Greece, Iceland, Ireland, Italy, Luxembourg, the Netherlands, Norway, Portugal, Spain, Sweden, Switzerland, Turkey, the United Kingdom and the United States. The following countries became Members subsequently through accession at the dates indicated hereafter: Japan (28th April 1964), Finland (28th January 1969), Australia (7th June 1971), New Zealand (29th May 1973), Mexico (18th May 1994), the Czech Republic (21st December 1995), Hungary (7th May 1996), Poland (22nd November 1996), Korea (12th December 1996) and the Slovak Republic (14th December 2000). The Commission of the European Communities takes part in the work of the OECD (Article 13 of the OECD Convention).

Publié en français sous le titre :
AU-DELÀ DU DISCOURS
POLITIQUES ET PRATIQUES DE FORMATION DES ADULTES

FOREWORD

In 1999, the OECD's Education Committee and the Employment, Labour and Social Affairs Committee launched a thematic review of adult learning. The review resulted from Ministries of education and employment reacting to calls for provision of lifelong learning for all, with special emphasis on improving employability in the labour market. The goal of the review was to analyse policy options within the different national contexts, specifically in terms of how to improve access to and participation in adult learning, and how an acceptable standard of quality and level of effectiveness could be ensured. Nine countries took part in the first round: Canada, Denmark, Finland, Norway, Portugal, Spain, Sweden, Switzerland and the United Kingdom (England). A number of countries have signed up for a second round of reviews, leading to a continuation of this activity.

The term adult learning, as used in the review, defines all aspects of adult education and training, and all learning activities undertaken by adults. The thematic review favoured a holistic approach by analysing the variety of purposes that adult learning served, be it personal or professional, remedial or re-skilling. Similarly, the learners' perspective was examined in terms of the different levels of opportunities which were available and supplied by any type of provider.

This comparative report provides an overview of the adult learning policies and practices within the participating countries and concludes by identifying a range of desirable features that make for successful adult learning systems. It draws heavily on background reports and country notes as well as information gathered through country visits and is the final exercise of the first round of the thematic review. The methodology followed is similar to that adopted in other thematic reviews conducted on behalf of the OECD Education Committee. Countries were required to prepare a background report, following a common outline, describing their adult learning practices. OECD expert review teams then visited each country, after which a country note was prepared summarising the teams' views and suggestions. These individual country documents and other relevant documents, can be found on the OECD Adult Learning website (*www/oecd.org/edu/adultlearning*).

National co-ordinators from each country, listed in Annex 4, and national steering committees were vital to the organisation of the country visits and the writing of the background reports. Their efforts were key to the success of this activity. Equally essential to the thematic review process, with their hard work and insights, were the OECD expert review teams, and especially the rapporteurs (also listed in Annex 4). They contributed to broad discussions during country visits and prepared the country notes. From the OECD Secretariat, Ms. Beatriz Pont, Ms. Anne Sonnet, and Mr. Patrick Werquin were authors of this report, with editorial assistance from Mr. Randy Holden. Statistical assistance was provided by Ms. Sophie Vayssettes and administrative assistance by Ms. Dianne Fowler. The project was carried out under the supervision of Mr. Abrar Hasan, Head of the Education and Training Division, and the late Mr. Norman Bowers and Mr. Raymond Torres, Head of the Employment Policy and Analysis Division. This report is published under the responsibility of the Secretary-General of the OECD.

TABLE OF CONTENTS

Tables

Figures

HIGHLIGHTS

Adult learning has taken on a much higher profile in the last decade, as OECD economies and ageing societies are increasingly knowledge-based. High unemployment rates among the unskilled, the increased and recognised importance of human capital for economic growth and social development – together with public interest in improving social and personal development – make it necessary to increase learning opportunities for adults within the wider context of lifelong learning. Depending on the country and context, these opportunities may be related to employment, to the need for basic skills or upskilling, or may respond to social and civic preoccupations. At the same time however, there are strong inequities in terms of access and provision.

It is therefore time to go beyond rhetoric and consider concrete policy answers to expand learning opportunities for all adults. The purpose of this publication is precisely to document the experiences of nine countries in this field.

Participation in adult learning

Percentage of population 25-64 years old in adult learning according to different reference periods

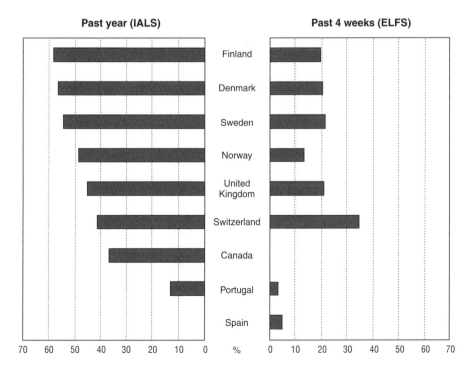

Note: Period of reference is one year for Switzerland in both surveys. Countries are ranked in descending order of total participation rate for IALS data.
Source: International Adult Literacy Survey (1994-98) and Eurostat, European Union Labour Force Survey (2001).

The problems

What is adult learning? The concept of adult learning adopted in this publication encompasses all education and training activities undertaken by adults for professional or personal reasons. It includes general, vocational and enterprise based training within a lifelong learning perspective. Throughout the nine OECD countries participating in this study there is a broad range of possibilities provided by the public and the private sector, education institutions, firms, commercial organisations, NGOs and other community organisations.

Participation in adult learning varies considerably across countries. In the Nordic countries, the United Kingdom, Switzerland and Canada, at least one out of every three adults participates in some training activity throughout the year (IALS). Similarly, in most of the Nordic countries and the United Kingdom at least one in five adults participated over a one-month period (ELFS). Spain and Portugal have lower participation rates.

Moreover, participation in adult learning is highly unequal among specific population subgroups. Younger adults, those with higher educational attainment, those with jobs or those employed in high-skilled occupations take greater advantage of or have greater access to learning opportunities than others. Age is important, as adults' rates of return to learning have been found to diminish with age and thus act as deterrent to learning. In most countries those aged 25-29 participate most, but active participation does continue until around age 50, at which point there is a considerable drop.

The persons who especially benefit from adult learning are those who have higher educational attainment levels – the higher educated continue learning throughout life. They are *aware* of the benefits, of the need for upgrading and reskilling, and are perhaps more motivated because of the potential returns. In short, learners are in most cases already convinced of the value of learning.

Adult learning by educational attainment

Ratio of participation rates at each educational level to the total participation rates for population 25-64 years old, 2000

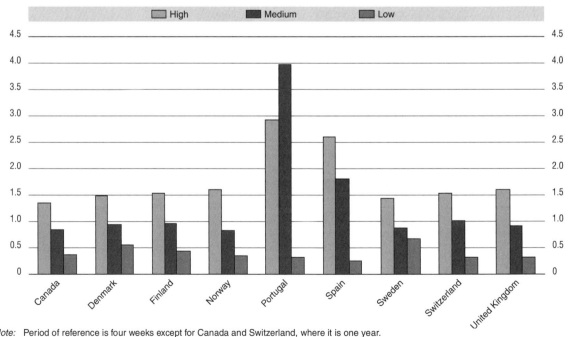

Note: Period of reference is four weeks except for Canada and Switzerland, where it is one year.
Source: Eurostat, European Union Labour Force Survey data except for Canada (1997 AETS data).

A high proportion of adult learning focuses on professional upgrading, as the enterprise is one of the main catalysts of training. More than 50% of those who trained did so with employer's support, and employers tend to choose investments from which they expect a high return. Thus training tends to concentrate on workers who are already qualified and enjoy relatively high professional status in large companies. This leaves out low-skilled or older workers, those in small companies, and those on temporary contracts. Larger firms train more, as do firms in the service sector, primarily social and personal services, financial intermediation and real estate.

There are different reasons for low and unequal participation rates. Time constraints are the reasons adults cite most for not being able to undertake learning, especially for non-vocational training. Reflecting work and family commitments, it is difficult to find time to engage in learning courses, especially for those unconvinced of the benefits of learning. Financial constraints are also mentioned as a barrier to undertake training.

Yet another reason is the fact that often, those adults most in need of education and training are also those least aware of that need or the benefits. Many low educated or low-skilled individuals believe their skills are good or excellent and thus do not see any need to improve. One of the important challenges ahead for policy makers, then, is to assist in revealing the benefits of learning and making learning easy and accessible for adults, especially for the low-skilled.

Even though there is some investment in adult learning from the public and private sectors, it is not enough. Even in the case of highly skilled workers, the return on investment for companies is risky; bearing in mind the possibility of "poaching" skilled labour in imperfect labour markets, companies often prefer to "buy in" skilled labour rather than invest in training. The lack of visibility of the benefits of training outcomes to companies or workers may also be an important factor.

Overall, there are barriers to participation in learning for adults. There is some evidence of unmet demand, with the existence of waiting lists for adult basic education courses in some countries

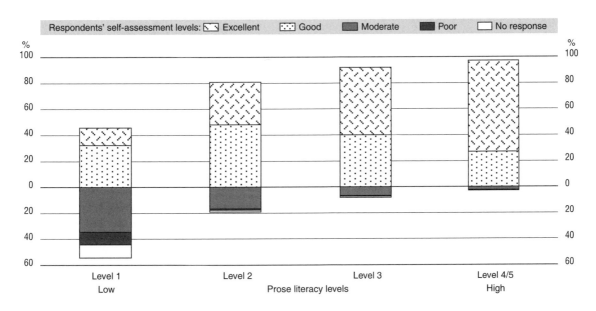

Self-assessment of reading skills by prose literacy level

Percentage of population 25-64 years old at each self-assessment level by prose literacy level, 1994-98

Source: International Adult Literacy Survey (1994-98).

visited. Hidden unmet demand is not as evident: people with low skills and low levels of education, populations living in distant or rural areas, people with psychological barriers to participation do not make their needs heard. Furthermore, there are institutional barriers: fragmented provision of learning opportunities means that there is a complex diversity of institutions – firms, trade associations, the public education system and private institutions – that provide learning but not in a transparent or coherent manner. There is a range of learning opportunities, but supply is fragmented and there are not enough incentives in place to reach those most in need.

The solutions

OECD Member countries have recognised the need for public intervention in this market, for equity and efficiency reasons. Overall, countries agree on the long-run goals, which include economic and non-economic reasons: the need to target low educational attainment and to intervene for social cohesion and economic growth, to reduce unemployment and for personal and social development. The development of democratic values and the improvement of skills to participate in the economy and labour market are all stated as vital reasons for government participation in adult learning.

Many countries mobilise a variety of resources to support the development of adult learning at different levels. Most have specific adult basic education to provide opportunities for higher educational attainment. There is a wide array of vocational training programmes to improve adults' ability to obtain employment. There are also efforts geared toward training for workers in companies by way of legislation, financial incentives and contractual agreements. The non-profit or community-based organisations are also important suppliers of learning opportunities for adults.

Countries have recently adopted a variety of approaches to target adult learning. These range from general action plans to increase learning opportunities for all adults to more specific programmes designed to upgrade skills, target particular adult sub-groups of the population, or increase training opportunities for those in the labour force. A number of these reforms are also geared towards improving the performance and results of adult learning in a more integrated or holistic approach that is learner-centred. Efforts have been made towards greater system efficiency through providing general frameworks for policy development, improving co-ordination among different (including social) partners, rationalising existing supply, focusing on cost-effectiveness, and taking greater account of individual needs. Decentralisation has been an important aspect of this process. Policy responses vary according to a country's economic and social contexts, the historical development of its education systems, and the political structures and systems in place.

The key: access and participation

Adopting an integrated approach to adult learning policies can address a diversity of issues concurrently. A comprehensive strategy can help OECD governments to improve adult learning opportunities, to raise the efficiency and quality of adult learning provision and ensure better coherence in the delivery of learning. The publication documents in depth desirable features that can shape an integrated approach to adult learning policies. Under the five key ingredients listed below some of the different policy approaches possible are provided.

1. **Measures and approaches directed towards *making learning more attractive to adults* can help increase participation.** As already shown, motivation is one of the key issues: learning has to be made attractive to adults. Specific desirable elements can be highlighted:

   - The use of pedagogical methods suited to adults rather than to the young. This implies learning that is learner centred and contextualised to make it relevant to adults' experiences. The *craft school workshops, trade schools and employment workshops* in Spain are a good example. Courses offered by Migros "club schools", a private initiative, play an important role in attracting adults back into learning in Switzerland.

- Flexibility in provision to suit adults' circumstances and schedules. The creation of modular systems, as has been done in Denmark, Switzerland and initiated in Portugal, can assist adults to study at their own pace. ICT and distance education can be effective tools to reach those hardest to reach in a flexible manner. The Mentor Programme in Spain is organised in local centres that provide anytime computer-based, audio-visual and telecommunication resources for adult learning.

- Outreach policies to reach adults who otherwise might not consider learning, or who have little motivation to learn. The availability of pertinent, up-to-date information, sound advice and guidance suited to the individual needs of adults is key to success. Adult Learners' Week in the United Kingdom, Learnfestival in Switzerland or Opintoluotsi open search service in educational information in Finland are good examples of outreach efforts. Community Access Programme sites throughout Canada are designed to provide adults with access to the information available on the Web.

- Recognition of prior learning. Assessing and giving credit for knowledge and skills acquired in work, home or community settings can ensure that adults do not waste time relearning what they already know. Portugal's national system for the recognition, validation and certification of school attainment and personal experience is a good practice in this respect.

2. **As learning is largely related to employment,** *measures to stimulate employment-related training,* **in enterprises, for workers and for the unemployed are important.** It may imply acting on several levels to overcome barriers, such as arranging and financing training, reconciling production time and training time, and putting the gains from training to profitable use. Among different key elements to be emphasised are:

- Practices to help workers overcome some of the barriers to training, including time and costs (through, *e.g.,* flexible time management). The rights to education or training leave from work in Finland and Norway are an important incentive for workers to undertake learning.

- Ensuring access to skills assessment and the possibility of skills development in firms for groups at risk – such as workers who are victims of restructuring, who did not have a proper initial education, or older workers. The Skandia company individual learning accounts initiative in Sweden is worth noting: workers payments into the accounts are matched by Skandia, and are tripled in the case of employees over 45 years old who do not have a higher secondary diploma. Other good practices have been found in enterprises in all visited countries.

- Public employment services that operate flexible models of public training programmes. Modules, tailor-made programmes, continuous admission and certification have been applied successfully in the public employment service in Norway or through the Vaggeryd-model for labour market training (named after the municipality where it was originally developed) in Sweden.

- Avoiding the sole criteria of quantitative results when financing training for the unemployed. It may lead to creaming in skills training, since the objective is immediate placement. Quality criteria must also be included in the call for tender.

3. ***Enhancing the financial incentives to invest in the human capital* of adults, at the individual and enterprise levels.** Financing of adult learning systems is a complex issue. Funding comes from both public and private sources in all the countries under review. And indeed the consensus seems to be that responsibility for financing should be shared among all partners, exploring co-operative financing mechanisms. In some cases, making individuals participate in the financing, if they can afford it, can also be applicable as a return on the benefits that they receive from participation. Different policy avenues are possible to enhance incentives to invest:

- The introduction of individual incentive mechanisms such as loans, grants or individual learning accounts. In Canada, some of these mechanisms have been used to stimulate adults to undertake learning opportunities. In the United Kingdom there is a broad range of financial support to encourage individuals to undertake learning throughout the country. In Finland, Norway and Sweden there are individual income support allowances complementary to free provision.

- Offering entitlements for learning or study leave during working hours. Alternation leave in Finland, for example, has a twofold purpose: employees can have leave from work, and unemployed job seekers can obtain work experience.

- The introduction of subsidies to private suppliers or to individuals. Compensation for part of the opportunity costs can help to attain an appropriate level of training. The Danish taximeter system, tax exemptions and subsidies for employer-financed training can be viewed in this light. Financial incentives can also be increased by allowing training to be treated as an investment for taxation purposes rather than an expenditure.

- The establishment of enterprise training levies or the setting up of national or sectoral training funds under specific conditions. The Development of Labour Promotion Act in Quebec, Canada to boost workers' qualifications, skills and performance through continuing training is a measure of the "train or pay" kind.

4. **Approaches to *improve the quality of adult learning* can greatly contribute to increase access and participation.** A number of these can focus on quality control and measurement of outcomes. Improvement can be achieved, for example, through better monitoring and evaluation; through improving statistical systems; through better accreditation systems; through better performance evaluation at the institution level; and through better monitoring of student outcomes and graduate destinations. Research in this field is imperative. Different elements may be highlighted:

- The introduction of quality assurance systems. The programmes EduQua in Switzerland and the Programme for Certification of Training Institutions (QUALFOR) in Portugal are interesting examples of monitoring. Many countries have also created institutes in charge of evaluating the quality of education and training, devoted exclusively to adult learning (such as the Norwegian Institute for Adult Education in Norway) or more broadly to all kinds of learning (such as the Danish Evaluation Institute in Denmark).

- Setting standards for service delivery and publicly certifying of the achievement of these standards. The *Investors in People* (IiP) label is awarded to companies that make a recognised training effort in the United Kingdom.

- Including evaluation as an integral part of policy design. Unfortunately, most evaluation of adult learning policies is limited to the measurement of the number of students taught and funding spent, with use of surveys to measure change and learning profiles. Broader evaluation tools to measure effectiveness of policies are not present in many country adult learning policies.

- Providing better support of policy choices requires research and analysis. National efforts in statistical and homogeneous data collection on participation and spending, and research and sharing of best practices at a national as well as an international level can contribute to improve quality of policies and programmes.

5. **Adopting *a co-ordinated approach to adult learning*, by bringing the relevant partners together.** Co-ordinating the activities of the different actors can help to rationalise scarce resources and contribute to more efficient public spending. Partnerships are useful tools, as is an outcomes-based approach. Countries are grappling with ways to develop comprehensive and integrated policy frameworks for adult learning. In contrast to the fragmented approach that can be observed in many countries, a holistic approach – encompassing both formal and informal learning as well as general education, vocational education and enterprise training – requires co-ordination. Key ingredients to a co-ordinated policy are:

- Developing a co-ordinated approach in the public adult learning system. Countries have worked towards increasing supply at different levels, rationalise and give coherence to the diversity of offerings, and co-ordinate the different actors involved. In most of these cases, that implies free or near-free provision of formal adult education or other educational opportunities. This is the case with the reforms introduced by Denmark, Finland, Norway and Sweden, and efforts undertaken by Spain and Portugal.

- Co-ordination within government, as well as between government and a wide range of non-government actors such as employers, trade unions, private and public educational institutions, and community groups. Examples of specific institutions to help co-ordinate adult learning policies include ANEFA in Portugal and the Learning and Skills Council in the United Kingdom.

- A balanced interaction between a top-down approach – in which governments define structures and financing procedures – and a bottom-up approach that enables local actors to provide feedback on the problems they face and the innovative solutions that they have found. The Adult Education Initiative in Sweden is an excellent example of this approach. Monitoring the implementation process of reforms is also essential.

- The promotion of partnerships. They have appeared in a number of countries as a means of co-operation and co-ordination. Examples are those developed in Canada or in the Economic Development Agency of La Rioja in Spain.

- Policy processes that co-ordinate well across the sectors and among the many actors involved, that incorporate rational funding mechanisms, and that build monitoring and evaluation into policy development all make systems more effective. These are the aims of the recent adult education and training reform in Denmark.

Such integrated policy frameworks also need to place the individual and the enterprise at the centre – in shaping incentives to participate; in funding mechanisms; in the design of adult learning programmes; and in determining outcomes. They need to make explicit the relative responsibilities of individuals, enterprises and governments within an overall framework. As in initial education, they need to balance goals of economic development with equity goals and social and personal development. They need to recognise the reality that many adults in OECD countries have at best completed lower secondary education; that they often have low levels of basic skills; and that many have been away from formal learning for some years. Overall, countries are moving in the right direction – but there is still a great deal of work to be done.

Chapter 1

INTRODUCTION

With the evolution toward knowledge-based societies, adult learning has taken on a much higher profile in the last decade. High unemployment rates, the increased and recognised importance of human capital for economic growth and social development, and changing economic contexts – together with public interest in improving social and personal development – have spurred an increase in learning opportunities for adults within the wider context of lifelong learning. There are broad learning opportunities in different contexts and countries for employment or personal purposes, for upskilling or for remedial purposes – but there are also strong inequities in terms of access and provision.

This publication analyses means for improving access to and participation in adult learning as well as its quality and effectiveness. It does so by reviewing current learning opportunities, the reasons for non-participation, and the different policies and approaches in place to improve both access and participation. It is based on information from nine countries that participated in this OECD thematic review on adult learning: Canada, Denmark, Finland, Norway, Portugal, Spain, Sweden, Switzerland and the United Kingdom (England).[1]

---

1. It should be understood that while throughout the report references are made to the United Kingdom, the thematic review in fact covered only England.

1.1. Purpose of the thematic review

Education and labour ministers had recognised the importance of lifelong learning opportunities for all.

The thematic review process began at the January 1996 meeting of OECD education ministers, who at that time argued that far-reaching changes were needed to make lifelong learning a reality for all: "Strategies for lifelong learning need a wholehearted commitment to new system-wide goals, standards and approaches, adapted to the culture and circumstance of each country." Recognising that adults encounter particular problems in participating in lifelong learning, the ministers called on the OECD to "review and explore new forms of teaching and learning appropriate for adults, whether employed, unemployed or retired". In October 1997, OECD labour ministers expanded on the message, adding a note of heightened importance. Identifying the adverse labour market consequences that can and do arise due to the lack of access to lifelong learning opportunities, they "underlined the importance of ensuring that lifelong learning opportunities are broadly accessible to all persons of working age, in order to sustain and increase their employability".

A cross-country thematic review would be of great value in analysing lessons from national experiences.

In 1998, the OECD and the US Department of Education co-organised an international conference, "How Adults Learn", to review recent research results and practices with regard to teaching and learning adapted to the needs of adults (OECD and US Department of Education, 1999). One of the conclusions from the conference was that a cross-country thematic review had valuable potential for identifying and analysing the lessons from different national experiences with adult learning, and for understanding how the policy and institutional environment could be made more supportive. At the end of 1998 the OECD Education Committee launched the Thematic Review on Adult Learning (TRAL) and, at its meeting in Spring 1999, the Employment, Labour and Social Affairs Committee requested that the TRAL be carried out as a joint activity of the two committees.

The result was the thematic review on adult learning.

The purpose of the thematic review is to analyse policy options in different national contexts for improving access to and participation in adult learning, as well as its quality and effectiveness. The review examines whether learning opportunities for adults are adequate and how adult education and training should respond to the labour market. The following are among the key issues covered by the review:

- Patterns of participation and non-participation in adult learning.
- Diagnoses of the problems that arise because of these patterns.
- Policy programmes and institutional arrangements used by countries for expanding learning opportunities for adults.
- Options that can be regarded as "good practices" under diverse institutional circumstances and how these can be applied more widely within and across countries.

1.2. Organisation and process

Nine countries volunteered to participate in the review...

A meeting of national representatives was held in June 1999 in Paris to discuss the proposed terms of reference and identify the countries interested in participating. Nine countries volunteered. The first visit was in December 1999 and the last one in November 2001.

At the meeting of national representatives an agreement was reached concerning the framework, scope and procedure of the review, and major policy issues for investigation were identified. The methodology involves the analysis, in a comparative framework, of country-specific issues and policy approaches to adult learning. A five-step procedure used for other thematic reviews in education was adopted:[2]

... which involved a five-step procedure.

- Preparation by the country of a background report.
- Preliminary one- or two-day visit to the country by the OECD Secretariat.
- A visit to the country by the review team.
- Preparation of a country note.
- Preparation of a comparative report.

Each participating country has prepared a background report on the basis of a common outline and data questionnaire. These reports provide a concise overview of the country context, current adult learning policies and provision, major issues and concerns, and available data. The preparation of the background report was managed by a national co-ordinator or team of co-ordinators, and guided by a steering committee that brought together experts and officials from both education and labour. The reports were written either by government officials or by commissioned authors. By providing a state-of-the-art overview and description of policy and provision in each participating country, the background reports have been important outputs of the review process. In several countries, it was the first time that such information had been brought together in one comprehensive document. Some of these reports have been published as such in the country. Their main purpose was to brief the expert reviewers prior to their country visit. As a consequence, they are designed to be descriptive; the analytical work is performed by the review team.

Background reports provided a state-of-the-art overview of policy and provision in each country beforehand.

Following the preparation of the background report and a visit by the OECD Secretariat to prepare the programme for the full visit, each participating country hosted a multinational team of two OECD Secretariat members and three reviewers (including the rapporteur in charge of co-ordinating the preparation of the country note) for a one- to two-week review visit. The visits, which were organised by government officials in co-operation with the OECD Secretariat, enabled the experts to study both education and labour market issues related to adult learning. The background report formed the basis for analysis, and the visiting teams discussed the issues with a wide range of stakeholders: government representatives, senior policy makers, officials in education and employment, trade unions, employers, representatives of training institutions, education professionals, non-governmental organisations and members of the research community. Usually there were field visits to institutions and organisations. A total of 27 external experts from 18 countries and four members of the OECD Secretariat took part in the nine review visits. This wide range of participants – with varied backgrounds in fields such as economics, education, political sciences and sociology – furnished a rich set of perspectives for analysing

Visiting teams then met with a wide range of education and labour market stakeholders in each country.

---

2. TRAL is the fourth thematic review of this sort. It follows similar studies undertaken on different subjects such as tertiary education (OECD, 1998), school-to-work transition (OECD, 2000) and early childhood education and care policy (OECD, 2001). Other thematic reviews currently in process are analysing attracting, retaining and developing effective teachers and the role of national qualification systems in promoting lifelong learning.

countries' experiences, while also facilitating cross-national discussions of policy lessons. The details of the national co-ordinators and members of the review teams are provided in Annex 4 and in the country notes.

Following these visits the review teams prepared country notes drawing together their analyses.

After each visit, the review team prepared a country note drawing together observations and analyses of country-specific policy issues. The qualitative assessments of the review teams have been supplemented by statistics and documents supplied by participating countries and the OECD. Data sources include the International Adult Literacy Survey (IALS), Labour Force Surveys (LFS), and Continuing Vocational Training Surveys (CVTS) (Annex 1 for more information on data sources). The country notes provide insights into current adult learning policy contexts, identify the major issues arising from the visit, and propose suggestions to improve policy and practice. In addition, each note highlights examples of innovative approaches with the goal of promoting cross-national exchange of good practice.

The descriptions and analysis included throughout this publication draw heavily upon the background reports and country notes. These reports are not individually cited in the text (unless directly quoted), but they can be found on the adult learning thematic review website together with other relevant material (*www.oecd.org/edu/adultlearning*). They offer rich contextual material on each of the participating countries; the country notes provide the review teams' assessments and policy suggestions.

This resulting publication does not rank countries but speaks of differences, similarities and implications.

This publication is the final output of the first round of this activity. In order to respect the diversity of policy approaches to adult learning, it does not attempt to compare countries in terms of better/worse or right/wrong, or to rank countries. Instead, the report seeks to analyse the nature of and reasons for similarities and differences in policy approaches across the nine participating countries, and to identify some of the possible implications for policy makers.

Adult learning is a very complex field for at least two reasons. First of all, there is no universally accepted definition of who is an adult learner or what is adult learning. In comparison with tertiary education or early childhood education, for example, the age range is very wide and the nature of the provision piecemeal. In this domain, the very concept of learning is itself complex. The second source of complexity has to do with the wide number of stakeholders, who sometimes have competing interests. This factor has made the tasks of the review team and the authors of this publication difficult. If the thematic review has been able to address different sets of issues in an integrated manner, it is because the process entailed having specialists from education and employment work together, both in the OECD Secretariat and in the participating countries.

The collaborative process has in fact encouraged knowledge and data sharing among all participants. The comparative methodology has encouraged those charged with making decisions regarding adult learning to reflect upon their own policy approaches and to be informed of successful policy initiatives in other countries or other regions of the same country. For instance, the project gave different government departments and ministries with responsibility for adult learning the opportunity to work together and exchange information and perspectives. It has also promoted collaboration and consultation between policy officials and other stakeholders in the field. The OECD Secretariat has worked closely with country authorities during the course of the review in preparing the reports, selecting the members of review teams, and developing the programmes for the review visits.

The intention of the comparative report has not been to provide carefully controlled data for in-depth research, but to provide illustrative material and insights into policy issues and trends identified in country reports and other sources. The collection of cross-national data in a short time frame has allowed for lessons from country experiences to be considered before national circumstances have changed. The short time frame, however, was not sufficient to address rather broad policy changes that occurred after the visits in some of the participating countries, particularly those visited toward the beginning of the review process (end of 1999 and beginning of 2000). These recent major policy changes demonstrate the growing importance accorded to adult learning in some of the participating countries, and even hint that the OECD review team's visits may well have contributed to moving the policy agenda forward.

The intention of this report is to provide illustrative material and insight into relevant policy issues.

1.3. Structure

Chapter 2 of this report provides the definitions and framework for the review and the rationale for the focus on adult learning. It lists the key issues that will be addressed in the subsequent chapters. Chapter 3 identifies patterns of participation in adult learning and assesses the needs and gaps in provision. Chapter 4 provides a summary of the general policies and priorities currently under way in adult learning in the nine participating countries. Chapter 5 analyses barriers to participation and different practices and incentives that can enhance motivation for learning in the labour market and other areas. Chapter 6 examines measures that can improve the quality of learning and outcomes through the use of appropriate pedagogy and modes of learning provision, teacher preparation and quality control. Chapter 7 analyses policy options to address problems of fragmented provision of services and inadequacies of delivery infrastructures. Chapter 8 provides a general overview of findings, key elements and features of a desirable adult learning system.

BIBLIOGRAPHY

OECD (1998),
   Redefining Tertiary Education, Paris.

OECD (2000),
   From Initial Education to Working Life: Making Transitions Work, Paris.

OECD (2001),
   Starting Strong: Early Childhood Education and Care, Paris.

OECD and US DEPARTMENT OF EDUCATION (1999),
   "How Adults Learn", Proceedings of the Conference held 6-8 April 1998, Georgetown University, Washington.

Chapter 2

ISSUES IN ADULT LEARNING

Adult learning is not a new idea, but one that has been evolving for centuries. Efforts are now under way to examine the issues in a lifelong learning perspective. The different views of what adult learning involves – including formal, informal and non-formal learning, learning for personal and professional reasons, full time or part time – make the analysis challenging. Taking account of all that adult learning implies is an important issue in public policy making because of the wide range of needs to be addressed and the range of actors and policy areas that are involved. This chapter describes the policy rationale and presents the key issues that were analysed for the comparative report – issues having to do with strengthening the incentives and motivation for adults to learn, improving the delivery of adult learning, and promoting a better integration of the supply and demand.

2.1. An old issue brought up to date

Retaining knowledge and acquiring further knowledge are concerns dating back to Condorcet.

Education should be universal, that is to say extended to every citizen. It should, in its various degrees, embrace the entire system of human knowledge and provide people, throughout their lives, with the ability to retain the knowledge they have and acquire more. People will be taught about new laws, agricultural observations and economic methods that they need to be aware of: they will be shown the art of educating themselves (Condorcet, 1792).

Condorcet's speech to the French National Assembly soon after the 1789 Revolution proves that lifelong learning is not a new idea – far from it.[1] Nor is adult learning. Key issues of concern to modern-day researchers and policy makers are mentioned in this speech, which dates back over two centuries: retaining knowledge, which is often associated with the idea that information and skills become obsolete when left unused, and acquiring further knowledge.

Folk high schools are an early example of adult learning based on demand.

It was in Denmark in the mid-19th century that adult learning was put into practice on a larger scale. Based on the ideas developed by N. Grundtvig and C. Kold, folk high schools[2] were set up in local communities based on demand. This was an example of a service launched in response to a more or less explicit need on the part of users. In those days small farmers were becoming increasingly important to the economy, and the folk high schools were designed to raise their political awareness. The idea gradually spread through northern Europe, and Grundtvig's precepts are still very much alive today in other countries. There are folk high schools throughout Norway and Sweden; they are the direct legacy of the schools founded in Denmark over a century and a half ago, in spite of some differences in the role they now play and in the way they operate.[3]

"Lifelong learning" has evolved into a holistic vision that accords greater weight to adult learning...

It was in the early 1970s that the notion of lifelong learning first came to be clearly and universally formalised (UNESCO, 1972; OECD, 1973). This work marked a turning point in adult learning[4] policy, since it recognised for the first time the need for periods of learning to take place throughout people's lives, not just in the early years. By the early 1970s the idea of lifelong learning was already a major advance on recurrent education. The first explicitly integrates education into a person's life cycle, whereas the second is sporadic and is merely for remedial purposes. Twenty years later (UNESCO, 1996; OECD, 1996), the concept of lifelong learning was further refined. The 1970s vision had emphasised adult learning at the expense of other phases of lifelong learning. The 1990s view established a holistic view of education and learning as a truly lifelong process ("from cradle to grave") that is, as stated, multidimensional. Adult learning, while a major feature of lifelong learning with which it is often confused, has long been the "poor relation" compared with other major domains, particularly formal education (primary, secondary and higher).

---

1. The reference is to "education in life" made in Plato's *Republic*.
2. *Folkehøjskole* in Danish, *Folkhögskola* in Swedish and *Folkehøgskole* in Norwegian. In English this is translated as folk high schools, but a more appropriate translation might be adult schools for liberal studies.
3. These adult education schools are described in Chapter 3.
4. Adult learning and adult education and training are used interchangeably throughout this publication.

Precisely because Condorcet's speech is so relevant to the modern world, it is also rather worrying. It shows that little has changed, and that many countries are probably still at the stage of mere rhetoric. In fact, one of the recurring comments heard during the review visits to individual countries was that the arguments developed over the past 25 years had not changed a great deal, in either substance or form. Major tasks of the thematic review, therefore, are to distinguish between rhetoric and genuine progress and to identify the ways to achieve further progress.

... but to what extent has that vision been realised?

2.2. Defining adult learning

No consensus on a single definition

Finding accurate definitions for "adult learning" and "adult learners" is not an easy task, for several reasons. One is that it is hard to define who an adult learner is – or, for that matter, what learning is. The definitions vary in terms of coverage, settings and age according to the country and, sometimes, to the regional authority or the type of programme (Box 2.1). As an example, formal learning is always included in the definition but non-formal and (especially) informal learning are less often so. The minimum age for defining the adult learner also varies: the lowest in some definitions is 16 if employed, for example in Spain and Portugal. In some other cases, it could be 17.5, 18, 19 or 25. Countries also differ in their coverage of non-vocational learning: Switzerland, for example, is preparing a law on adult learning that deals with vocational training only.

Lack of agreement on definitions can lead to a lack of comparable data...

The lack of consensus on a single definition is a problem of deeper significance. There are insufficient comparable statistical data on adult learning, largely due to the lack of a coherent definition across countries or even within a country. One example comes from Canada, where no single definition is applicable in all provinces. The participation rate in adult learning in 1998 was 27.7%, according to the Adult Education and Training Survey (AETS). That same year, however, the New Approach to Lifelong Learning Survey (NALL) revealed that 96.7% of Canadians feel that they engage in some sort of informal learning in their everyday life. Another example: some countries provide a breakdown of participation by age, but the key information for definitional purposes of whether or not a person is returning to learning or is still in the initial system may be missing. Available data on adult learning are very patchy and not easily comparable across countries, which can hinder policy making (Annex 1 contains information on data sources).

... which can in turn hinder policy making.

Different forms of adult learning

Some of the definitional problems stem from the variety of forms and settings of adult learning. For the purposes of this report, and to take the debate forward with a view to developing policy recommendations, three major, non-mutually exclusive distinctions need to be made:

- Whether or not learning is formal – to some extent this entails defining what learning is.
- Whether it is undertaken for personal or professional reasons.
- Whether it is on a full-time or part-time basis.

Box 2.1.   **Institutional definitions of adult learning in the nine countries of the thematic review**

Canada: Adult learning covers vocational training and general education. Age and time spent since leaving initial education and training are the main criteria, but these vary according to the province, ministry and programme. There is no reference to the type of learning. However, situations differ from one province to another. Newfoundland and Labrador, Nova Scotia, New Brunswick, Ontario, Saskatchewan, Alberta and British Columbia do not have an official definition for adult learners. Four provinces (Prince Edward Island, Quebec, Manitoba and the Northwestern Territories) state that they do.

Denmark: Adult learning covers vocational training and general education as well as formal, non-formal and informal learning. All adult learning activities are defined in contrast to initial education and training, which is confined to youth. There is no one definition of adult learning, but all facilities providing adult education courses are clearly identified; adult learners therefore can be said to be those who are enrolled there. There is mention of age especially in two respects: 1) general adult education at lower secondary level and preparatory adult education at an even lower level (18 years is the minimum entry age for basic general adult education, corresponding to the age at which schooling in the initial system at that level is no longer open to participants); and 2) adult vocational education and training (VET) and basic adult (vocational) education (25 years is established as the minimum entry age to post-compulsory vocational education and training, so as to avoid having financial income or student recruitment efforts play the dominant role in education decisions). 17½ years is the minimum age for entering a "folk high school".

Finland: Adult learning covers vocational training and general education as well as formal and non-formal learning. The definition of adult learning was contingent on the nature of the host institution and education/training provision rather than on the learner's profile. Until recently, learning has to be organised specifically for adults to be viewed as adult learning. Nowadays the definition is more based on learners' profile and also takes informal learning into account, for those 25 and over.

Norway: Adult learning covers vocational training and general education as well as formal, non-formal and informal learning. The definition therefore encompasses all the settings, whether formal or not, in which learning can occur. On the age side this generally means 19 and over, 19 being the age limit for students in secondary education and not enrolled in a higher education facility.

Portugal: Adult learning covers vocational training and general education as well as formal, non-formal and informal learning. However, the ministries of education and labour do not use the exact same definition even if the two jointly set up the National Agency for Adult Education and Training (ANEFA). The agency's definition initially covered those over 18 but now includes those aged 16 and over in work.

Spain: Adult learning covers people over 18 who have left initial education and training, and those over 16 who are in work. It includes vocational training and general education, which are defined in relation to provision and individual situations. Adult basic education refers to education for basic skills to function in today's society. Training is related to work and comprises initial regulated vocational training provided by the ministry of education, occupational training for the unemployed arranged by the public employment services, and continuing training to qualify and requalify workers.

Sweden: Adult learning is defined in relation to education/training provision rather than individuals. An adult learner is therefore someone who participates in some form of education organised and provided in an adult facility (*e.g.* municipal learning centre, folk high school, learning circle, jobseeker scheme, etc.), regardless of age. On the other hand, self-learners and those who learn in the workplace or at university, for instance, are not covered by the definition. 20 would appear to be the threshold age.

Switzerland: Adult learning covers any learning process that enables adults to develop their skills, increase their knowledge and upgrade their general and vocational qualifications, or to switch to a new form of employment better matched to their own needs and those of society. There is little or no scope for non-vocational learning. In Swiss law and in practice, learning is virtually synonymous with vocational training, even if the term "general training" appears in some places. There is no mention of age.

United Kingdom (England): An adult learner is a person engaged in education and training outside the formal initial education system. Policy tends to target those aged 19 and over. The type of learning concerned includes formal education or training leading to a qualification and a range of informal learning opportunities that can be significant sources of skill or knowledge development. The focus is now broadening to encompass informal (as well as formal) learning and non-vocational (as well as vocational) learning.

Source: Definitions are taken from the country background reports (*www.oecd.org/edu/adultlearning*).

Formal, non-formal and informal learning

Formal, non-formal and informal learning are terms that have emerged from work by UNESCO on lifelong education and the knowledge society, which culminated in the report *Learning to Be: The World of Education Today and Tomorrow* (UNESCO, 1972). To simplify matters, this report uses the most recently developed definitions, adopted for European Union work (Bjørnåvold, 2000 and 2001):

- *Formal learning* is defined as taking place in an organised, structured setting. It is clearly identified as a learning activity. One example is *formal instruction – i.e.* primary, secondary and higher education – or vocational training. This kind of learning, by its very nature, leads to certification, by the ministry of education, a professional branch, or another ministry (usually labour, social affairs, industry, agriculture or defence).

- *Non-formal learning* refers to organised activities that are not explicitly identified as learning activities but that have a major learning component. This means, for instance, that it does not lead to qualifications or certification. It may occur within the workplace or outside. This type of learning supplements more formal learning.

- *Informal learning* occurs by chance or during everyday activities (work, family life, leisure, etc.). Another term used is experiential learning (learning through experience). It is not provided through any formal structure. Typically, self-learners using new ICTs, television or radio, for instance, participate in informal learning if these activities do not constitute part of an organised course or programme. It may be useful, for the purposes of policy making or argument, to break down informal learning into planned and unplanned learning. In the former, people set aside time for informal learning, whereas in the latter they are not conscious of acquiring knowledge. Informal learning is sometimes presented as the only real process of active lifelong learning.

Learning for personal or professional purposes

Another major distinction further complicates the picture. A number of different factors (*e.g.* the types of funding available) often make it necessary to clarify whether the training is for professional or personal reasons. This distinction does not necessarily hold over time, but it is relevant when the decision to learn is taken. Initial motivation for non-professional reasons could well eventually lead to interest in a particular career or facilitate access to a specific job.

The personal/professional distinction applies particularly when the decision to learn is taken

Learning for private, social and/or recreational purposes or for reasons not directly related to work is an important facet of lifelong learning, and falls within the scope of this thematic review. It also adds something to earlier concepts such as recurrent or remedial education, which is heavily influenced by the idea of making up for initial underachievement. The background reports and country notes drawn up for the review and country visits reveal that non-vocational aspects, including learning related to citizenship,[5] democracy and general well-being are much in evidence.

---

5. Citizenship is here taken to mean entitlement to social goods created by the state and institutions, for the benefit of all. These include education, learning and health care.

It should be remembered that while people are learning all the time, not all types of learning can receive equal attention from those who provide adult learning. For roughly the same reason, not all forms of learning can be addressed in this report. Informal learning in particular will only be viewed through examples because of lack of data or focus on those issues during the review visits.

Full- or part-time learning

Part-time learning interferes less with lifestyles, and so is the more common avenue for adults.

This third and final distinction is very significant and raises many issues important to adult learning. Full-time learning, the basis for many of the calculations used to measure return(s) to investment in education and/or training, requires that adults take time off from other activities – mainly employment, which means not earning wages. It generally involves adults returning to formal education, normally higher education or specialisation courses. Part-time learning is more compatible with other life situations, such as working. Adults thus do not need to cease to earn wages, but have to find time in their schedules to arrange for learning. Part-time learning is a more common avenue for adults, as the investment is not as time- or resource-intensive and is more compatible with working.

The adopted definition: resumption of learning

There may well be no point in reaching agreement on one single definition. However, the review's terms of reference define potential adult learners as *adults aged 25 to 64 who have left initial education and training*. This definition serves for comparison, throughout this publication, when statistics or figures are available in the countries concerned. When analysing policy issues and measures within a country, on the other hand, there is no real need to adopt a precise, universal definition.[6] The important point is that the adults in question returned to some kind of learning activities at some point after having left initial education and training.

2.3. Why adult learning is important

Describing objectives is simpler than defining terms.

As seen above, there is considerable complexity in pinpointing a comprehensive and agreed definition of adult learning. The objectives that adult learning policies pursue, on the other hand, can be described easily in broad terms: they must ensure high levels of adult participation in education and training activities while preserving equity among individuals and subgroups of the population, with high-quality programmes that are efficiently resourced.

There are several reasons why, in recent years, adult learning has become an important item on the policy agenda. Education and training contribute to the human capital of individuals and make them more efficient workers as well as better-informed citizens in a knowledge society. More specifically, the increased interest can be put down to a number of factors. In the economic domain there are possible benefits of increased employability, greater productivity and improved-quality employment. In the social domain, one can include individual well-being and increased social returns such as

---

6. For instance, 16 and 19 would be more relevant ages in the United Kingdom and Norway, respectively. In addition, Portugal opted for a review of the issues involved with low-qualified individuals only.

better health, lower incidence of crime, etc. There are as well the political benefits of improved civic participation and a strengthening of the foundations of democracy. All these aspects are closely linked, and described in greater detail below. The rest of the chapter will then describe the main policy issues examined in this report. Before turning to the main issues, it is worth noting that the general context is provided by the wide range of adult learning needs, whether those of the employers, workers, or simple citizens.

A *wide range of needs*

Adult learning cannot be understood or approached in the same way as initial learning. The range of needs is wider and more complex. Historically, the system of adult learning can only be described as highly fragmented and an inadequate response to problem areas and needs that have not often been explicitly articulated. Adult learning has involved public intervention, mainly because some of those needs are not always met by the market. As a consequence there are many gaps in adult learning provision, partly due to market failures. It is important, as a starting point, to keep the range of adult learning needs in mind:

The market alone has not been able to meet a wide range of complex needs.

- Vocational training needs in the workplace. These may relate to cutting-edge technology for highly skilled workers – a field not covered by the thematic review – or more classic needs to update knowledge and know-how. Although there are no fully reliable data, there is evidence that employers provide most of the training of this type, compared with the public or non-governmental organisations.

- Basic education needs (reading, writing and arithmetic). This refers mainly to "second-chance" or recurrent education, for those who have left the initial education system without basic skills (Levels 1 and 2 in Figure 2.1). Clearly, the lack of basic literacy skills can severely limit an individual's civic participation and ability to reap benefit from the opportunities society has to offer.

- Special needs of low-paid workers. Research evidence shows that workers with average or above salaries have good access to training opportunities, as have the unemployed through public training systems. Workers at the lowest wage level tend to be overlooked.

- Workers in small firms do not receive as many training opportunities as workers in larger firms, as it is usually difficult to arrange and to cover workers who are training. Similar situations occur for workers in insecure and short-term contracts.

- Immigrants as a group have specific needs, especially with regard to language training and cultural adaptation.

- Other target groups. Some countries visited have substantial native populations, such as the Lapps in northern Europe or First Nations in Canada, whose education and training needs are not readily met by the general system of provision because that system does not cater to the many special problems of these groups.[7]

---

7. The very notion of pedagogy or a cognitive process among members of Canada's First Nations has very little to do with what those terms mean in relation to groups of European origin.

Figure 2.1. **Literacy levels in selected countries**

Percentage of population aged 25-64 at each prose literacy level, 1994-98

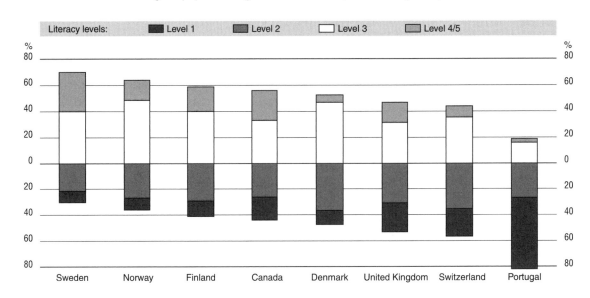

Note: Countries are ranked in increasing order, by the proportion of the population in Levels 1 and 2.
Source: International Adult Literacy Survey (1994-98).

- Disabled workers. Their needs cannot be easily met by a general-purpose system of provision either.
- The training needs of women and men, may as a group, also differ. This issue requires further analysis however, as evidence shows that in a number of countries, women participate slightly more in learning activities than men.
- Geographical variables also impact on the diversity of learning. In some cases, training needs outside major urban centres are not readily met except by distance learning. In almost half of the countries visited during the review, there was a severe demographic imbalance of training provision owing to, *e.g.*, climatic factors and a highly dispersed population (Canada, Finland, Norway and Sweden).

Designing a comprehensive system of adult learning is complex mostly because the needs are so diverse for different sections of the population. At the same time, learning needs can vary within a given group of the population. Hence, it is difficult to identify the type of provision needed simply in terms of the broad characteristics of the population groups. Developing a good and detailed knowledge base on population subgroups is, therefore, one of the key requirements for policy making.

Adult learning contributes to human capital and to economic growth

Human capital plays an important role in the process of economic growth...

One aspect of the importance of adult learning is its contribution to human capital. While the size of the contribution of human capital to economic growth is the subject of considerable debate, there is little question that human capital is a key factor. An OECD study (2000) sets the average long-term impact of one year's additional education on per capita output at between 4 and 7%. This is still a wide range, which is partly due to the lack of consensus on how best to measure investment in human capital; most studies focus on the growth effect of initial education, rather than on the possible contribution of adult learning. However, despite the divergences in the methods of measurement used and the orders of magnitude of the impact, there is consensus that human capital plays an important role in the process of economic growth.

Adult learning is also part of human capital, and there are grounds for expecting that it will contribute to human capital accumulation and growth. Individuals who have left the initial education and training system can strengthen their human capital through adult learning in all sort of settings, whether formal or not. Adult learning may help improve workers' skills and productivity, especially useful in periods of rapid technological change. Also, it is often argued that adult learning enhances employability and workers' ability to cope with job loss. In other words, investment in the human capital of workers may help mobilise labour resources, thereby supporting the growth process (OECD, 2002b). The necessary reliance on human capital in all economic sectors in the nine countries under review calls for a good understanding of how human capital is acquired and kept alive. Research on the contribution of adult learning to human capital could certainly help governments in their investment decision processes.

... and adult learning is undeniably part of human capital.

All adults are potential workers... if properly qualified

Considering that economic growth and employment creation is at the forefront of the preoccupations of all governments, it is of paramount importance to ensure that the largest possible share of the population is available for work. Adult learning programmes can increase the size of the available pool. This is especially important because the large fraction of the population that is not working (young people, retired people, other non-participants in the labour market) or not always working full time (unemployed, part-time workers) is likely to increase for at least two reasons: the strengthening of the knowledge economy and the ageing of the population.

The knowledge economy has once again made basic skills a necessary condition to cope with everyday life in general and to enter the labour market in particular. The International Adult Literacy Survey (IALS) shows that the level of basic skills needed to function well in today's societies is greater than generally thought. Even in countries with better results for prose literacy for instance, one-quarter of the population does not reach the basic required level of attainment, which has been defined as Level 3 (Figure 2.1). The cross-country comparison of average scores from the IALS shows considerable diversity in how adult skills are distributed among country populations. On the one hand, countries like Canada have high average levels of literacy but also a wide spread of literacy skills around the average score. Other countries, like Denmark or Norway, exhibit a narrow spread around the average score. These differences in literacy patterns across populations are closely linked to differences in the models of education and training of these countries (OECD and Statistics Canada, 2000).

Basic skills are once again necessary to enter the knowledge economy's labour market.

Some skill shortages concern the lack of potential workers and some the lack of workers with appropriate skills.

In some countries, the knowledge economy has also caused severe skill shortages in some sectors of the economy. Shortages can be of two types.[8] In the first case, the employer demand for labour is not met; there is an insufficient supply. In the second case, the employer cannot find the appropriate characteristics among the available supply as the level of qualification may not be optimal for an individual firm or the economy as a whole. Adult learning policies can contribute to an improvement of the situation in the labour market by addressing both types of shortages at the same time – in the former case by helping non-participants in the labour market to find a job, and in the latter case by providing appropriate education and training to meet the requirements of enterprises.

There are solid arguments for adult learning...

The necessary training or retraining of the labour force goes far beyond the need to fight against skill shortages. There is a need for adult learning throughout the economy and the population to improve countries' human capital, prepare for the knowledge economy, and curb the side-effects of the ageing of the population. This provides a good rationale for adult learning.

... relating to human capital, the knowledge economy and the ageing of the population.

In regard to ageing of the population, data show that the size of older populations is increasing in all the countries under study and will continue to increase (Figure 2.2). It is clear that an important segment of the general population and the workers concerned have left initial education and training a long time ago, a period that increases with the ageing of the population. This underlines the need for retraining policies, on the grounds that educational attainment was lower at the time of that initial departure. It is also argued that knowledge and skills deteriorate if not used, and that technological progress entails an updating (Figure 2.3).

Retraining of populations and individuals for economic change

Adult learning policies can help address the phenomena of multiple job and career changes...

Unemployment affects low-skilled or low-qualified individuals to a greater extent than it does other workers. This fact provides one more rationale for adult learning policies that can aim to improve skills and the qualifications of potential workers. Unemployment is not, however, the only rationale for adult education and training. Technological change presents the labour force[9] with a challenge. The very notion of a career is changing: job tenure has decreased and temporary employment has grown in a considerable number of OECD countries in the past two decades (OECD, 2002a). Education and training is needed to cope with multiple job and career changes by providing new skills that contribute to greater versatility and mobility of workers. There are also those individuals who want to change jobs, occupations and/or professions for reasons of personal choice and career advancement.

---

8. Skill shortage is here defined as the scarcity of certain skills among workers who ought to carry out particular tasks and/or master specific techniques, whether relating to manual know-how or cognitive knowledge. This is a commonly accepted definition that does not cover, for instance, what Oliver and Turton (1982) have shown to be characteristics that employers refer to as skills, namely reliability, autonomy and stability.

9. Those who are in work, looking for work, or both.

Figure 2.2.   **Ageing of the population**

Evolution of the 45-64 year-olds as proportion of total population, 1950-2020

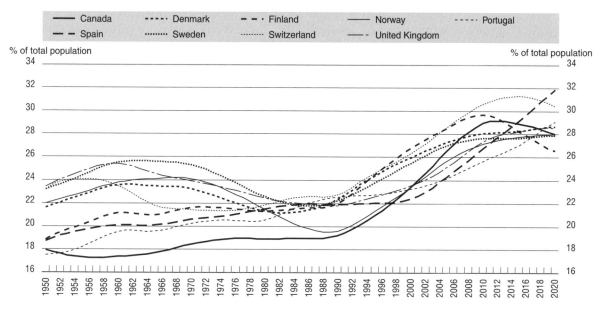

Source: United Nations (2001).

Figure 2.3.   **Younger generations are more educated**

Percentage of adults with at least upper secondary education by age group, 1999

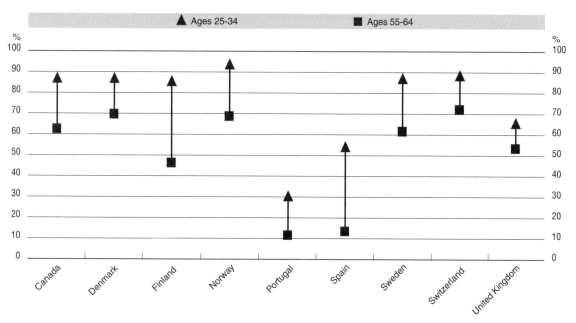

Source: OECD (2001b).

... help furnish the potential for innovation...

Yet another rationale for high levels of participation in adult learning is the probability that many of the occupations that will appear over the next 15 years are not yet invented. Innovation of this type might be encouraged if the population at large – those in as well as out of the labour force – were to attain a certain level of skills. There is, of course, no certainty that cutting-edge and/or specific vocational training alone is conducive to innovation. However, a general increase in skills attainment might create a conducive environment in which innovation could thrive.

... and help refit the labour force as traditional skills and structures disappear.

In any event, the erosion or complete disappearance of some occupations – with technical change and industrial restructuring – is already making it necessary to retrain workers and adapt their skills. Adult learning policies are the only tools available to refit the existing adult labour force to the changing skill requirements of the economy. Even in the more durable occupations, new work patterns and practices are leading to the introduction of periods of learning to allow people to adapt to new skills; these may not often top the list of hiring criteria, but they do in fact figure into final hiring decisions (OECD, 2001a, Chapter 4).

Learning for functioning in today's society

It can help society benefit from the new technologies...

The challenges are not confined to the workforce, because in the nine countries under review, technology has clearly become part and parcel of individuals' everyday lives. Using interactive television, cash dispensers, Internet or email, for instance, requires skills that most adults have not been taught, particularly during their initial education. In addition, new ICTs have rendered writing skills more necessary than during the age of the telephone, for example.

... and even make for a better society.

Adult learning also receives attention because it can affect every facet of one's life. It raises issues ranging from individual welfare and betterment to citizenship and democracy. There is evidence, for instance, that some find it hard to administer the right dose of medication to a child because they cannot correctly read the label on a bottle or calculate the dosage. There are also interesting correlations between political variables (such as women in parliament) and literacy proficiency (OECD and Statistics Canada, 2000). Many surveys have shown that one reason why adults, or pensioners, return to learning is to help their children or grandchildren with their schoolwork.

2.4. Key issues

Patterns of participation and provision

To set the context for examining the key issues, it is useful to describe the existing situation in terms of the basic characteristics of the participants, providers and the mode of provision. Chapter 3 offers an overview of existing patterns in the countries reviewed. With regard to patterns of participation, some of the key questions addressed in that chapter are:

- Is there imbalance in the participation rates in terms of gender, age, country of origin, occupational status?
- What *are* the patterns of participation? What are the main reasons individuals have for learning?
- What are the characteristics of the training provided by the employers?

When dealing with the mode of provision, the key questions are:

- What are the types of provision and providers? What are the respective roles of providers?
- Is classroom-based teaching still the prevalent way of teaching adults?
- Is the learning enterprise a reality?
- What is the private/public breakdown in terms of adult learning providers?
- To what extent is distance learning a solution? Is it widely used?

Countries' policies and practices

The patterns described in Chapter 3 do not appear in a vacuum but are closely related to existing policies and practices. Chapter 4 presents an overview of country policies and practices, including the degree to which adult learning is important for the policy agenda at the national level. The chapter addresses, among others, the following questions:

- What are the policy approaches to adult learning across the nine reviewed countries?
- Are there general strategies to increase learning opportunities?
- What are the tools of these policy strategies? For example, what reliance is placed on national qualification systems, quality assurance, financing mechanisms, use of benchmarks such as upper secondary level?
- What is the division of roles between the national level and decentralised levels in the development and implementation of policies?
- How is co-operation and partnership among different actors and stakeholders organised?

Strengthening the incentives and motivations to learn

Existing literature on adult learning has identified the inadequacy of incentives and lack of motivation to learn as key barriers to participation in adult learning. Chapter 5 addresses these issues from two perspectives, the more general situation applying to all training and the more specific context of the labour market, for employed and unemployed adults. The enterprise is a significant provider of training and it is essential to assess how incentives can be improved in this context. Hence the following relevant questions:

- Has the perceived value of learning been sufficient to generate adequate levels of participation – *i.e.* social values and citizenship on one hand and economic benefits (better employability and increased productivity) on the other?
- What specific mechanisms have been shown to work well in practice, and which specific approaches have not worked well: training levy schemes, a legal obligation for companies to finance training, loans or grants, allowing time for training within the enterprise, general training programmes for the unemployed?
- What approaches have proved efficient in public employment service training programmes? General rather than targeted, incorporating on-the-job components in training? Which good practices have been found to reach the long-term unemployed?

- What incentives and motivations have proved useful in improving participation in adult learning: better information about learning opportunities; wider room for personal fulfilment; opportunities for collective self-help; greater autonomy in decision making; wider civic involvement; a wider range of cultural activities?

- What specific barriers need to be removed in order to increase participation (poor scheduling, lack of daycare centres for children, inadequate financing, inadequate support from the employer or the family)?

- What is the experience with approaches providing new incentives such as right to study leave and the options of individual learning accounts?

- How can incentives be tailored to meet the population segments most in need: target groups within non-learners, groups at risk, workers in SMEs, unemployed people?

Improving the delivery of learning to adults

Incentive and motivation are two keywords in the field of adult learning. While Chapter 5 analyses those issues in general and in the labour market, Chapter 6 deals with one specific approach to motivating individuals to learn: improving delivery. It outlines different dimensions of delivery that are key to the interests of the learner and the smooth functioning of the adult learning system. Delivery here is taken in a broad sense, embracing all the components of the adult learning system, including the enterprise and the teacher. A comprehensive approach is essential in ensuring a conducive environment to adult learning. To assess how well such an approach is being put into practice, the chapter addresses the following questions:

- How can the learning and teaching methods be tailored to meet the specific needs of adults? If there is a specific pedagogy that is suitable, what are its key features? Is it possible to create or invent adult learning activities that are really learner-centred? How can education and training be made useful to the participants?

- How can a conducive general environment be created (infrastructure, targeted approach)? Under what conditions do non-vocationally oriented learning activities improve accessibility to vocational activities? Is sufficient effort given to investigating how particular groups of adults learn most effectively?

- How can appropriate co-ordination be ensured between research findings and their use by the policy makers? Can routine assessment of programmes – before, during and after – help in spotting inefficient or ineffective learning activities?

- How effective are some of the tools most often used: recognition of prior learning, flexible organisation such as modularisation, certification of current learning? Have some specific ways of delivering learning proven useful: distance learning, e-learning, non-classroom-based learning?

Promoting a better integration of supply and demand

Providing a coherent and transparent system is an important step in creating an environment conducive to adult learning. Another element that needs to be considered is better integration of supply and demand, which is taken up in Chapter 7.

In all the countries visited for the thematic review, there is a broad range of providers of adult learning activities. One of the key barriers for adults to resume learning activities after a long gap is the lack of simplicity and/or transparency of the system. On the other hand, a certain degree of complexity is sometimes made necessary by the wide range of needs. In this case, a good system of information and guidance is also required. What can be done:

- To reduce fragmented provision of adult learning services and increase support infrastructure?
- To take fuller account of learners' needs and enable would-be learners to come forward and participate in learning programmes?
- To make institutions work together? To encourage partnerships at all levels?
- To regulate education and training markets so as to take account of the demand for learning?
- To ensure that would-be learners have easy access to complete and reliable information and guidance on the full range of learning opportunities?
- To use the system and the infrastructure (support services, for example) to reduce inequalities (by educational attainment for instance) and extend opportunities to those adults hard to reach?

Adult education and training is a subject that raises important topics for international debate, because of the diversity of individual country experiences and policies. Even if not all experiences are transposable beyond national borders, it is always instructive to see what works elsewhere, how it works and why. The following chapters review major policy issues and solutions in each of the nine countries visited. More exhaustive national analysis can be found in the individual country notes. It goes without saying that it is particularly hard to take the full measure of all the problems during just a short visit, however intensive and well organised. The real problem is to put into perspective everything seen and heard, and then accurately weigh all the views and arguments in order to describe and analyse as faithfully as possible the actual situation on the ground. Clearly, people learn everywhere, all the time. This report consequently had to focus on the most obvious advances in fields where some formalisation is possible. Questions such as the recognition of prior learning and informal learning could not be dealt with thoroughly here, but will be addressed specifically in the OECD thematic review on national qualification systems.

Going beyond the rhetoric, it is likely that learning deficits will persist. In fact, the chapters that follow attempt to describe how countries are trying to overcome such deficits. But they are also to some extent analytical, in that they try to see why, and in what settings, innovative solutions work.

BIBLIOGRAPHY

BJØRNÅVOLD, J. (2000),
  "Making Learning Visible: Identification, Assessment and Recognition of Non-formal Learning in Europe", CEDEFOP, Thessaloniki, July.

BJØRNÅVOLD, J. (2001),
  Assessment and Recognition of Non-formal Learning in Europe: Main Tendencies and Challenges, Communication prepared for the OECD-KRIVET International Conference on Adult Learning Policies, 5-7 December, Seoul, Korea.

CONDORCET (1792),
  "Rapport à l'Assemblée nationale" (Report to the National Assembly), Paris.

OECD (1973),
  Recruitment Education: A Strategy for Lifelong Learning, Paris.

OECD (1996),
  Lifelong Learning for All, Paris.

OECD (2000),
  OECD Economic Outlook, Vol. 68, December, Paris.

OECD (2001a),
  Education Policy Analysis – Education and Skills, Paris, April.

OECD (2001b),
  Education at a Glance – OECD Indicators, Paris.

OECD (2002a),
  OECD Employment Outlook, July.

OECD (2002b),
  "Supporting Economic Growth through Continuous Education and Training – Some Preliminary Results", ELS working paper, OECD, Paris.

OECD and STATISTICS CANADA (2000),
  Literacy in the Information Age, Final Report of the International Adult Literacy Survey, Paris and Ontario.

OLIVER, J. and J. TURTON (1982),
  "Is there a Shortage of Skilled Labour?", *British Journal of Industrial Relations*, Vol. 20, pp. 195-200.

UNESCO (1972),
  Learning to Be: The World of Education Today and Tomorrow, Report of the Commission chaired by E. Faure, Paris.

UNESCO (1996),
  "Learning: A Treasure Within", Report to UNESCO of the International Commission on Education for the Twenty-first Century, Paris.

UNITED NATIONS (2001),
  "World Population Prospects 1950-2050 (The 2000 revision)", Population Division, Department of Economic and Social Affairs, New York.

Chapter 3

PATTERNS OF PARTICIPATION AND PROVISION: ASSESSING NEEDS

This chapter offers an overview of patterns and profiles of participation and provision in adult learning across the countries included in the thematic review. It shows how adults who follow learning activities do it mostly for employment-related reasons and in short training spells. Learning concentrates in specific subgroups of the population, such as those with higher educational attainment, employed in white-collar high-skilled occupations or working in larger firms or those at the forefront of the knowledge-based economy. The broad range of adult learning providers includes private, public and quasi non-governmental institutions, with enterprises playing a vital role in the process. There are similar patterns of participation across countries – and therefore similar gaps in provision for specific groups of adults who might require further learning opportunities.

3.1. Profiles of participation in adult learning

Issues of definition make it difficult to render a clear picture of adult participation in learning.

Providing a clear picture of adult participation in learning activities is quite challenging. Not only do perceptions differ with regard to what can be considered learning within and across countries, but participation itself can be measured in different ways. Some surveys might focus on vocational training, or on training provided by enterprises; others include learning for personal reasons, some may also include informal learning. The differences in reference periods for learning activities also render the analysis difficult. Learning can cover different periods – a week, a month or throughout the whole year – and so not be comparable across countries. The definition of an adult learner also varies. It is a matter of who is considered an adult in different countries, and whether adults who have not left the education system are included as adult learners or not (Table 2.1 reviews different country definitions). Some surveys might also focus on the supply side, that providies data on courses and participants, while others offer information about people following training. These issues of definition and methodology are important for a chapter that provides a profile of participation. The different sources available will be used to provide a general picture of adult learning in as comparable a manner as possible across countries[1] (Annex 1 for details on sources used for this publication).

Participation rates vary greatly across countries.

Adults participate in learning processes in all countries, although the percentages differ significantly (Figure 3.1). According to the International Adult Literacy Survey, more than one in two adults participated in Finland, Denmark, and Sweden. In Norway, the United Kingdom and Switzerland participation ranged from 48 to 40%. In Canada it was more than one in three. Portugal had the lowest rate of the countries that participated in this survey.[2] It is important to note here that the survey was taken between 1994 and 1998, depending on the country, and participation rates may have varied since then due to economic and socio-demographic factors such as those listed in Chapter 2.

The participation rates registered by the European Union Labour Force Survey (ELFS) are generally lower (ranging between 3 and 24%) than those from the IALS, mainly due to a difference in reference periods – four weeks for the former and one year for the latter. In Sweden, the United Kingdom, Denmark and Finland, one in five adults has received training in the month prior to the survey. The distribution of countries in the ELFS follows a ranking similar to that in the IALS with the exception of the United Kingdom. The Nordic countries, Sweden, Denmark and Finland, have the highest and similar participation rates, followed by Norway. The United Kingdom's higher ranking could be due to increased efforts in training undertaken in recent years with

---

1. A number of efforts are under way at the OECD to harmonise this information. The working party on employment and unemployment statistics has already tried to assemble an overview of the data variations and establish a framework for harmonisation of training statistics (OECD, 1998). The INES network launched a project to develop an International Continuing Education and Training Module (OECD-Module) in April 2001 and work is in progress to try to achieve comparability of data across OECD countries on adult learning and training statistics.
2. Spain was the one country among those in the thematic review that did not participate in the IALS.

Figure 3.1. **Participation in adult learning by gender**

Percentage of population 25-64 years old in adult learning by gender according to different reference periods

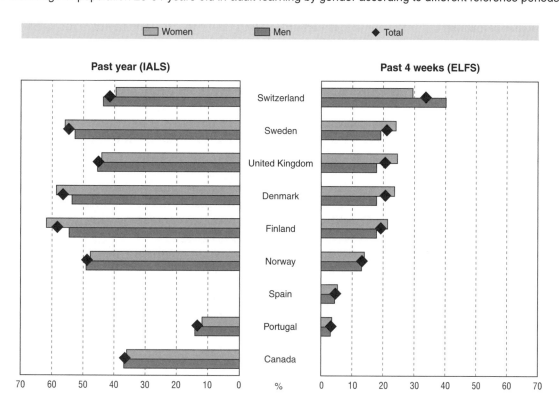

Note: Period of reference is one year for Switzerland in both surveys. Countries are ranked in descending order of total participation rate for ELFS data.
Source: International Adult Literacy Survey (1994-98); Eurostat, European Union Labour Force Survey (2001).

the establishment of learning participation targets (7% reduction in non-learners between 1998 and 2002) since the ELFS refers to the year 2000 and IALS data for the United Kingdom refer to 1996. Norway has a slightly lower participation rate than other Nordic countries. Spain and Portugal have the lowest rates.

Country rankings remain similar according to different data sources and reference periods. The Nordic Countries and the United Kingdom are followed by Switzerland and Canada. In these countries, at least one out of every three adults participates in some training activity throughout the year according to the IALS, while the ELFS shows that at least one in five participates in training over a one-month period. Spain and Portugal show lower participation rates.

Country rankings do not vary widely according to sources.

Participation rates seem to have generally increased from 1995 to 2000, but this does not hold for all countries. According to the ELFS, in Finland, Denmark, Spain, Switzerland and the United Kingdom, adult learning has increased by 15% while in Norway and Sweden there has been a downturn in the past year. Portuguese participation rates have remained stable (data not

Not every country shows an increase in participation.

shown). Canada experienced a decreasing tendency from 1991 through 1997 (Statistics Canada and Human Resources Development Canada (2001).

The number of learning hours received varies less.

There is less variation across countries in learning hours received than in the rate of participation. The number of hours per participant according to IALS data ranged from around 135 in Switzerland and the United Kingdom to 190 in Finland and Norway, to over 200 in Canada and Denmark. According to OECD Secretariat data available for the thematic review, more than half of participants in Finland, Canada and Norway took courses that lasted less than 50 hours each, while between 10 and 15% took courses that were over 200 hours. In general, this would indicate that the majority of adult learning focuses on short learning processes.

There are extensive and intensive models of training.

Some differences are visible when employment-related training is considered. Figure 3.2, based on the results of the Third European Survey on Working Conditions in 2000, shows the average number of training days financed or arranged by the employer during the last twelve months. This number ranges from 30 days in Spain to 9 days in Finland. A comparison of the participation rates and average training days reveals two models of investment in training: an extensive model, which provides a fairly low volume of training to a large number of workers (Denmark, Finland, Sweden and the United Kingdom); and an intensive model, which concentrates more training efforts on a smaller number of people (Portugal and Spain). This

Figure 3.2. **Participation and average days of training**

Percentage of people in training and average days of training, 2000

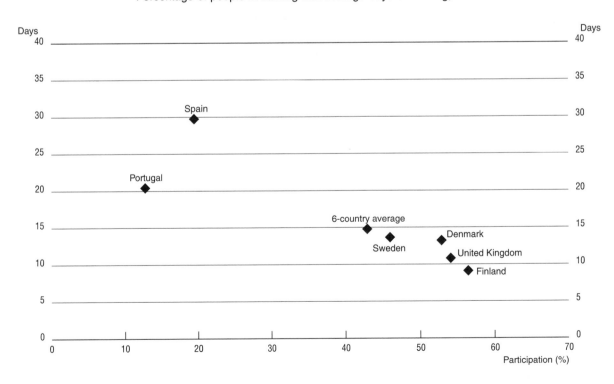

Source: European Foundation for the Improvement of Living and Working Conditions, Third European Survey on Working Conditions, 2000.

© OECD 2003

contrast has already been noted by the OECD in a study (1999) which also placed Norway among countries with the extensive model, and Switzerland and Canada somewhere between the two.

The sections that follow examine different trends in participation in adult learning. The analysis shows some common patterns, particularly a tendency for learning to be concentrated among certain groups and inequalities of access across the board. The implication is that efforts have to be undertaken to increase the opportunities for others who do not have access to learning. The rest of the chapters in this publication provide an analysis of the different country approaches to increasing these opportunities for their populations.

No substantial gender imbalances

There are no substantial gender differences in participation in adult learning (Figure 3.1). According to the ELFS data, women train at slightly higher rates than men, except in Switzerland, especially unemployed and younger women (not shown). Similar patterns were found in the IALS data, with higher participation by women in Nordic countries in Sweden, Denmark and Finland, slightly higher for men in Canada, Norway and the United Kingdom and much higher in Switzerland for men. There seem to be differences when comparing sources of financing for training but they vary according to the survey. In the IALS, employers are found to be the leading sources of this support for men, while self and family were the most common sources of funding reported for women (OECD and Statistics Canada, 2000). This could be because there are more women undertaking learning for personal reasons or adult basic education, as was evidenced throughout country visits. However, according to a different source, the European Survey on Working Conditions, training paid for by the employer had higher female representation in most countries (Table 3.2).

Gender differences in participation are minor.

Younger adults train more

Younger cohorts participate in learning more than older cohorts (Figure 3.3). In all countries, but especially in Portugal and Spain, adults aged 25 through 29 have the highest participation rates. For the 30-49 age groups, training rates decrease across countries. After age 50 there is a considerable decrease in participation, with the lowest rates for those 60 to 64 years old. Data gathered through the thematic review show that adults over 65 also undertake training, although the rates are quite low.[3] In Canada, Norway and Switzerland, between 6 and 16% of those 65 through 69 years old receive some kind of training. In fact, countries are making greater efforts to increase adult education for retired people. Different universities and institutions are creating special programmes for the elderly, as presented in the next section.

Participation rates are lower for older population.

The decline in participation rates after age 50 is partly explained by economic returns to learning. A recent OECD study that analyses investment in human capital through post-compulsory education and training (OECD, 2002) concludes that for younger people there are strong labour market benefits and high rates of return to investments in training. For older adults,

To some extent the post-50 decrease is a question of economic returns.

---

3. OECD Secretariat questionnaire on Adult Learning.

Figure 3.3. **Participation in adult learning by age groups**
Percentage of population 25-64 years old in adult learning by age according to different reference periods

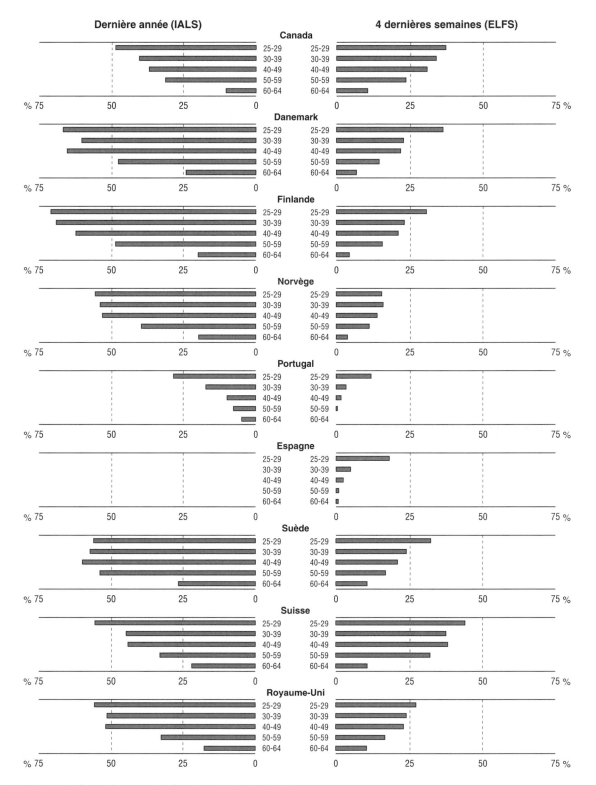

Note: Period of reference is one year for Canada and Switzerland in both surveys.
Source: International Adult Literacy Survey (1994-98); Eurostat, European Union Labour Force Survey (2001) except for Canada (1997 AETS data).

on the other hand, there are certain disincentives to pursue post-compulsory education and training. The opportunity costs of forgone earnings will be significantly higher for older adults if education requires time out of work. Furthermore, the eventual return in the form of higher earnings from formal education or training at older ages may be subject to uncertainty. It may require changing employers, which might cause a loss of seniority benefits or employer-specific skills. Another disincentive is the fact that the remaining length of working life implies a shorter period of time to amortise the investment costs for the training programmes, and it might even eliminate all financial gains from such investment.

The effects of some of these factors may not, however, be large as expected. These are indeed important reasons for adults not to undergo learning, but the fact is that most of adult learning programmes do not focus on formal post-secondary education. Figure 3.1 and Figure 3.2 present evidence that most of adult learning is short in duration and that it focuses on professional or career upgrading. Less than 20% of those who train do so to obtain a university degree or college or vocational diploma. Furthermore, findings from the thematic review show that adult learning processes may be organised around working schedules or within working hours by the employers, so that they do not normally conflict with work or other life situations. Therefore, the opportunity costs for older adults may not be as high as the above study estimates: learning does not imply taking a long period off from work, and there are financial assistance arrangements to overcome the potential high opportunity costs.

High educational attainment/literacy and training are complementary

The level of education reached is one of the most relevant variables in relation to adult learning. Those with highest educational attainment train most, except in Portugal (Figure 3.4). Similarly, in each country, people with the lowest levels of educational attainment have the lowest learning participation rates. Patterns of participation are similar across countries except for Portugal and Spain. In these two countries, those with secondary- and tertiary-level education have learning rates much higher than the average. Those with low levels have the least learning opportunities in all countries, but especially in Canada, Norway, Portugal, Spain, Switzerland and the United Kingdom.

Those with highest educational attainment train most and vice versa.

These patterns suggest that education and adult learning are complementary. Those who are more educated receive more training, participate in employment that requires high skills use, and therefore have the chance to reinforce their training (OECD, 1999).

The same pattern holds when analysing participation in training and literacy levels (Figure 3.5). Rates are much higher for people with higher literacy levels. Again, there is a virtuous circle. An analysis of education and literacy levels of knowledge workers[4] showed that those who are either highly

The same pattern holds in relation to literacy levels, again suggesting a virtuous circle.

---

4. Described as those who are participating in the knowledge-based economy. This definition, developed with IALS data, refers to those who are employed in white-collar high-skilled occupations and perform a set of tasks that revolve around creating and processing information. For more information see Box 4.2 in OECD (2001a) for different definitions of knowledge workers.

Figure 3.4. **Adult learning by educational attainment**

Ratio of participation rates at each educational level to the total participation rates for population 25-64 years old,[1]
2000

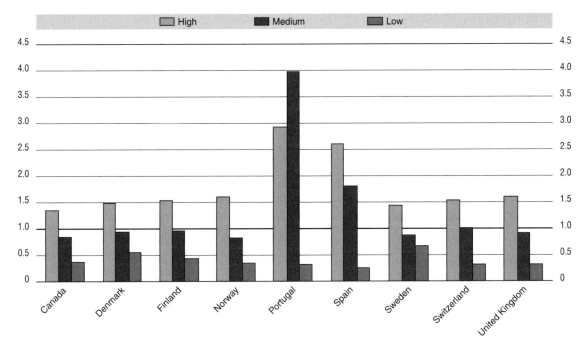

1. A ratio superior to 1 implies that the proportion of persons in adult learning in the specific category is above the average country participation rate; a ratio between 0 and 1, below the average rate.
Note: Period of reference is four weeks except for Canada and Switzerland, where it is one year.
Source: Eurostat, European Union Labour Force Survey data except for Canada (1997 AETS data).

educated or highly literate may well acquire the necessary skills and competencies to become knowledge workers through means other than formal education. Knowledge workers were found to participate in training more than all other workers, revealing that participation in training can be viewed as both a result and a cause of being a knowledge worker.

Growing migratory pressures and learning

Learning for immigrants has now been accorded a higher priority.

Growing migration rates spurred by globalisation and skills shortages in a number of OECD countries may have helped to raise the importance of learning for immigrants. A number of countries visited for the thematic review have developed vocational training programmes designed especially for immigrants.

Data for training by citizenship or place of birth show some differences across countries; all but the United Kingdom have higher participation in learning by national populations. Among the countries for which there is such statistical information, Switzerland and Spain show the largest differences between immigrant and native-born populations (Figure 3.7). A different analysis of immigrants and native-born people with difficulties in their reading abilities in 20 IALS participating countries showed that the training

Figure 3.5. **Adult learning by literacy levels**

Percentage of population 25-64 years old in adult learning by document literacy levels, 1994-98

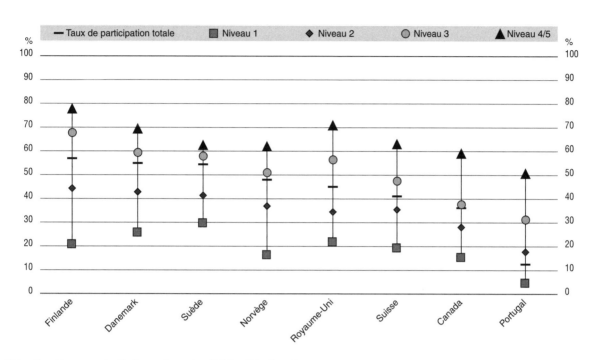

Note: Countries are ranked in descending order of total participation rate.
Source: International Adult Literacy Survey (1994-98).

rate of the immigrants at risk was higher than for the native-born population (NORD, 2001). However, immigrant populations tend to be heterogeneous and there are strong variations in their educational attainment and social and employment situation. Some countries have a large share of highly educated people among immigrant populations, so learning opportunities may vary according to need and other factors.

Learning for personal or professional reasons?

One of the strongest links to adult learning is the world of work. Among the different reasons stated for undertaking adult learning, most are employment-related. On average, according to most surveys, three out of four people who learn participate in job-related education and training in some form or another. This implies that labour market considerations weight heavily in individuals' decisions to undertake learning.

Most reasons for undertaking adult learning are employment-related...

The IALS shows that learning is mostly for career or job-related reasons; more that 60% of adult learners are in this category (Figure 3.6). Data for Canada also showed that at least 70% of training was job-related.[5] There are, however, a number of countries in which high proportions of the

... although many learners in Finland, Sweden and Switzerland cite other reasons.

------

5. The Adult Education and Training Survey (AETS).

Figure 3.7. **Adult learning by residence situation**

Ratio of participation rates by residence situation to the total participation rates for population 25-64 years old,[1]
2000

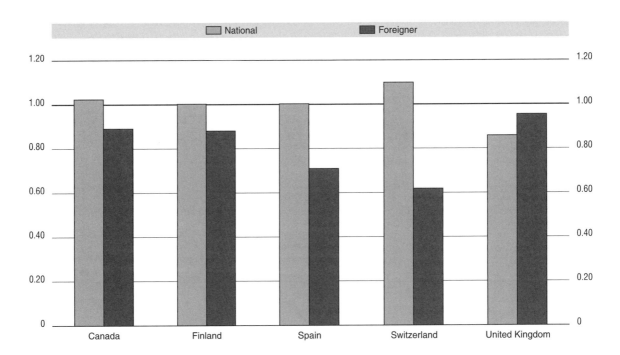

1. A ratio superior to 1 implies that the proportion of persons in adult learning in the specific category is above the average country participation rate; a ratio between 0 and 1, below the average rate.
Source: OECD Secretariat questionnaire on Adult Learning. See Annex 1 for details.

population undertake training for personal or other reasons: in Finland, Sweden and Switzerland, this type of learning may be closely linked to goals of personal development, active citizenship and democratic values. It is also the case that people who are pursuing remedial education, a basic literacy level or primary or secondary education can state they are doing so for personal reasons. Data from the ELFS (not shown) also reveal differences in reasons for participation, although they cannot be compared to IALS data. From a diversity of listed reasons, adapting to technological change, obtaining a promotion and upgrading acquired skills were the three main ones for learning for more than one in two adults in Denmark, Finland, Sweden and the United Kingdom. Learning for general interest was given high priority in Spain, Portugal and Sweden. In those first two countries and Denmark, the proportions in initial education or training were also high.

Actually, the divide of personal/professional motivation is not so clear-cut.

However, a number of issues need to be considered for a clearer understanding of the reasons for taking training. It can be difficult to distinguish between what is job-related education and training and what is not. Language courses, for example, might be followed for personal reasons while the skills obtained are useful for professional purposes. The divide of personal/professional motivation is not so clear-cut, *e.g.* in the case of training

Figure 3.6. **Reasons for adult learning**

Percentage distribution of adult learners 25-64 years old by reason, 1994-98

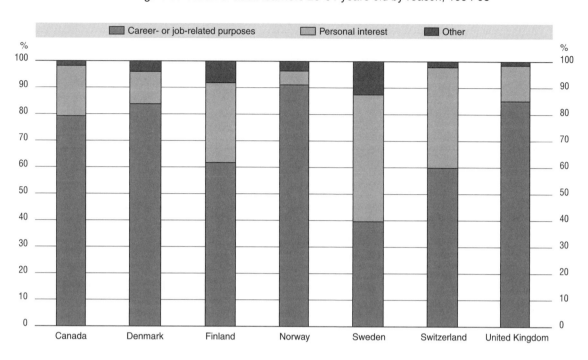

Source: International Adult Literacy Survey (1994-98).

to adapt to technological change, such as learning to use the Internet or other technological software for work or personal reasons. Learning designed to increase employability can also increase individual confidence and willingness to engage actively in society. Also, training for personal reasons can affect one's position in the labour market, and give individuals the capacity to influence their own opportunities at work. In fact, some studies have found that general knowledge courses have a stronger impact on firm productivity than firm-specific training (Barrett and O'Connell, 1999). Furthermore, most surveys focus on job-related training, and the questions specifically relate to those opportunities. There is also the issue of what people recognise as learning; they may not include some learning processes that could be considered as such.

An analysis of the enrolment patterns of adult learners can help clarify that issue. According to the IALS, at least half the training participants were involved in learning for professional or career upgrading (Table 3.1). In the countries for which data are available, only between 5 and 10% of the people who received training were seeking a university degree or college diploma, and vocational diplomas or apprenticeships presented even smaller rates. The goal of an elementary school diploma ranked lowest, with rates of less than 3% in most countries. It should be noted here that in some of the countries there were nonetheless waiting lists for adult basic education

Few learners are enrolled in adult basic education courses, although that could be due to lack of availability.

47

Table 3.1. **Adult learners by type of learning undertaken**
Percentage distribution of adult learners 25-64 years old by type of learning, 1994-98

	University	College	Trade-vocational or apprenticeship	Elementary or secondary school	Professional or career upgrading	Other
Canada	6.7	3.6	6.6	2.4	61.2	19.4
Denmark	2.0	2.5	3.5	0.2	68.7	23.0
Finland	4.5	0.9	1.4	0.5	77.2	15.6
Norway	2.8	3.4	1.4	0.2	82.1	10.1
Sweden	5.4	2.1	2.4	0.3	..	89.8
Switzerland	2.0	0.2	7.7	..	54.8	35.4
United Kingdom	2.9	2.3	5.3	1.9	22.6	65.1

Source: International Adult Literacy Survey (1994-98).

courses. That could imply that if there are not many people following these courses, it could be because of lack of availability. Finally, there was a high proportion of survey respondents who noted they were taking "other" types of courses in Sweden and the United Kingdom.

Learning depends largely on adults position in the labour force.

As the major reason for participation in adult education and training is job-related, the individuals' situation with respect to the labour force is extremely significant. The incidence of training depends on whether people work or not, what sector of the economy they work in, their occupation, and the nature of the employment or the enterprise they work for. Most active labour market policies are geared to training of the labour force so as to improve productivity, assist the unemployed in finding work and help those in the low wage groups to raise their skills and wage opportunities.

Firms are aware of the benefits of human capital.

The benefits of human capital, which includes formal initial education as well as adult learning, in the labour force, have been highlighted in a large number of studies. Firms use training as a means to obtain higher worker and firm productivity, as a large number of research evidence has proved (Finegold and Mason, 1996, Barret and O'Connell, 1999, Lounds, 1999, Dearden, Reed and van Reenen, 2000). Firms also use training to adapt to technological changes (Dybowski, 1998, Kiley, 1999), or to introduce changes in workplace practices and adapt workers' skills to new requirements (Green, Ashton and Felstead, 2001; Osterman, 1995). Adults also benefit from training, as it may improve their employability, reduce the risk of unemployment, and may contribute to greater mobility or higher wages.

In most countries, both the employed and unemployed participate more than those who are out of the labour force.

Different patterns emerge from the analysis of learning incidence by labour force situation (Figure 3.8). What is most evident is that both the employed and unemployed have higher training rates than those who are out of the labour force in most countries, except for Sweden. While there are similar participation patterns across countries included in the IALS, there are cross-country variations according to the ELFS. In Canada, Finland, Switzerland and the United Kingdom the employed have the highest training rates, followed by the unemployed and by those out of the labour force. In Denmark, Portugal, Sweden and Spain the ratio is higher for the unemployed as well as for those not in the labour force, rather than the employed. In Norway, the employed and unemployed have similar participation patterns.

Figure 3.8. **Adult learning by labour force status**

Ratio of participation rates by labour force status to the total participation rates for population 25-64 years old,[1]
2000

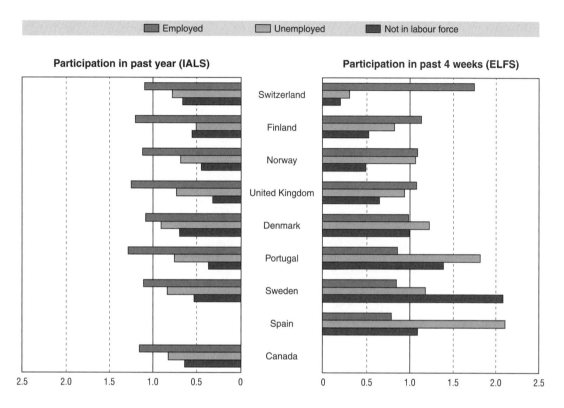

1. A ratio superior to 1 implies that the proportion of persons in adult learning in the specific category is above the average country participation rate;
   a ratio between 0 and 1, below the average rate.
Notes: Countries are ranked in descending order of total participation rate of employed population for ELFS data.
      Period of reference is one year for Switzerland in both surveys.
Source: International Adult Literacy Survey (1994-98); Eurostat, European Union Labour Force Survey (2001).

These differences across training rates of the unemployed can be due to the impact of targeted active labour market policies or different policies geared towards increasing training for the unemployed. In general, employment and unemployment rates have changed since 1994 and labour market training programmes or others might have played a role at different periods of the economic cycle. There are also differences according to data sources, especially in time frames, which might have affected training rates by labour force status: the IALS took place between 1994 and 1998 for different countries, and the ELFS in the second trimester of the year 2000.

Targeted active labour market policies may account for differences across training rates of the unemployed.

The high ratio of participation for out of the labour force populations' reveals that countries may have chosen policies geared towards personal development, active citizenship and democracy. Also, Denmark, Portugal, Spain, and Sweden have devoted major efforts to raising the educational level of adult populations through adult basic education programmes.

Higher-skilled occupations and service sector employment receive more training

Participation rates are highest for workers in white-collar high-skilled occupations.

In almost all countries, participation rates are highest for workers in white-collar high-skilled occupations, normally those that require higher education attainment levels. They include legislators, senior officials and managers, professionals, technicians and associate professionals. Together with white-collar low-skilled occupations, which include clerks and service workers, they make up for the largest proportion of training of the employed labour force (Figure 3.9). Within blue-collar occupations, adult participation rates in training are higher for high-skilled than low-skilled jobs in all countries except Portugal and Spain, where the reverse is the case. The strongest inequalities in participation are found in those two countries and Switzerland.

Workers in service sector jobs have higher probabilities of receiving training.

The ratio of participation by economic sectors of activity (data not shown) reveals that workers in service sector jobs have higher probabilities of receiving training than workers in other sectors. Within the service economy, adults working in social and personal services, financial intermediation and real estate sector, followed closely by the electricity, water and gas supply sector participate more than others.

Figure 3.9. **Adult learning by occupation**

Ratio of participation rates by occupation to the total participation rates for population 25-64 years old,[1] 2000

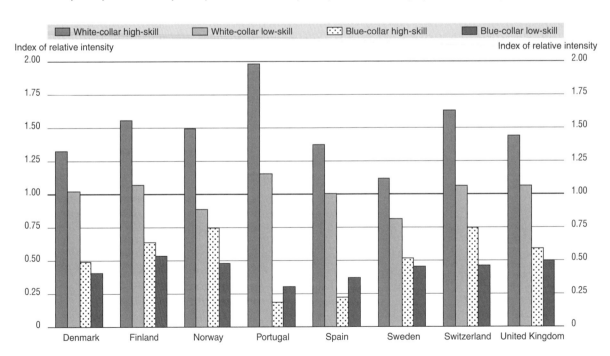

1. A ratio superior to 1 implies that the proportion of persons in adult learning in the specific category is above the average country participation rate; a ratio between 0 and 1, below the average rate.

Note: Period of reference is four weeks except for Switzerland, where it is one year.

Source: Eurostat, European Union Labour Force Survey (2001).

Firms and training

Firms or enterprises represent a large sector of the training market, on the demand as well as on the supply side. Approximately two out of every three persons who undertook training did so with employer support, implying that employers provide most support for training (Table 4.1 and Statistics Canada and Human Resource Development Canada, 2001). These data vary by countries: Canadian and Swiss employers give lower than the average support, and Norway and the United Kingdom much higher than the average. However, the employer share was higher than 50% in all thematic review countries. It is also interesting to know whether the training was suggested by the employer or by the employees. The evidence shows that most of the training that received financial support from employers was suggested by them, although most employee-suggested training was also financed by the employer (NORD, 2001). Given that firms have such a major role in training, it is important to analyse the specific characteristics of firms that train.

Firms have a major role in training...

The published Second Continuing Vocational Training Survey (CVTS2, Eurostat) shows that the percentage of enterprises that organised continuous vocational training varied between 96% in Denmark to 22% in Portugal. However, defining what enterprise training is or may be can vary. Alongside participation in courses structured along formal apprenticeship lines on company premises or in external institutions, a considerable proportion of workers' training is in-house, non-formal or informal. It is called on-the-job training and it is not easy to distinguish from the learning process inherent in the work experience. In fact, the CVTS2 signals a high percentage of training enterprises and distinguishes between those that offer continuous vocational training courses and those that offer other forms of training, which can include conferences or workshops, job rotation or exchanges, and normal work tools or self-learning (Figure 3.10).

... although on-the-job training is not easy to distinguish from the learning process inherent in the work experience.

The results of the Third European Survey on Working Conditions clearly show the difference between opportunities to learn at work and participation in more structured training in an employment context (Table 3.2). Thus, while 56% of Portuguese workers say that they have the opportunity to learn new things in their job, only 10% of them have had training paid for or organised by their employer during the last twelve months. The difference between these two proportions is high in the six countries of the thematic review which participated in this survey, especially in Portugal and Spain. The difference between learning and taking formal training places additional significance on measures to recognise and validate vocational skills and experience for experienced workers, especially in countries where formal kinds of learning are little used. According to the CVTS2, participation in courses (participants as a proportion of employees in enterprises providing CVT courses) was generally quite high in all countries, ranging from 36% in Denmark to 63% in Sweden. In Spain and Portugal, participation rates were higher than the percentage of enterprises providing training, so that in those that provided courses, nearly half of the employees attended them.

Opportunities to learn new things on the job are more frequent than employer-paid or -organised training.

There are inequalities in adults' access to learning, depending on the initial level of education as well as many other demographic and socio-economic characteristics. These differences in access are similar to those in overall adult education, with higher proportions of training going to women,

The self-employed and workers in micro-enterprises have the least access to training.

Figure 3.10. **Training enterprises and type of training**

Percentage of enterprises that train by type of training, 2000

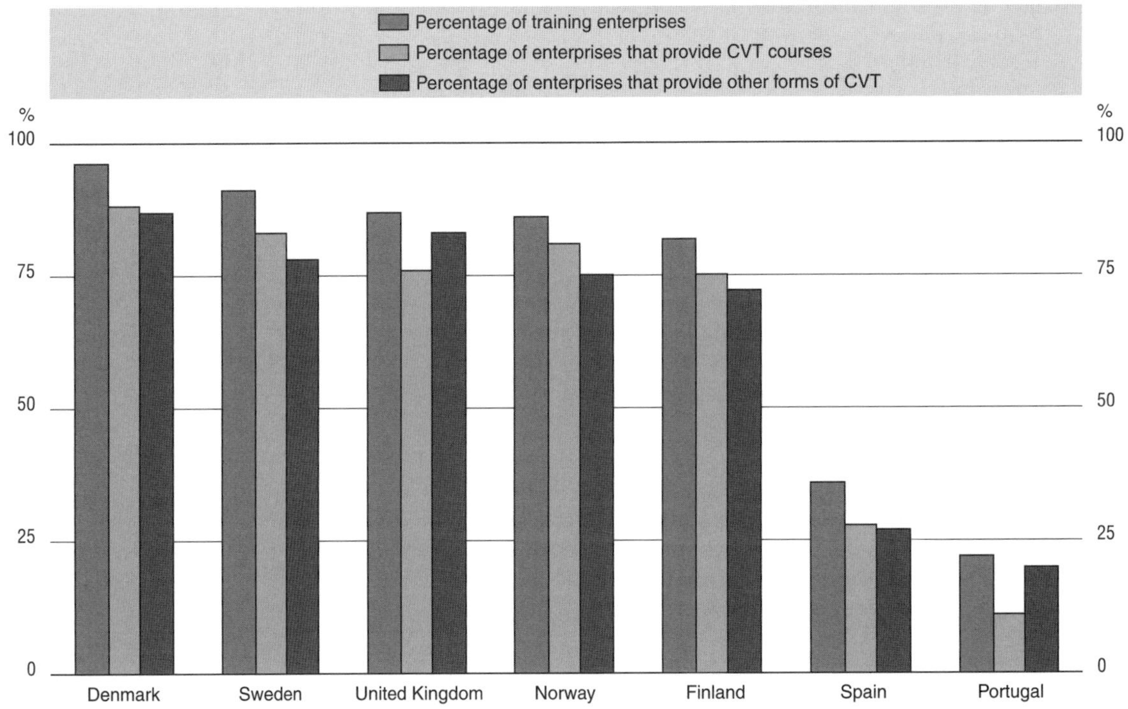

■ Percentage of training enterprises
□ Percentage of enterprises that provide CVT courses
■ Percentage of enterprises that provide other forms of CVT

Source: Eurostat, New Chronos Database, CVTS.

younger cohorts and those in larger firms. As shown in Table 3.2 and Figure 3.11 the incidence of training decreases with the size of the enterprise. Table 3.2 shows that the groups with the least access are the self-employed and workers in micro-enterprises, except in Spain and Portugal where it is the 55-64 age group. On the other hand, the fact of having a temporary contract is not a handicap to training, except in Finland and Sweden. There is a large difference in access in all countries between those who are self-employed and those who are wage earners, which is also linked to the size of the firm.

It appears that firms at the forefront of the knowledge-based economy offer more training possibilities.

In addition, there is some evidence from a number of studies that the firms at the forefront of the knowledge-based economy offer more training possibilities for their employees. These are firms that have implemented organisational changes and introduced new technologies, both factors that have been associated with higher productivity growth. An Australian study showed that firms that have undergone workplace reforms have shown a rise in relative labour productivity[6] (Crockett, 2000). In fact, high-skilled labour, physical capital and new technology are found to be complementary.

---

6. These reforms include formal training, semi-autonomous groups, income bonus schemes, quality circles or team building, staff appraisal, total quality management, computer-integrated management, skills auditing and just-in-time.

Table 3.2.   **Differences in training paid for or provided by the employer**
Ratio of participation rates to the total participation rates, 2000

	Denmark	Spain	Finland	Portugal	United Kingdom	Sweden
Participation rate[1]	52%	18%	54%	10%	50%	44%
Learning new things at work	87%	65%	92%	56%	77%	83%
Ratios of the participation rate of each category to the total participation rate						
Gender						
Men	0.93	0.96	1.02	0.99	0.98	0.92
Women	1.08	1.08	0.97	1.01	1.03	1.08
Age group						
25-34 years	1.00	1.29	1.00	1.66	1.07	1.01
35-44 years	1.05	1.12	1.05	0.96	0.98	0.92
45-54 years	1.06	0.87	0.96	1.04	1.03	1.08
55-64 years	0.73	0.22	0.97	0.15	0.60	0.96
Type of contract						
Permanent	1.05	1.17	1.11	1.35	1.11	1.06
Temporary	1.05	1.16	0.77	1.79	1.09	0.89
Interim	0.78	0.61	. .	. .	1.11	1.16
Apprenticeship and other programmes	1.28	2.11	0.24	4.73	. .	0.67
Unknown	0.75	0.60	0.77	0.24	0.55	0.69
Status						
Self-employed	0.66	0.66	0.81	0.31	0.44	0.63
Wage and salary earners	1.02	1.12	1.04	1.26	1.09	1.05
Firm size						
Less than 9 employees	0.65	0.62	0.83	0.51	0.68	0.76
100-499 employees	1.07	1.08	1.10	1.50	1.11	1.07
More than 500 employees	1.26	2.73	1.34	2.56	1.25	1.33

1.   The question asked is: "Over the past 12 months, have you undergone training paid for or provided by your employer, or yourself if you are self-employed, to improve your skills, or not?"
Source: European Foundation for the Improvement of Living and Working Conditions, Third European Survey on Working Conditions, 2000.

Analysis of firm-level practices shows a strong correlation between information technology, human capital and workplace organisation (Bresnahan and Brynjolfsson, 1999; OECD, 1999). Other studies have found links between the introduction of ICTs and the demand for skills or skills upgrading (Baldwin *et al.*, 1997; Berman, Bound and Machin, 1997; Machin, Ryan and van Reenan, 1996). At the same time, enterprises that adopt new workplace practices (such as teamwork, flatter management structures and job rotation), which are also found to have more highly skilled workforces, are prone to train their workers more than other firms (Pil and Macduffie, 1996; Gittleman, Gorrigan and Joyce, 1998; OECD, 1999). According to a European survey analysing firms and training (the EPOC survey), while 39% of firms that implemented new work practices provided training, only 27% that did not implement new work practices did so. Other surveys across OECD countries have consistently shown that the incidence of training is higher in firms that adopt new work practices than is the case in other firms (Arnal *et al.*, 2001).

Higher wages, more training?

The distribution of wages by training shows that training rates are higher for top wage earners, according to IALS datas (Statistics Canada and Human Resource Development Canada, 2001). In all IALS countries, the bottom 40% of wage earners received less training that the top 60% of wage earners. There was a significant and positive relationship between adult education

Training rates are higher for top wage earners...

Figure 3.11. **Adult learning by firm size**

Ratio of participation rates by firm size to the total participation rates for population 25-64 years old,[1] 2000

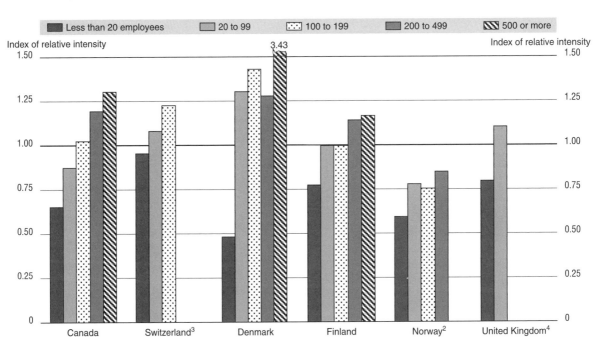

1. A ratio superior to 1 implies that the proportion of persons in adult learning in the specific category is above the average country participation rate; a ratio between 0 and 1, below the average rate.
2. 200 or more employees instead of 200 to 499.
3. 100 or more employees instead of 100 to 199.
4. Less than 25 instead of less than 20; more than 25 instead of 20 to 99.
Source: OECD Secretariat questionnaire on Adult Learning. See Annex 1 for details.

participation and average wages. This evidence can be explained in several different ways. Training rates are mediated by occupations or by industrial sectors where workers are employed. And there is a relationship between wages and occupations: high-skilled occupations, which also have higher training incidence, offer higher wages. Also, it might be easier for people with higher wages to purchase training.

... and training itself seems to have a significant positive impact on wages.

Other evidence has shown that training may also lead to higher wages. According to one study in the United Kingdom, training has a significant positive impact on wage growth, even after controlling for its endogeneity (Arulampalam and Booth, 1998). Another study in the United States showed that formal training has a significant positive impact on wages, after controlling for endogeneity of training as well (Loewenstein and Spletzer, 1997). Yet another study in the United States found that company training and outside seminar work had a positive impact on wages (Veum, 1995). An OECD study (1999) showed that in many countries, training had a significant and positive relationship with wages and that the earnings gains from training are higher for some categories of workers who are less likely to be trained. But the relationship between wages and training is not a simple one. The question of causality has not yet been sufficiently resolved and requires further analysis.

3.2. The supply of adult education: different modes of provision

There are different models of provision that include a broad range of actors across the board, from public or private to non-governmental organisations. Some provide broader training opportunities, some focus more on vocational training, others on basic literacy or other learning opportunities.

Adult learning providers include public, private, and NGOs.

The provision of adult learning across the thematic review countries reveals a quite complex system of training suppliers, with a relatively high number of diverse institutions – private, including the enterprise, and public – or different patterns of co-operation, making systems quite opaque. The role of informal learning is also important but will not be taken into consideration in this section because provision is based mostly on individual development. Distance education, especially education based on new technologies, is of growing importance in adult learning, as the use of the Internet and e-learning contribute to dissolving barriers across countries and allows for new providers to enter this market. However, a number of providers of distance education have expanded their barriers to the virtual world, and are therefore considered in their relevant initial categories.

Distance learning, the Internet and e-learning have allowed new providers to enter this market.

It is difficult to distinguish between providers of education, because a provider can be considered the physical institution where the education is undertaken or the institution that requests the training be undertaken or that finances it. Firms or the public sector can provide training, but it can be taken in commercial institutions, special training centres or even university or college campuses that are hired for the purpose. Furthermore, the lines between the private and public sector are fading, as different institutions that provide training want to amortise their investment costs in physical capital (training machines, space, etc.). A number of public vocational training centres visited during the review have or are in the process of following this line by leasing their classroom facilities for private enterprise training. Especially at the local level, there is good co-ordination among the different partners involved in training. Firms can obtain the use of public training facilities while the public sector can learn from firms' experiences. The following sections review the different types of providers of adult learning in a broad sense.

Classroom instruction is still thriving

In terms of physical space and methods for learning, one can distinguish classroom instruction, instruction in a working environment, distance learning, workshops, etc. The ELFS data show that classroom instruction is by far the most important mode of provision in all countries, with almost more than half of people training doing so in that setting (Table 3.3). The only exception is the United Kingdom, where there are similar rates for those in class and for those receiving instruction in a working environment. This is followed by instruction in a working environment and both work experience and complementary classroom instruction in Finland, Norway, Sweden and Portugal. Distance learning is high in proportional terms in Sweden, the United Kingdom and Spain.

The classroom remains the most frequent setting for instruction.

Participation rates in different types of learning vary according to labour force status, except in Portugal. More detailed analysis of the ELFS data, not shown here, reveals that most inactive and unemployed populations follow classroom instruction as the main route for adult learning, especially in

The type of learning pursued can be linked to labour force status.

Table 3.3. **Adult learners by mode of provision**

Percentage of adult learners 25-64 years old by mode of provision, 2000

	Classroom instruction	Instruction in a working environment	Instruction combining both work experience and complementary classroom instruction	Distance learning, correspondance courses	Self-learning	Conferences, seminars, workshops
Denmark	80.1	. .	2.8	1.2	. .	15.9
Finland	53.3	12.8	12.0	2.4	1.9	17.6
Norway	64.5	24.2	8.7	2.6	. .	. .
Portugal	81.4	4.1	8.4	0.4	. .	5.7
Spain	73.0	1.6	1.9	6.6	12.8	4.0
Sweden	48.5	22.6	11.3	17.5	. .	. .
United Kingdom	41.8	43.3	2.2	8.8	3.1	0.7

Source: Eurostat, European Union Labour Force Survey (2001).

Table 3.4. **Supply of adult learning**

Percentage distribution of training by type of training, 1994-98

	Percentage of training or education given by					
	University or higher education establishment	Further education college	Commercial organisation[1]	Non-profit organisation	Company	Other
Canada	12.0	13.5	22.0	12.3	31.5	8.7
Denmark	4.5	34.4	20.6	13.0	20.1	7.4
Finland	12.9	19.7	19.6	10.9	33.7	3.2
Norway	19.7	7.1	32.3	8.6	23.8	8.5
Switzerland	7.2	0.2	18.4	11.2	17.0	45.9
United Kingdom	6.6	14.8	26.8	5.5	38.3	8.1

1. Includes producers or suppliers of equipment.
Source: International Adult Literacy Survey (1994-98).

Denmark and Norway. In Spain, Sweden and the United Kingdom, most inactive populations also used the classroom as the main venue, but there were variations across the employed and unemployed populations.

Employed populations train in a working environment, while unemployed populations use a combination of work experience and complementary classroom settings. These are more in tune with active labour market policies that focus on giving the unemployed training together with work experience. The United Kingdom, Sweden, Portugal and Finland used this mode to a larger extent.

Distance learning is used in Sweden for those in the labour force, employed and unemployed, and to some extent for those employed in Spain and unemployed in the United Kingdom.

Broad range of suppliers

Table 3.4 reflects the variety of adult learning suppliers. Employers stand out as the main providers of training in most countries, except for Denmark and Switzerland.

Canada and the United Kingdom have similar patterns: firms are the predominant suppliers, followed by commercial organisations and further education colleges. Switzerland is a special case in that it has the highest incidence of training in the category of "other" provider. The private and not-for-profit sector is quite large in this country. In Denmark, Finland and Norway, special adult education centres, including universities, higher education establishments and further education colleges play a more important role than in other countries.

Learning enterprises

Across countries, between 20 and 25% of training takes place in the firm on average, with the exception of United Kingdom where there have been efforts to make training part of the culture of firms; there the figure is almost 40%, a large amount that reveals the increasing role of the firm in providing training. The results presented in Figure 3.10 also indicate the role of the enterprise in training. Larger firms use training as an incentive to attract potential workers and train employees for their specific needs. Most of the larger enterprises visited during the reviews have created their own training centres within the firm. As they were not finding the skills they required in the labour market, it was more efficient for them to design and implement their own training programmes.

Between a fifth and a quarter of training takes place in the firm.

Larger firms have a number of advantages in providing training. They have internal job markets that can allow employees internal mobility, because jobs that match new qualifications can be obtained through training. It also facilitates workers remaining with the firm because of internal connections, familiarity with the culture, and the possibility of establishing long-term careers. Enterprises also benefit from the internal mobility of their workers. Long-term planning allows an upgrading of employee skills in accordance with changes in the firm. Finally, economies of scale in training are associated with greater efficiency, because of the use of space and other resources, the number of trainees and the development of more firm-specific skills and courses, which can also contribute to the development of internal networks that can bring their own intangible benefits. Also, larger firms have organised unions that can also facilitate training plans for employees.

Training provided by larger firms offers advantages to both the firm and the employee.

The knowledge-based economy has increased the importance of training within firms. As a tool for adapting to technological change and for developing new workplace practices and other firm-specific skills, firm-based training is effective. The concept of "learning enterprises" has become popular across knowledge-based sectors. It is especially the larger enterprises that are able to define their own training programmes and design workers' training trajectories. More and more, human resources departments are creating their own training divisions.

"Learning enterprises" in the knowledge-based sectors are able to define their own training programmes.

Commercial organisations

The role of private providers is important in the adult learning market. Their role differs across the countries visited. In some, private providers offer courses that give formal qualifications, while in others they focus on non-formal qualifications. Some private providers, for instance consultancy firms,

Private providers offer courses leading to both formal and non-formal qualifications.

supply training such as computer courses, management training and personal development.

Depending on the country, private providers can benefit from public financial assistance in different ways. In Norway for example, they may offer courses in which students can receive financial assistance from the State Education Loan Fund. In Sweden, almost half of all labour market training is carried out by private educational providers and approximately one-third by Lernia (formerly the AmuGruppen), a state-owned educational company.

Temporary employment agencies also offer training...

Training has also been introduced by temporary employment agencies. Companies of this kind often provide temporary workers with a free general basic education for word processing or spreadsheets for example. Autor (2000) sought to explain this practice, which at first sight seems inconsistent with the classic market paradigm. He suggests that training plays a role in telling temporary work agencies about the skills of workers who approach them and in their selection. A rapid assessment of individuals' skills and their achievements in basic computer knowledge enables them to serve their clients' needs in a more positive way.

... and are experimenting with new methods.

The temporary employment agency sector is also experimenting with new training methods. In the last few years, with a shortage of certain skilled workers, these agencies have competed with firms through measures to attract skilled temporary workers, especially by signing training agreements with them. They are particularly interested in validation of work experience. Indeed, through successive assignments, temporary workers accumulate know-how but only derive unconnected experiences which are not easy to sell in the labour market where diplomas and certificates count for a great deal. That is why validation of work experience provides recognition and certification of professional experience, especially valuable to temporary workers with few formal qualifications.

Adult education institutions

The variety of institutions providing adult education is extremely broad.

There is a broad range of public or semi-public institutions across countries that target supply of adult education and training. They may vary in terminology and in types of training provided. These can be higher education establishments such as universities or polytechnics, colleges, vocational institutions and specialised liberal education institutions and special schools for adult basic education and upper secondary schools. The variety of institutions providing adult education is extremely broad and contributes to the opacity of the existing system.

College and university campuses provide a large proportion of public adult learning programmes in some countries.

The role of college or university campuses is important in the United Kingdom, Canada, Denmark and Finland, because they provide a large proportion of public adult learning programmes. Community colleges and other types of campuses, including adult learning schools, are one of the methods through which public provision reaches potential participants. These can be generally centred on provision of less vocationally oriented diplomas or non-degree granting, such as literacy programmes. Students can enrol for retraining, to upgrade training, or for basic skills instruction in community colleges, further education colleges in the United Kingdom, and polytechnics in several countries. These adult education institutions also provide language instruction for immigrants. In Spain there has been an increase of adult learning in universities, especially in postgraduate degrees and in programmes for the elderly, with nineteen universities having such programmes.

Community colleges

In Canada, community colleges offer career-oriented and technical training, as well as university transfer programmes and general education leading to diplomas or certificates. The private colleges (or schools) in Canada comprise what has been referred to as an alternative system for skills training for adults. British Columbia has both community colleges providing one- and two-year diplomas, and university colleges providing these diplomas as well as a limited number of university degrees. There is a vast array of programme options such as one-year certificate and two-year diploma programmes in occupational areas. Students can go on to university if they want, either through transfer agreements or through the university college option; most colleges offer various forms of co-operative education combining working and learning, an attractive option for many adults; and all colleges offer adult basic education (though waiting lists are long). Colleges also tend to have special programmes for specific groups, like social assistance recipients and aboriginal students.

Further education colleges

Further education colleges focus on providing education opportunities for people after compulsory schooling age. In England, they make up the largest education sector for those past compulsory schooling age, with approximately 4 million students each year, or around 7% of the population. Responsibility for funding the sector lies with the Learning and Skills Council, and of the students on council-funded provision 82% are adults. There are currently 403 colleges made up of general further education and tertiary colleges, sixth form colleges, agriculture and horticulture colleges, art design and performing arts colleges, and specialist colleges.

Folk high schools

Folk high schools are widespread in Sweden, Denmark, Norway and Finland. In Sweden they are generally run by popular movements and NGOs, although some are run by local authorities and county councils. They do not have standard curricula, and each school makes its own decisions regarding teaching plans. Boarding is an important part of the study environment. In addition to tuition, many schools offer cultural and leisure activities. In some places folk high schools are day schools, especially in the larger cities. Subjects and courses vary substantially. Some teach arts and crafts, others may teach how to be a recreation leader, and some may offer music. But in most, a large proportion of the studies are focused on core subjects such as language, mathematics and social studies, corresponding to what is taught at secondary school or in municipal adult education. These courses may also qualify students for higher education at university.

Folk high schools, which decide their own curricula, offer basic education courses as well as cultural and leisure activities.

Denmark has approximately 100 folk high schools, although they are very different from the traditional folk high schools in their philosophy. These are private schools organised as private foundations that decide on the content and form of the teaching themselves. They offer adult students (over

17½ years of age) general education and may within that framework give individual subjects or subject groups an important place. The concept of "general education" means that the aim of the schools is personal development: they offer long courses (of 5-32 weeks' duration) and short courses (of 1-4 weeks' duration) and they do not hold any examinations or tests. The average age of the students in the long courses is 22-23 years; it is considerably higher in the short courses, which take place in the summer season.

Adult education-specific institutions

Adult education institutions, usually run by local authorities, provide basic adult and upper secondary education.

There is a broad array of adult education-specific institutions across countries. These are run by education authorities, normally at the local or municipal level, and provide basic adult education and upper secondary education.

Finland has over 262 adult education centres that provide general and interest-oriented education. Although originally created for adult vocational training, they evolved to offer learning opportunities for the entire adult population. Most centres (around 90%) are owned by municipalities. There are general upper secondary schools for adults, who can complete basic and general upper secondary education and take matriculation examination and also study individual subjects, mainly languages.

In Sweden, municipal adult education centres are widespread and play an important role in the provision of compulsory and upper secondary level education for adults. They have been the main focus of the recent Adult Education Initiative to provide upper secondary education to those adults who lacked it.

In Spain, most public adult learning is provided in adult education centres, run by autonomous regional governments (secretariats for adult education or the like), by municipalities or by local authorities, and includes both formal and non-formal education. Sometimes these specific adult education centres have their own buildings, and sometimes they share their physical space with other public education centres.

Vocational training centres

Vocational training centres have mainly targeted the unemployed, but many are now expanding their role to accommodate all adult learners.

Almost all countries have specific vocational training centres for young people or for adults. These provide general vocational training courses and are the main instruments for active labour market policies for the unemployed. However, during the 1990s and even recently, they have been changing their role in some countries. They are opening up not only to cater to the unemployed, but also to provide in-service training for companies or training for other purposes.

AMU in Denmark is the adult vocational training system, designed to offer participants vocational skills and to solve restructuring and adaptation problems on the labour market. Vocational education and training aiming at enhancing adults' competencies is also offered within the VET programmes (Adult VET, VET single subjects offered as open education, basic adult education). In Finland there are 48 Vocational Adult Education Centres, which can be linked to a limited company, a foundation, municipalities or a joint municipal authority. They were originally created for the training of the unemployed but have evolved to offer vocational learning opportunities for the entire adult population. In Norway, technical schools are public schools owned and managed by the counties. The main purpose of technical schools is to provide education for persons having a relevant trade or journeyman's certificate and a minimum of two years' background in a specific trade covered by the Education Act. Technical schools provide training that builds on the existing practical experience of students. Simultaneously, they provide leadership education.

In Spain, the INEM has a large network of specialised vocational training centres for the unemployed. These can be specialised INEM centres or private providers that have special arrangements with the Ministry of Labour or with the autonomous regional governments to be "collaborative centres". A similar initiative has been created in the United Kingdom. The Centres of Vocational Excellence aim to address skills deficits by creating a network of quality, specialist provision tightly focused on skills needs of business and industry across a range of occupations. They plan to develop new and enhance existing vocational provision nationally, by sectors, regionally and locally, and will seek to give a greater number of individuals from all backgrounds access to quality vocational training.

Non-profit or community-based organisations

A less visible and largely undocumented contribution to adult learning is made by a range of community-based organisations. They are established to address special issues (such as adult literacy), or to meet the needs of special groups (such as immigrants, the rural poor, persons with physical or learning disabilities, members of specific ethnic or cultural groups, displaced workers, or adults with low levels of literacy). Typically, local agencies or advocacy groups identify unmet needs, and then seek funding from public institutions. They exist in most of the countries reviewed and can include institutions like employer associations, voluntary organisations or trade unions. They represent around 10% of the training market.

Community-based organisations address special issues and meet the needs of special groups.

In Canada for example, adult basic education is largely provided in community-based organisations, even though curricula and syllabuses are being developed within formal educational institutions. The advantages of these programmes are that they exist in the communities where their students live, and instructors can come to know their students. They are not "school-like" and may be more welcoming to individuals who lack a history of success in school. They provide different types of social and moral support and sometimes help with other services (housing or health, for example), in addition to literacy instruction. Community-based programmes are also committed to holistic approaches, including citizenship and community education.

In Canada they are the setting for most adult basic education.

A specific non-profit model of educational institutions can be found in Switzerland, under the name of Migros "club schools"(Box 7.3). These are "education clubs" that form a large network of comprehensive training centres under the aegis of an agro-food distribution company. They started in 1944 with language courses for adults and broadened in the 1950s to handicrafts, arts and sport. Since then, the clubs have extended their coverage to more vocational subjects. One example is computing, with Microsoft diploma courses for adults. Languages account for 40% of all courses, leisure-related subjects 34%, and business courses 20%. They are open to private individuals and firms alike. Funding comes partly from enrolment fees and partly from

Migros "club schools" in Switzerland began with language courses and broadened their scope to include business and leisure-related courses.

the "cultural 1%" contribution which makes up the shortfall between teaching revenues and the centres' operating costs, which amount to tens of millions of Swiss francs every year.

Study associations in the Nordic countries offer learning opportunities ranging from formal education to study circles.

Study associations are also an important network of adult learning supply and have a strong tradition in Nordic countries. They are based on popular enlightenment traditions, based and organised by people's own institutions, and organise a broad array of adult education opportunities, from formal education (except in Denmark) to study circles. They can be backed and supported by various popular movements and non-governmental organisations. For example, political parties run a study association sponsored by women's, youth, sports, trade and other organisations supporting the party in question. On the other hand, many centres wish to underline their independence from party politics. Their background organisations may then include various organisations that have not committed themselves politically, such as the Christian Study Centre run by organisations close to Finland's Evangelical Lutheran Church, and the Swedish Study Circle Centre (in Finland), which caters to the needs of the entire Swedish-speaking minority.

In Norway, education and training organised by study associations has its origin in the tradition of popular enlightenment. The associations are voluntary, covering a variety of ideological interests as well as the interests of the disabled. Study associations are responsible for organising education unrestricted by the set curricula and examinations of the public educational system. They determine their own study plans and the professional content of the courses. Study associations offer their courses to members as well as to the general public in all parts of the country. The most common way of organising adult education is to establish so called study circles with five to ten participants, with or without a teacher. Study associations can also organise formal education.

Adult and Community Learning helps tackle disadvantage, exclusion and neighbourhood renewal.

Adult and Community Learning (ACL) in the United Kingdom occurs in a variety of settings, including community-based and informal venues. Often it does not lead to a formal qualification. Its wide range of provision helps tackle disadvantage, exclusion and neighbourhood renewal as well as contributing to creating a culture of commitment to learning.

Popular universities in Spain aim to promote social interest, education, training and culture.

Popular universities operate in more than 240 municipalities in Spain. Their objective is to promote social interest, education, training and culture, and to improve the quality of life for the individuals and the community. They report directly to the cities, communities, or non-profit-making associations, developing a mediator's role between the administration and the citizens. Given their close ties to the cities, their programmes, activities and services are focused on meeting the local citizens' educational and cultural needs and, in particular, to contributing to personal and social change.

Distance and virtual learning

Some traditional distance learning institutions are shifting towards providing education in the virtual world.

Almost all countries reviewed have traditional distance learning institutions and have set into motion new virtual learning institutions for adults. In fact, a number of traditional distance learning institutions are shifting towards providing education in the virtual world. E-learning has the potential to provide new learning models for adults who reject the traditional classroom provision. It also has the ability to overcome barriers that adults face in terms of time and space by granting a certain degree of flexibility in learning. It can help increase access, bringing learning opportunities to remote geographical areas and to adults who are faced with daily constraints to learning. The process is slowly taking off: while the initial stages brought about many new providers, there is a focus now on trying to use ICT effectively for adult learning delivery. Efforts are under way to design e-learning quality content for adults; the quality of courses seems to be a problem since current virtual offerings are still at the early stages of development.

In most countries there have been public efforts geared towards the establishment of virtual centres for adults. In Finland, virtual studies are possible for all education levels. Norway has the NKI Distance Education and Norway-net with IT for Open Learning (NITOL). In the United Kingdom, the University for Industry/learndirect aims to drive up demand for learning, to help adults improve their employability by acquiring new knowledge and skills, and to help businesses become more competitive. It is developing learning materials that allow people and businesses to learn in "bite-sized chunks", online through the Internet at a pace and at times that suits them, at learning centres, at home or at work. The Mentor Programme in Spain is a web-based learning forum for adults to study a broad range of educational activities. It is an open system based on modules which can be followed at home or in specific classrooms located throughout the country.

Countries have been working toward establishing virtual centres for adult learning...

There has also been an increase in the number of private providers that are focusing on e-learning. Some are providing IT skills while others focus on tertiary education, and there is a broad provision of company training through e-learning. One example, a private virtual learning enterprise named smartforce (*www.smartforce.com*) provides training by purchase in information technology; business; e-business; management; healthcare learning; and environmental, safety, and health training. Virtual corporate universities and regular virtual universities that provide post-tertiary degrees have also been created. More and more, the borders across different types of provision are blurring and virtual platforms are trying to cater to a large diversity of needs.

... and private providers have been focusing on e-learning as the means for delivering tertiary education and company training.

Efforts also seem to be under way to try to expand collaboration between the private and the public sector for the adoption of good learning practices in terms of network infrastructure, access to hardware or internet connectivity, and digital content. A new OECD activity on ICT and education policy will explore a number of these issues further. Focusing on initial and adult education, it will analyse how education policies can help to ensure that the use of ICT leads to positive educational outcomes: better teaching, improved learning, fairer access to educational opportunities. It will explore how ICT is influencing the ways that educational institutions operate, and how ICT is influencing educational policies.

A new OECD activity will explore how education policies can ensure that good ICT learning practices lead to positive outcomes.

3.3. Trends, needs and priorities

The analysis of participation in training as the representation of demand, together with an analysis of the overall supply of learning, can provide a general overview of the situation of adult learning in the countries reviewed. Some broad patterns of participation across countries were observed.

Overall country groupings emerge

The Nordic countries, with Canada, Switzerland and the United Kingdom, have high overall participation rates in adult learning.

- The Nordic countries, together with Canada, Switzerland and the United Kingdom, have high overall participation rates in adult learning. In most of these countries, except Canada, participation rates have increased over time, revealing the continued investment in adult learning.

- Spain and Portugal have lower participation rates and there is no considerable increase over time in adult learning. It seems to be a growing field, with the entry of new providers into the market. These two countries have similar participation rates and similar patterns of training across the board. They have stronger inequalities in terms of access to training as compared to other countries, except for the unemployed, showing the strong impact of the European Union active labour market policies. The fact that Spain did not participate in the IALS makes comparative analysis somewhat more difficult.

- Canada and the United Kingdom reveal a similar pattern of distribution of training, with wide inequalities and a large private sector involvement focused on vocational purposes. Switzerland follows a similar predominantly private provision pattern, but there is a large provision for non-vocational purposes in which the private sector is involved. In these countries there seem to be broader differences between those who receive training and those who do not.

- The Nordic countries have a social model of distribution of learning opportunities, which seems to be geared towards reaching a larger proportion of adults. There are fewer inequalities than in other countries in training rates across different indicators such as age, educational attainment, occupational status or even wages. This performance can be due to the type of delivery systems of adult learning, the role of popular movements, the quality of initial education systems, or the general commitment to public provision of education. According to a comparative study of the Nordic adult education systems, the general high participation rates in adult education cannot be attributed to high levels of public support for adult education. However, public support seems to be a significant factor in the provision of adult education for the low-skilled population or those with lower schooling or literacy levels. It could be the case that public support for the disadvantaged groups is the main defining characteristic of Nordic approaches to adult education (NORD, 2001).

Who is left out? Training gaps

The evidence presented in this chapter reveals that there are groups that are over-represented and groups that are under-represented in training. There are inequities in access and participation in learning according to different socio-demographic, personal and economic factors. The specific groups that do not participate in learning vary across countries, but they include the following:

- Those with the lowest educational attainment and lowest literacy levels. These can be elderly populations or dropouts from the educational system.

- Populations over 50 years old in most countries.

- Long-term unemployed people with low educational attainment.

- Workers in small and medium-sized enterprises who have difficulties in accessing training opportunities. Lack of replacement during training time can be a factor.

- Workers in blue-collar occupations who have very few opportunities for training.

- There are wage-related inequalities in access to adult education. Lower-wage earners participate at much lower rates than high-wage earners. Part of the issue here is that employer-based training tends to be concentrated on high-skilled occupations and well-educated employees.

There are inequities in participation in learning according to different socio-demographic, personal and economic factors.

There are specific profiles that can be characteristic of those groups that do not receive training opportunities. A good example could be older workers in blue-collar low-skilled occupations, earning the lowest wages (in, *e.g.*, construction or low-skilled services). Yet another example would be an unemployed low-skilled person between 40 and 60 years old living in a rural area.

Are these low participation rates in adult learning due to lack of access to training opportunities? Across countries, a large fraction of those who did not take training would have wanted to participate. Chapter 5 shows that among a wide array of reasons for not undertaking learning, the most frequent was lack of time in all reviewed countries. Another frequent reason is the lack of financing or funding for learning. Together with reasons relating to family responsibilities, these can be marked as the most important factors for not learning, but only for those who would have liked to. The unavailability of a training course was a reason included in a number of responses, but not a major one – implying that lack of supply does not seem to be a major problem. For enterprise provision of training, according to the CVTS2, more than 70% of enterprises that did not provide training, did not do so because the existing skills of their employees were appropriate or they recruited people with the required skills. A smaller proportion stated that the employee workload did not allow them to provide training. It can also be a matter of distribution: the provision of adult learning across countries reveals a quite complex system of training suppliers, with a relatively high number of diverse institutions – private (including the enterprise) and public – and different patterns of co-operation. But finally, there is a broad array of potential learners who, apart from time or the availability of financial resources, require motivation to return to learning: those who did not have success in their schooling experiences, or who do not see the real, positive difference it can make in their lives.

Low participation rates in adult learning appear to stem mainly from the lack of three things: time, financing, and motivation.

BIBLIOGRAPHY

ARNAL, E., W. OK and R. TORRES (2001),
"Knowledge, Work Organisation and Economic Growth", Labour Market and Social Policy Occasional Paper No. 50, OECD, Paris.

ARULAMPALAM, W. and A.L. BOOTH (1998),
"Learning and Earning: Do Multiple Training Events Pay? – A Decade of Evidence from a Cohort of Young British Men", Warwick University and Essex University, mimeo.

AUTOR, D.H. (2000),
"Why Do Temporary Help Firms Provide Free General Skills Training", NBER Working Paper No. 7637, National Bureau of Economic Research, Cambridge, MA.

BALDWIN, J.R., T. GRAY and J. JOHNSON (1997),
"Technology Induced Wage Premia in Canadian Manufacturing Plants during the 1980s", Working Paper No. 92, Micro-Economics Analysis Division, Statistics Canada, Ottawa.

BARRETT, A. and P.J. O'CONNELL (1999),
"Does Training Generally Work? The Returns to In-Company Training", IZA Discussion Papers No. 51.

BERMAN, E., J. BOUND and S. MACHIN (1997),
"Implications of Skilled Biased Technological Change: International Evidence", NBER Working Paper No. 6166, National Bureau of Economic Research, Cambridge, MA.

BOUDARD, E. (2001),
Literacy Proficiency, Earnings and Recurrent Training: A *Ten Country Comparative Study*, Institute of International Education, Stockholm University, Stockholm.

BOYER, R. (2001),
"Promoting Learning in the Enterprise: The Lessons of International Comparisons in the Light of Economic Theory", Communication prepared for the OECD-KRIVET International Conference on Adult Learning Policies, 5-7 December, Seoul.

BRESNAHAN, T.F. and E. BRYNJOLFSSON (1999),
"Information Technology, Workplace Organisation and the Demand for Skilled Labour: Firm Level Evidence", NBER Working Paper No. 7136, National Bureau of Economic Research, Cambridge, MA.

CROCKETT, G. (2000),
"Can we Explain Australian Productivity Growth? Some Evidence from the AWIRS", University of Tasmania School of Economics Discussion Paper 2000/04.

DEARDEN, L, H. REED and J. van REENEN (2000),
"Who Gains when Workers Train?", The Institute for Fiscal Studies Working Papers WP00/04.

DYBOWSKI, G. (1998),
"New Technologies and Work Organisation: Impact on Vocational Education and Training", in M. Tessaring (ed.), *Vocational Education and Training – The European Research Field*, Background Report 1998, Vol. I, CEDEFOP, Thesaloniki.

EUROSTAT (2000),
European Labour Force Survey, Brussels.

EUROSTAT (2001),
New Chronos Database, CVTS2, Brussels.

FINEGOLD, D. and G. MASON (1996),
"National Training Systems and Industrial Performance: US-European Matched-Plant Comparisons", Paper prepared for the conference "New Empirical Research on Employer Training: Who pays? Who benefits?", Cornell University.

GITTLEMAN, M., M. GORRIGAN and M. JOYCE (1998),
"'Flexible' Workplace Practices: Evidence from a Nationally Representative Survey", *Industrial and Labor Relations Review*, pp. 99-115.

GREEN, F., D. ASHTON and A. FELSTEAD (2001),
"Estimating the Determinants of Supply of Computing, Problem-solving, Communication, Social and Teamworking Skills", *Oxford Economic Papers*, Vol. 53, July.

KILEY, M. (1999),
"The Supply of Skilled Labour and Skilled Biased Technological Progress", *The Economic Journal*, No. 109, October, pp. 708-724.

LOEWENSTEIN, M.A. and J.R. SPLETZER (1997),
"Belated Training: The Relationship between Training, Tenure and Wages", US Bureau of Labour Statistics, September, mimeo.

LOUNDS, J. (1999),
"Labour Productivity in Australian Workplaces: Evidence from the AWIRS", Melbourne Institute Working Paper No. 19/99.

MACHIN, S., A. RYAN and J. van REENAN (1996),
"Technology and Changes in Skill Structure: Evidence from an International Panel of Industries", Center for Economic Performance, Discussion Paper Series, London School of Economics and Political Science.

NORD (2001),
Curious Minds: Nordic Adult Education Compared, Copenhagen.

OECD (1998),
"Harmonisation of Training Statistics", Paris (*www.oecd.org/edu/adultlearning*).

OECD (1999),
"Training of Adult Workers in OECD Countries: Measurement and Analysis", OECD *Employment Outlook*, Paris, June.

OECD (2001a),
"Skills for the Knowledge Economy", *Education Policy Analysis*, Chapter 4, Paris.

OECD (2001b),
OECD *Science, Technology and Industry Scoreboard: Towards a Knowledge-based Economy*, Paris.

OECD (2001c),
"The Characteristics and Quality of Service Sector Jobs", OECD *employment Outlook*, Paris, June.

OECD (2001d),
"Thematic Review on Adult Learning: Highlights, Emerging Issues and Lessons to Date", Paris, (*www.oecd.org/edu/adultlearning*).

OECD (2002),
"Investment in Human Capital through Post-compulsory Education and Training", OECD *Economic Outlook*, December 2001, No. 70, Paris.

OECD and STATISTICS CANADA (2000),
Literacy in the Information Age, Paris and Ottawa.

OSTERMAN, P. (1995),
"Skill, Training, and Work Organisation in American Establishments", *Industrial Relations*, Vol. 34, No. 2.

PIL, F.K. and J.P. MACDUFFIE (1996),
"The Adoption of High-Involvement Work Practices", *Industrial Relations*, Vol. 35, No. 3, pp. 423-455.

STATISTICS CANADA and HUMAN RESOURCE DEVELOPMENT CANADA (2001),
"A Report on Adult Education and Training in Canada: Learning a Living", Ottawa.

VEUM, J.R. (1995),
"Sources of Training and Their Impact on Wages", *Industrial and Labour Relations Review*, No. 4, pp. 812-826.

Chapter 4

OVERVIEW OF COUNTRY POLICIES AND PRACTICES

As part of the wider perspective of lifelong learning, adult learning has in recent years slowly begun to be mainstreamed into education and human resource policies. It is now clearly recognised as an important tool for equity and social cohesion, for economic and social development in knowledge-based societies, for reducing unemployment and skills shortages, for personal development, and for furthering citizenship and democratic values. This chapter will show that all countries visited for the thematic review have taken some type of specific policy measure targeting adult learning at the national level. These range from general action plans to increase learning opportunities for all adults, to more specific programmes designed to upgrade skills, target particular adult sub-groups of the population or increase training opportunities for those in the labour force. A number of these reforms are also geared towards improving the performance and efficiency of adult education in a more integrated approach that is learner-centred. Efforts have been made towards greater system efficiency through providing general frameworks for policy development, improving co-ordination among different (including the social) partners, rationalising existing supply, focusing on cost effectiveness, and taking greater account of individual needs. Decentralisation has been an important aspect of this process.

Overall, the analysis reveals that adult learning has indeed reached national policy-making agendas. Common patterns emerge, such as approaches to step up learning opportunities for individuals, to providing basic educational attainment to those who do not have it, to bringing about a holistic approach focusing on potential learners and to recognising informal and non-formal learning processes. Policy responses vary however, according to economic and social contexts, the historical development of education systems, and political structures and systems in place. From the diversity of policies and practices, it is difficult to understand the overall country funding arrangements in place and whether they have reached the multiplicity of objectives established. The role of the enterprise in funding training is quite important in this respect. Finally, it is important to provide better, more clearly defined intermediate objectives and better means of measuring the efficiency and effectiveness of different programmes and approaches in light of those objectives.

4.1. A diversity of objectives for public intervention in adult learning

The degree to which countries decide to invest resources depends on whether they feel it is necessary to devote public efforts to stimulating adult learning and whether there should be public intervention in adult education markets or whether they should be left to the private sector. Chapter 2 has evoked a number of reasons – economic, social and personal – for a step-up in skills development. Chapter 3 has shown that a large proportion of adult learning is supplied by the private sector (firms or commercial organisations). Do these growing requirements for skills and the high proportion of private sector learning imply that governments should participate in the supply of learning for adults? Public spending is limited and the fact that investment in learning can bring private returns to individuals and higher productivity for firms questions the degree to which the public sector should finance these types of investments.

Most governments have seen the need for public intervention for a variety of reasons.

The analysis of policy objectives reveals that countries participating in the thematic review believe in the need for some degree of public intervention. Most countries have explicitly articulated their reasons for public involvement, as can be seen in Table 4.2 (at the end of the chapter). At an individual level, country policy statements call for education for personal, professional and social development. At a macro level, equity and social cohesion, the inequity of market outcomes, the development of democratic values and the improvement of skills to participate in the economy and labour market are all stated as vital reasons for government participation in adult learning. Furthermore, an overarching and more recent goal has been the development of knowledge-based societies. Overall, countries agree on the long-run goals, which include economic and non-economic reasons: the need to target low educational attainment and to intervene for social cohesion and economic development, for unemployment purposes and for personal and social development. They believe in the role of adult learning for redistribution and growth. These objectives are seen as important enough to formulate specific policies; most governments therefore believe that intervention in the adult learning market is justified.

Federal systems may categorise adult learning as a regional responsibility.

Countries with a federal system might not include national objectives for adult learning because they are the responsibility of regional governments. In fact, in Canada and Switzerland, national adult learning policies have been part of labour market policies because they are situated at the national policy-making level, while education policies are the responsibility of the provinces or cantons. However, there have been recent efforts to embrace adult learning in the national policy-making agenda. In Canada, the Innovation Agenda (2002) includes two complementary green papers: "Knowledge Matters", addressing Canada's skills and learning challenges, and "Achieving Excellence", dealing with Canada's innovative capacity. Switzerland is in the process of passing a bill that will target adult vocational training in a more comprehensive manner.

In some countries, there are separate policies for vocational and general adult education.

In Spain, there are separate educational and vocational policies for adult education. From the educational perspective, there is a focus on access, upskilling and participation in the social, political and economic realms of life. From a labour market perspective, there is a strong focus on vocational training for reducing unemployment and on labour market training for employed populations. In Portugal, separate objectives were established by the education community and by the social partners together with the government, but they focus on combating low skills.

Denmark, Finland, Norway, Sweden and the United Kingdom have a broader vision of the concept of lifelong learning for personal, professional, economic and social reasons, made explicit under one single document or policy (Table 4.2). These countries focus on ensuring adequate learning opportunities for all adults. Learning is seen as important from an economic perspective of increased productivity, but also from a more personal and social perspective concerned with social and democratic values and attitudes. All view adult learning as necessary for workplace, society and individual development, although some countries then focus more on training for labour market purposes.

Certain countries place adult learning in the wider, overall policy context of lifelong learning.

This vision of adult learning as part of lifelong learning has been adopted in a number of countries and has formed the basis of a number of government initiatives. It was embraced in 1996, when OECD education ministers adopted "lifelong learning for all" as a guiding framework for their education policy. They included adult learning as key in ensuring that all individuals have the knowledge and skills to fully participate in society throughout their lives. Their policy framework implies that adult learning and lifelong learning should be embraced from a learner perspective.

OECD education ministers support "lifelong learning for all" as a guiding principle.

4.2. Country policy approaches to adult learning

As shown in Table 4.2, most countries reviewed have taken specific policy actions or measures at the national level geared towards adult learning. These range from defining general action plans to targeting adult education and skills needs and passing broad legislative initiatives for developing adult learning, to other operational issues that involve institutional or structural rearrangements.

Policy measures vary from general action plans, specific targeting to operational issues.

Most country policies are focused on improving the opportunities for upskilling or reskilling of adult populations through different approaches. Canada's recent skills and learning agenda highlights the importance of lifelong learning for personal well-being and continued economic growth; Denmark's Adult Education Reform (2000) aims to tie together in a single coherent and transparent adult educational system the different training categories; Finland's Joy of Learning (1997) is a comprehensive reform of adult education; Norway's Competence Reform (1999) also spelled out a long-term initiative to expand learning opportunities for adults. Portugal prepared a strategy for the development of adult education (1998) aiming at greater access for low-educated people. It also signed an agreement on employment, labour and education and training policy (2001) between the government and the social partners to consolidate an adult education system within a coherent strategy to raise skill levels. Spain's National Vocational Training Programme (1998-2002) aims towards flexibility and adults' access to training across different settings. Sweden recently passed a new law on adult learning and has mainstreamed the Adult Learning Initiative focused on increasing skills. The Learning and Skills Act (2000) in the United Kingdom is focused on raising the skill levels of English adults. Switzerland's development of their vocational training law will try to ensure equal training opportunities to all.

Most focus on improving opportunities for upskilling or reskilling of adult populations...

71

... using different approaches, separately or in combination.

There are a diversity of approaches that countries have taken towards reaching these goals. These different approaches, listed below, are not mutually exclusive:

- *Emphasising demand through financial incentives*: Some countries have focused on introducing individual incentive mechanisms to stimulate adults to undertake learning opportunities. These include grants, loans, individual learning accounts and other individual financial incentives such as income support for studies or study allowances. In Canada, loans, grants and tax incentives have been used to stimulate individual demand. In the United Kingdom there is a broad range of financial support to encourage students to undertake learning throughout the country. In Finland, Norway and Sweden there are income support allowances complementary to free provision.

- *Emphasising demand through non-financial incentives*: There are other important mechanisms that have been used to stimulate demand; in many cases they are complementary to financial incentives. The rights to education or training leave from work in Finland, Norway and Portugal are an important incentive for workers to undertake learning. Most countries have also initiated plans or activities towards assessment or recognition of informal or prior learning as an incentive to bring adults back into learning. Portugal has created a national system of centres that recognise, validate and certify skills.

- *Focusing on supply*: Countries have worked towards developing the public adult learning system so as to increase supply at different levels, rationalise and give coherence to the diversity of offerings, and co-ordinate the different actors involved. In most of these cases, that implies free or near-free provision of formal adult education or other educational opportunities. This is the case with the reforms introduced by Denmark, Finland, Norway and Sweden, and efforts undertaken by Spain and Portugal. Most of these countries have focused on increasing access and improving public provision. Some have tried to rationalise different supply available by sharing institutions or resources. Some countries have also undertaken work to improve adult teachers' skills so as to improve supply.

- *Stimulating supply and demand*: In some countries the focus has been on creating mechanisms that can help stimulate the adult learning market by targeting both supply and demand. Some countries have funded infrastructure for educational suppliers, or assisted the private market through incentives or subsidies. Others have provided or assisted in providing information, orientation and guidance concerning learning opportunities (such as "learn festival" in Switzerland or Opintoluotsi open search service in educational information in Finland). The introduction of a quality assurance schemes [EduQua in Switzerland or Investors in People (IiP) in the United Kingdom] has also contributed to allowing the private sector to take an active role. The introduction of subsidies to private suppliers, the Danish taximeter system,[1] tax exemptions and subsidies for employer-financed education or tax

---

1. The government gives grants to cover the education and training costs of institutions according to the number of full-time equivalent students completing training.

levies for learning and training can also be viewed in this light. Social partners have become involved in stimulating vocational and enterprise-based training in most countries. Greater decentralisation and transfer of decision-making power to the local level have also been key.

There are also different approaches towards labour market training. In some countries it has been included within the broader concept of adult learning. In Denmark for example, the adult education reform tries to bring continuing training and further education together into a single coherent system. In Sweden, the Adult Education Initiative was financed by reallocating funds from passive labour market measures to active education and training programmes in the ministry of education. In other countries, ministries of labour sometimes have separate strategies for labour market training, including training for the unemployed and for employed adults. In Spain, the creation of a National Vocational Training Programme has focused on the development of a cohesive system of vocational training, leaving basic or general education as a separate issue. In a number of countries, these objectives are established separately from general adult education objectives, and their policy measures or approaches are viewed separately.

Approaches also vary with regard to labour market training.

However, what has been common to all countries is the activation of labour market policies, or the increased importance accorded to training and other active measures as opposed to reliance on passive reception of unemployment benefits. Some countries have introduced a training insurance scheme to assist the unemployed for the loss of unemployment benefits during training. Other countries have made training mandatory during unemployment spells. Another instrument has been alternation leave or job rotation in place in Denmark and Finland: in the latter, an employee goes on training leave (from 90 to 359 days) and a registered unemployed jobseeker fills in for him/her.

Generally, active measures are preferred over passive reception of unemployment benefits.

Learning in the enterprise has also been included in some national policy approaches but not in others, although in most countries there is some type of support for this learning. Support models and structures vary. In Spain, the Canton of Geneva, Switzerland and the region of Quebec, there is a tax levy on workers and enterprises for funding learning in the enterprise. In Denmark, training is channelled through training leave and is publicly financed. In Finland, there is a tax levy directed towards compensating income loss for employees who participate as a means of advancing or maintaining their vocational skills. In Norway, there is tax exemption for employer-financed education. A recent agreement between the social partners in Portugal (2001) establishes an individual entitlement to a minimum amount of training for all workers (20 hours per year to be increased over time) and a minimum annual volume of training, which has been set at 10% of all workers.

There is also support for learning in the enterprise, provided through a variety of structures.

Towards a holistic view of adult learning?

Although different forms and patterns of institutional arrangements exist in adult learning across OECD countries, there is a general trend towards a more holistic approach to adult learning in a lifelong learning perspective, as can be seen from most of the recent reforms. Some countries already had a broader concept of adult learning in its early stages, although it was limited to adult basic education and literacy or other programmes not directly related to the labour market. Until the adoption of a lifelong learning vision, adult

Prior to the lifelong learning approach, education and labour market policies were separate domains.

education and training policies had been fragmented efforts to target specific needs of adults. There had not been sustained efforts towards mainstreaming adult education into general education policies. And most importantly, education and labour market policies remained isolated from each other. However, the increasing unemployment rates in the early 1990s, the growing requirements for high-skilled workers linked to the development of the knowledge economy, and the increased awareness of the importance of human capital have slowly moved adult education to the political forefront.

Since then adult education has shifted to adult learning: a more systemic, adult-centred view.

These developments have stimulated a shift from the concept of adult education towards that of adult learning, in a more systemic adult-centred view. In fact, in a number of countries recent policies in adult learning represent a shift towards increasing opportunities across the board in a lifelong learning perspective. As shown in Table 4.2, Canada's recent measures are directed at increasing overall participation. Denmark, Finland and Norway all embrace the broad spectrum of learning opportunities for all. Sweden's new parliament supports individual learning for all, as does the United Kingdom, which seeks to stimulate participation in different learning activities. There is a growing effort to give coherence to the many scattered and diverse programmes and courses for adults. The concept of education is broadening to include formal, non-formal and informal learning as reviewed in Chapter 2, as well as a broad range of educational strategies. This approach offers a more systemic view of learning, and includes the diversity of demand for and supply of learning opportunities as part of a whole system. It places the learner at the centre and includes all the different types of learning that adults undertake. It also covers the multiplicity of objectives that adults may have in learning, be it for professional, personal or social reasons. The approach also represents an increased effort to rationalise adult education and give it a national coherence within education and labour market policy agendas. If all of this seems more of an objective than a reality at present, countries are nonetheless moving in this direction with efforts to develop coherent or co-ordinated approaches or *systems* of adult learning.

Most countries support vocational-oriented training more than they do general adult learning.

While this holistic vision is being developed in country approaches, there is greater support for vocational-oriented training as opposed to general adult learning in most countries, a development reflected in levels of participation. There is some debate about this division, especially in the Nordic countries, but there still remains a dominance of learning for labour market purposes and of vocationally oriented conceptions of lifelong learning. A number of the reforms are especially focused on vocational training, such as those in Portugal, Spain and Switzerland, mainly targeting legislative reforms. Also, most Nordic countries' reforms have had as main aims the development of training systems to attend to economic and labour market developments. The European Social Fund (ESF) and a European Employment Strategy to provide funding for increased training to reduce unemployment in European countries have also contributed to this focus.

There have been efforts to shift that trend in support of democratic values.

There are also some attempts to shift these tendencies in countries' policy statements, including expressions of support for the development of democratic values and other non-vocational practices. For example, in Switzerland, private training providers have shifted away somewhat from more vocational purposes toward more civic concerns, and the role of the federal government in consolidating vocationally oriented education has caused strains with those who believe that non-vocational forms should also be included. In Norway, the Competence Reform will maintain a connection to the tradition of providing adult education for its own sake, and the study associations that provide the majority of adult learners have their roots in liberal rather than vocational study. Both Norway and Sweden have folk high schools with non-vocational traditions, and Sweden also has active study circles. In Sweden, the Adult Education Initiative targeted a reduction in high unemployment rates by increasing the educational attainment of the unemployed to secondary level education so as to improve their position in the labour market. In the United Kingdom, the Learning and Skills Council (LSC) has recently brought together the planning and funding of all post-compulsory education and training into a single body. Overall, while the scales appear to be tipped toward vocational rather than non-vocational purposes, there seem to be increased efforts to broaden the focus and provision in a more comprehensive approach.

The establishment of a European area of lifelong learning, initiated by the European Union Memorandum on Lifelong Learning, is also reflecting this shift towards a holistic vision of adult learning. It aims to bring together within a lifelong learning framework education, training and other important European policies such as youth, employment, social inclusion and research policy (European Commission, 2001). It calls for a more coherent and efficient use of existing instruments and resources to achieve a European lifelong learning area that includes a whole spectrum of formal, non-formal and informal learning for employment-related aspects, as well as active citizenship, personal fulfillment and social inclusion. The creation of the Grundtvig programme (2000 to 2006) is evidence of the heightened attention given by the Commission to adults within lifelong learning (Box 4.1).

The EU has called for the creation of a European area of lifelong learning.

A more comprehensive view of adult learning within lifelong learning is not, however, a fully realised concept. This is in part a result of the different forms of supply, which come from a policy fragmentation that exists both at a vertical and horizontal level.[2] Coherence and co-ordination have been lacking at the national level over the years, and adult learning has not been a priority on many governments' agendas until recently.

Fragmentation poses a challenge to realising a holistic approach within lifelong learning.

Remedial or second chance programmes: A priority

A clear policy decision in most reviewed countries is to support basic skills instruction (Table 4.2). Most countries have a broad range of adult education schools or initiatives targeting the attainment of basic educational levels for adults, either primary or secondary. These are mainstream programmes included in education ministries' general policies, and represent the most

Ensuring that adults have at least the minimum level of basic skills is a priority in most countries.

---

2. These levels depend on and reflect, to a large extent, the administrative and political configuration of the state. Vertical integration would imply that adult education and training programmes are well integrated within the formal education system at initial, secondary and tertiary level, and that informal and non-formal learning is taken into consideration as part of the adult education process. Horizontal integration refers to how the different partners that contribute to the design and implementation of adult education policies work together or co-ordinate their planning or activities to provide coherent adult education policies.

Box 4.1. **Adult learning in the European Union: The Grundtvig programme**

The Grundtvig programme places the adult learner at the centre. Equal attention is given to students in the formal and informal systems. Grundtvig aims to enhance the options available for lifelong learning and improve the quality of adult education within the European dimension.

The following main goals have been distinguished:

- The promotion of European partnership and co-operation between bodies offering adult education.
- Improving the education and training of persons who teach in adult education.
- Promotion of product development and other outcomes.
- Continuing the debate on lifelong learning and dissemination of good practice.

The campaign directs itself towards adults with special educational needs and/or adults who lack basic skills. Groups that are difficult to reach such as adults who live in deprived areas within nations or areas suffering from socio-economic disadvantages also make up important target groups for the programme. The organisations eligible to apply for in the programme therefore cover a fairly large range: adult education institutions (formal and informal), universities, socio-educational and socio-cultural organisations/institutes, non-government bodies, libraries, museums and local communities, etc.

Source: European Union, Grundtvig, *http://europa.eu.int/comm/education/socrates/adult/overview.html*

---

clear adult education delivery mechanisms. However, to strengthen remedial opportunities there have been a number of specific programmes designed to facilitate the attainment of a minimum level of education by adults. Countries with high overall levels of attainment have focused on upper secondary education and vocational education, while those with lower levels have focused on adult basic education and primary-level education. The extent to which each country supports these varies, but all have a diversity of arrangements towards this objective. The role of the International Adult Literacy Survey in detecting low literacy levels in all countries has been important to raise awareness of this deficiency; a number of such policies were designed after the IALS results were published.

Basic skill instruction has been a special priority in Canada with literacy programmes, and in the United Kingdom (as part of a UK national intervention for improving adult literacy and numeracy skills). Denmark, Norway and Sweden have all created national-level programmes that try to increase skills by offering primary or secondary education and other provisions to adults. The Adult Education Reform, the Competence Reform and the Adult Education Initiative are all programmes that target the increase of adult learning at a national level. In Portugal, the creation of ANEFA is also geared to create opportunities for low-qualified adults. In Spain, the provision of primary and secondary education for adults, directly or through open call exams, can also be viewed in this light. In general, the importance of adult basic education programmes has been recognised, but the existence of waiting lists in a number of countries visited reveals that efforts undertaken so far are not enough.

Approaches to inequities in access

There are a number of programmes that respond to government's concerns for equity. As shown in Chapter 3, there are groups that are under-represented in adult learning programmes, with fewer opportunities of access and participation. Countries have designed different solutions. They may have targeted programmes of spending, subsidies for groups with special needs, special outreach programmes, easier access to courses for specific groups, and in a few cases special institutions (*e.g.* for aboriginal people in Canada). Barriers to participation in mainstream educational programmes can be eliminated, for example by providing childcare to working mothers or transportation in rural or suburban areas, or expanding access to education grants and loans (Grubb, 2001). The specific groups targeted in public policy vary in different countries, but overall there are public programmes targeting the following.

There are various measures to assist groups under-represented in adult learning programmes.

The unemployed and the long-term unemployed. Special measures have targeted the unemployed and the long-term unemployed in all forms of adult learning, vocational and non-vocational. The long-term unemployed tend to have lower levels of education, and active labour market policies have focused on training them for the job market. However, a number of policies with employment targets have had the effect of "cherry picking", or selecting those that have the highest chances of finding a job whether they have training or not. The Swedish IT programme (SWIT) aimed at meeting particular competence-shortages in the labour market, and described as a success, has been cited as an example.

There are measures geared to the unemployed, immigrants, the low-skilled, or the handicapped.

Immigrants. In a number of countries, increasing immigration rates are contributing to an increase in language and culture immersion programmes. This is an effect of equity concerns but also in response to changing labour force requirements and skills shortages. Countries have recognised the need for immigrants to obtain working knowledge of the country where they live if they are to integrate and participate fully in the labour market and in society. Sweden has a strong Swedish for Immigrants programme (Sfi), while Denmark also has Danish as a second language for adult foreigners. The Finnish Broadcasting Company YLE provides Finnish for both Finns and foreigners. In Spain, recent immigration inflows have caused an increase in public and NGO provision of Spanish language and culture courses. Figure 3.7 in Chapter 3 has already shown learning rates by residence situation, revealing that in some countries the differences in learning participation are not so large, but in others, such as Switzerland or Spain, participation is much lower.

The low-skilled. As can be seen in Table 4.2 and the section above, a large proportion of measures or reforms taken in countries have been directed towards providing opportunities for increasing the educational attainment for those with low skills. The Swedish Adult Education Initiative, the efforts in Portugal, or in Norway with the right to basic or to upper secondary education, and in the Danish reform are good examples. Furthermore, most countries have a broad variety of adult education institutions that provide upskilling opportunities for adults.

Low-income groups. One of the main approaches to increase motivation and participation in adult learning is through financial incentives. Most public programmes involve either the creation of free provision or the development of financial assistance mechanisms for those who cannot fund their own learning. Most of the financial arrangements focus on formal learning or education directed to obtaining a certificate. However, from the participation rates and profiles seen in Chapter 3, inequities in participation remain, as it is those with the highest educational attainment and those with higher wages participate more in adult learning.

Rural or remote dwellers. There is an imbalance between programmes available in urban *versus* rural areas. Similarly, the efforts to enhance competition among providers generally have worked only in urban areas, where there are multiple providers, and not at all in rural areas where provision of adult education is scarce. Different delivery methods have tried to target these inequities, as shown in Table 4.2, but the results are unclear. In Saskatchewan (Canada), for example, there have been efforts to develop regional colleges in rural areas where students then go into technical institutes in urban areas. In Finland (and other countries) there have been efforts to develop distance learning methods to overcome the isolation of rural areas, though the lack of availability of computers for older groups and low-income groups has hampered this process. In the more remote communities in Spain, there are also efforts to bring adult education close to home. In countries that have federal government structures, such as Canada or Switzerland, there are regional differences in access to adult education. In Canada, residents of remote communities and poorer provinces (like the Maritimes) tend to have less access; in Switzerland the German-speaking cantons have the greatest access and the Italian cantons the least. In these cases the only cure for regional imbalances is for the federal government to play a greater equalising role.

Handicapped individuals. There are a number of adult learning programmes geared towards the handicapped, especially those using available information and communication technologies. All countries have substantial numbers of disabled or handicapped individuals, and they often lack access to public services such as education. Although the focus of the thematic review has not been on handicapped people, the review teams have seen a number of inspiring programmes across countries. In Sweden for example, a visit to a school from Municipal Education for Adult with Learning Disabilities (*särvux*) was enlightening. Handicapped adults were learning to use advanced ICT technologies to read and write.

From supply-led to demand-driven education and training

There has been greater recognition of and response to demand.

From the analysis of the different reform measures taken by countries, a tendency towards greater recognition of and response to demand through different policy approaches can be observed. However, evidence has not shown clear institutionalised mechanisms for detecting needs, as can be seen in the evaluation column of Table 4.2. Most adult learning has been supply-driven, with learning opportunities largely relying on replicating the formal education system used for young people to serve the needs of adults.

However, as economies and societies evolve, changing learning needs of adults need to be taken into account. The International Adult Literacy Survey (IALS) was one international effort that drew attention to the magnitude of the lack of skills in adult populations throughout OECD countries in a comparative manner. However, it is unclear that countries use systematic means to detect demand. In recent years, countries have made increased efforts, and in fact a number of country policies state the need to recognise demand and to broaden learning opportunities for adults.

Different mechanisms employed to gauge demand have involved decentralisation of decision making to the regional level and to the education provider level. These can be viewed as a response to provide greater access and to foster a broader variety of learning opportunities for adults. The wider use of individual incentive mechanisms can also be seen as recognition that individuals will choose what is best for them. Such arrangements, however, can serve to exacerbate inequities, as those who have higher educational attainment are usually those who follow more training. Therefore, countries also use compensatory mechanisms to assure equal access opportunities for those groups that are under-represented in training, such as those mentioned in the previous section.

Individual incentive mechanisms designed to widen access and opportunity may in fact exacerbate inequities.

There seems to be a need for national policy agendas to take the recognition and detection of demand as an important instrument in policy design (Pont, 2001). The Danish 10-item plan includes the development of provision based on demand, and the recent Swedish parliament goals also include provision for adjusting education to individual needs.

A *shift from process to outcomes*: national qualification systems

Another way in which some governments have tried to provide a holistic approach to adult learning, as well as incentives for adults to learn, is through the introduction of national qualification frameworks. The recognition of all kinds of learning can motivate adults back to learning; qualification frameworks offer the possibility of progression routes and equivalencies within education systems (OECD, 2000a); and, through credit transfer and established equivalencies, they can make it easier for individuals to have skills and competencies acquired in one sector recognised in another. Countries are looking towards their qualifications systems as a means of promoting lifelong learning for all, but the impact of different policy instruments within qualifications systems – including qualifications frameworks – needs more clarification. A new OECD Directorate for Education activity is analysing these issues more in-depth across OECD countries (OECD, 2002a).

Qualifications systems that recognise competencies can fuel adults' motivation to return to learning.

From an institutional point of view, the definition of common criteria for the outcomes or results of training processes can be an important tool to make different institutions work towards the same goals, giving them (and individuals) the flexibility to design their own education pathways. Qualifications frameworks are regarded as potential powerful steering mechanisms for developing more open and effective systems of lifelong learning.

If different institutions share the same goals, learners will be freer to design their own pathways.

Countries are experimenting with different types of qualifications structures that can cater to adult learners. Finland has had a qualifications framework since 1994, based on competence-based examinations irrespective of where the knowledge and skills are acquired. Portugal and Spain are in the process of defining national qualifications frameworks, the latter through the creation of the National Institute for Professional Qualification (INCUAL) to accredit qualifications. In the United Kingdom the National Vocational Qualification (NVQ) is a unified system of vocational qualifications, and efforts are currently under way to bring together general and vocational qualifications under one unified system. Modularisation, or the division of qualifications into small units, falls within this framework and is

Modularisation of qualifications allows for the recognition of individualised "skills profiles".

viewed as positive for adult learning. It allows for an individualised pace of learning and for the recognition of individualised "skills profiles".

Recognition of informal and non-formal learning

Recognition of informal and non-formal learning, which occurs outside formal settings...

The recognition of informal and non-formal learning that adults undertake has been included in a number of country approaches towards adult learning. In fact, some countries are in the process of developing and implementing methodologies and systems for the identification, assessment and recognition of non-formal learning. It has been viewed as a tool for realising lifelong learning systems, as it can give learners credit for learning undertaken throughout different settings and contribute to the development of individualised career paths. It can also be a valuable tool for motivating individual learners. It can avoid repeating education processes and contribute to shortening them: adults can therefore begin learning at the level that reflects their actual competencies, not based on their formal qualifications. These approaches can thus support more flexible education, training and learning careers, making it possible for people to better afford education and training (Bjørnåvold, 2001).

... allows adults to begin learning at the level that reflects their actual competencies.

Sweden has recently begun developing general systems for assessment of competencies that have been acquired outside formal learning settings together with the social partners. While the social partners seem to be more concerned about the utilisation of competencies developed in working life, the interest of the government seems to be more focused on the need to make public educational institutions more flexible (to open the system up for immigrants and adults with long working experience, and to reduce costs). And while the social partners seem to strive for a more balanced recognition of formal and non-formal learning, the government initiatives aim to use the formal, school-based qualification as the standard according to which other competencies should be measured and valued (Bjørnåvold, 2001 and OECD, 2001c).

Canada has prior learning assessment at an institutional level across the country; British Columbia has developed guidelines that cover prior learning assessment and recognition (PLAR) of both the K-12 system and of adult education. In Denmark an important goal of the Adult Education Reform is to create a coherent system of recognition for training supervised by the ministry for labour. In Norway, documentation and recognition of informal and non-formal learning is one of the key elements in the Competence Reform, through which the government is trying to develop a national system for the documentation and recognition of non-formal learning. The parliament has approved a measure whereby an adult over 25 years old can access university studies with the approval of his/her non-formal learning. In Finland, each institution providing education and training leading to a qualification must see that the student has the opportunity to obtain competence-based qualifications as part of the programme. However, despite the fact that one aim of the system was to facilitate public recognition of the competence of adults with long work experience in particular, it is the younger generations who have mostly obtained the qualifications. In Portugal, the creation of a national system for the recognition, validation and certification of school attainment and personal experience will develop key competency benchmarks in areas such as language and communication, ICT, everyday mathematics, employability, and citizenship.

Evaluation of outcomes and quality assurance

Evaluation and quality control should be integral components of adult learning systems, as they can contribute to more efficient and effective policy making. Evaluation of outcomes can guide policy makers to choosing the most appropriate adult learning programmes for specific objectives. The importance of understanding the results and effects of learning is imperative for all stakeholders, from learners to investors. To obtain a consensus and maintain commitment and sustainability of the policies over the long run, it is important to measure the efficiency and the returns. Quality assurance mechanisms can also contribute to controlling public and private spending in adult education. However, the extent to which countries have recognised this is still limited. There have been recent efforts by some countries to include it as part of their adult learning reforms; most countries state that there is a need for improved evaluation of outcomes and results.

The importance of understanding the results and effects of learning is imperative for all stakeholders.

Evaluation is crucial to develop satisfactory policies, and should be an integral part of policy design. It can help detect adult learning needs and whether they are being met or not. Evaluation can also contribute to rationalising limited resources and to better co-ordinating different actors across the board. Unfortunately, most evaluation of adult learning policies is limited to the measurement of the number of students taught and funding spent (Table 4.2, outcomes measurement). Some evaluation can be found at the local or regional level but information is not carried through to the national level. There has been widespread use of surveys, such as labour force surveys, to measure change and learning profiles. In Finland for example, adult education surveys are conducted every five years to provide a picture of educational needs and participation in adult education. However, the Finnish state that steering and monitoring measures aiming to utilise the adult education system to achieve government objectives for education, labour, social and industrial needs often prove inadequate and call for the expansion of person-based data collection (OECD, 2001b).

Some evaluation is performed locally or regionally but the information is not carried through to the national level.

More evaluation has been focused on public training programmes than on any other type of adult learning. Some evaluation studies show that public training programmes appear to work for some target groups but not for others. Having the answers to such questions is important for appropriate policy design. Martin and Grubb (2001) have found four crucial features in the design of public training programmes: *a*) the need for tight targeting on participants; *b*) the need to keep the programmes relatively small in scale; *c*) the need to have a strong on-the-job component in the programme; and *d*) the need for the programme to result in a qualification or certificate that is recognised and valued by the market.

Public training programmes have been evaluated more than any other type of adult learning.

Quality assurance can also be seen as part of an efficient and effective adult learning system. In countries with a larger public provision of adult learning, there are public institutions in charge of quality control and evaluation. In Sweden, the National Agency for Education takes on this role, while in Spain there is an Education Inspector Directorate at a national level. The Adult Education Reform in Denmark establishes the task of quality

Quality assurance is another key element in any efficient and effective adult learning system.

assurance at different levels, including the overall adult education and training system, the education or education programme level, and the institutional level. The Danish have created an Evaluation Institute, which is an independent institution under the ministry of education. Its tasks include external examination of individual education programmes under the ministry of education, assessment of coherence between various educational programmes, development and innovation related to evaluation techniques and methods, and collection of national and international experiences with education evaluation. An example of a recent measure in this direction is the Adult Learning Inspectorate (ALI) in the United Kingdom, a new non-departmental public body with responsibility for quality assurance. It will inspect provision for people aged 19 and over in further education colleges, for enterprise based training for all age groups, New Deal, adult and community learning, University for Industry/learndirect, as well as education and training in prisons. All providers of adult literacy and numeracy provision funded by the Learning and Skills Council or a local authority will be inspected by the Office for Standards in Education (OfSTED) and/or the ALI.

Government may prove a reliable quality controller.

In countries where there is a large private provision of learning, the national government can play a role in assuring and improving quality, as there is concern about the role of private training providers. In Canada, for example, the review team was made aware of a private institution that closed in a fortnight and disappeared in a province where there was no control over private training providers. Countries have established different mechanisms for quality control. The EduQua system in Switzerland is a quality assurance mechanism for training institutions that assures learners of the quality of the institution. The Investors in People in the United Kingdom follows a similar pattern.

Resourcing and financing issues[3]

Adult learning financing can be a shared endeavour.

In all countries reviewed, adult learning is a shared endeavour undertaken by the public as well as the private sector. According to IALS data, training is mostly financed by the enterprise or by private individuals; a small proportion of learning is financed by the public sector. These data need to be interpreted with caution: some respondents are often not clear on where the financing for their training comes from because it is not transparent. For example, enterprise training might be publicly funded but the employees might not be aware of this financing arrangement.[4] Training financed by individuals might also include loans and grants, which are public mechanisms to stimulate learning.

A large proportion of learning for the unemployed and those not in the labour force is government financed.

Figure 4.1 shows that most training undertaken by employed people is financed by the enterprise, while the government funds a large proportion of training for the unemployed. A significant proportion of training of those not in the labour force is also government financed. This shows the role of active labour market policies and the strong country policy focus on reducing

---

3. Further in-depth research on this issue has been undertaken as part of the OECD activity on financing lifelong learning. See findings in OECD, 2000b and 2001a.
4. This is the case of Norway, where participants in labour market training are registered as paid for by the employers for coding reasons, but it would be correct to classify them as funded by the government.

Figure 4.1. **Sources of adult learning financing by labour force status**

Percentage distribution of financing by labour force status for population 25-64 years old, 1994-98

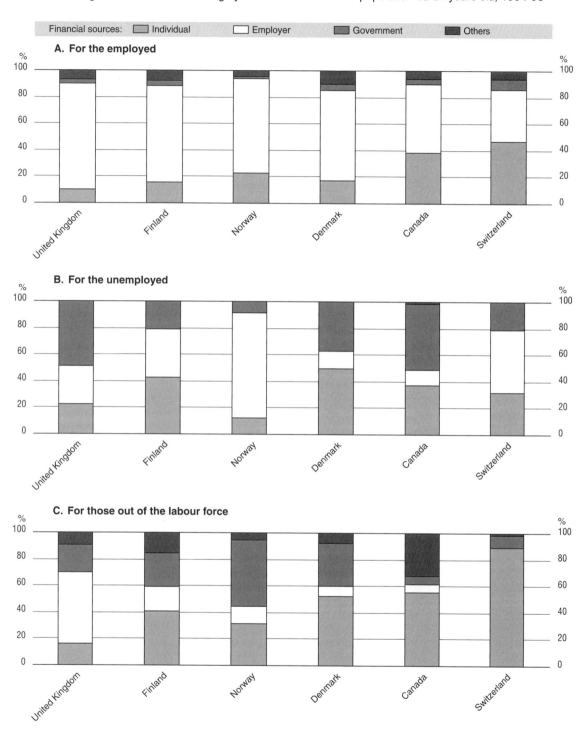

Note: Countries are ranked in descending order by employers' funding of training of those who are employed.
Source: International Adult Literacy Survey (1994-98).

unemployment rates and assisting those with difficulties in the labour market, especially in Canada and the United Kingdom. It also seems that people who are not in the labour market benefit from training more in countries with a public system of adult education such as Denmark, Norway or Finland, although there is not enough information for all countries and it is therefore difficult to compare. Still, a large proportion of learning for those out of the labour force is financed directly by individuals.

It is difficult to provide an overall picture of spending on adult learning.

Data on financing adult learning are challenging to say the least. It is difficult to provide an overall picture because of the complex and varied nature of the programmes and their differences across countries in financing arrangements, as can be seen in the broad variety shown in Table 4.2. The different modes range from direct financing to educational institutions, to suppliers of education, to indirect funding, to individual financial assistance mechanisms. Furthermore, adult learning includes general adult education, vocational adult education, basic skills education, general non-vocational education, labour market training for the unemployed or those at risk, and enterprise-based training. It can also include informal training. In some countries, these are separate areas of activity spread across ministries of education, employment and finance. As there is also a high degree of decentralisation, regional and municipal authorities are also involved. The private sector, especially the enterprise, also plays an extremely important role in adult learning. Sources of funding are therefore diverse and it is difficult to provide a homogenised picture of spending on adult learning.

A few countries participating in the thematic review provided overall information on public or private financing for adult learning. Denmark's data show that around 1% of its GDP was spent on adult learning in 1998 – or around 13% of that country's total educational budget. In Finland, education administration public funding of adult education was 0.59% of GDP in 2001. In Spain, the total spending in adult learning, which includes basic adult education, vocational occupational training, work-training programmes and continuing vocational training, adds up to approximately 0.4% of GDP. This is a rough estimate, and includes training by enterprises and by the public sector from the education and the labour side. In Sweden, data presented gave a figure of 4.9% of GDP on adult learning in 1998, although this includes in-service training, which can be private or publicly funded. It represents 44% of the total educational spending in Sweden. Overall, however, it is difficult to provide a complete picture, as there are different concepts involved in each country.

There is more comparable data on labour market training expenditure.

OECD data on active labour market policies expenditure, which are comparable across countries, show that overall spending on labour market training ranges from 0.05% of GDP in the United Kingdom to 0.84% in Denmark in 2001 (Table 5.1).

Public financing arrangements play a small role in the provision of training in enterprises.

There are also data available on financing of Continuing Vocational Training (CVT) courses for some of the reviewed countries (Table 4.1). They reveal that between 1.2% and 3.6% of overall labour costs of enterprises that provided training were invested in training. The total cost per employee ranged from over 600 PPS per employee in Portugal, Spain and the United Kingdom to 1 124 PPS in Denmark. The United Kingdom, with the highest labour cost overall, had low cost per employee, perhaps due to a policy of

Table 4.1. **Costs of training courses in enterprises**

Costs of training in PPS[1] per employee and costs of training courses as a percentage of total labour costs of all enterprises, 1999

	Denmark	Finland	Portugal	Spain	Sweden	United Kingdom
Direct costs	642	419	342	242	518	507
Labour costs of participants	481	358	338	389	415	143
Contributions (+)	23	10	1	87	4	44
Receipts (−)	22	30	38	50	31	31
Total	1 124	758	642	668	907	662
Costs as % of total labour costs, 1999	3.0%	2.4%	1.2%	1.5%	2.8%	3.6%
1993	1.3%	. .	0.7%	1.0%	. .	. .

1. Purchasing-power standards (PPS): costs are indicated in PPS to allow for price differences between countries. The PPS conversion factors indicate how many national currency units the same quantity of goods and services would cost in individual countries.

Source: Eurostat, New Chronos Database, CVTS.

more extensive *versus* intensive participation. What is important to note is that the receipts from national or other funding arrangements were low in most countries as measured in PPS per employee, with the highest proportions in Spain and the United Kingdom followed by Denmark. Included here are public financing arrangements for enterprise-based training, revealing the small role they play in financing and provision of adult learning for those in enterprises. In fact, there is a strong association to be noted between the enterprises' spending in training and overall participation rates.

An interesting analysis using IALS information for Nordic countries has shown that overall, there is no relationship between the level of public support for education and training and training participation rates across countries (NORD, 2001). According to this study, it would appear that the observed high levels of adult education participation in the Nordic countries should not be attributed, at least not directly, to high levels of public support for such activities. There were other countries with relatively high rates of participation in publicly supported adult education, but these had overall levels of participation much lower than the Nordic countries. There were also other countries with low support and high overall participation rates.

The association between participation in and public support for adult education is not clear cut...

A slightly different picture emerges if the incidence of participation among some of the main target groups of publicly supported adult education is examined. When analysing the levels of training of the low-skilled and the odds of receiving public subsidies for it, there is a relationship between the level of public support and the incidence of adult education for the low-skilled. This high level of public support for education and training has increased the training rate of the low-skilled and it might well be that it is here where public spending can make the largest difference.

... except when it comes to the low-skilled.

It is not the level of public resources alone that determines overall learning performance, but the participation of and funding by firms and how public funding is used. The distribution of learning supply, the role of firms and the efficiency of the adult learning system, together with other social, cultural or historical factors, have a strong impact on participation rates. In terms of public resources, it is a question of whether public funding is appropriately directed to provide the right incentives for adults to engage in

Countries are using a variety of public approaches and financial arrangement.

adult learning, especially for the low skilled. Information gathered from the countries reviewed and presented in Table 4.2 shows that countries are using a variety of public approaches and financial arrangements to improve access to and participation in adult learning:

- *Basic adult education* is generally financed by education ministries. In most countries reviewed, there is free adult education for those who want to attain basic education levels. Ministries either have their own provision or give subsidies to private providers for accepting students into their programmes. In some countries where these opportunities are not available, there are loans or grants. There are sometimes subsistence funds for those undertaking learning, or trainees can receive unemployment benefits or similar types of assistance. There is also the possibility of offsetting the wage losses linked to education and training.

- *Labour market training for the unemployed or those at risk.* This is the most organised or homogeneous sector in terms of financial arrangements. It is normally ministries of labour that have special schemes to enhance the employability of those unemployed. Most funding is generated at the national level and there are different arrangements available, from public provision of vocational training for the unemployed to individual funding for unemployed who can purchase their training in private institutions. In a number of countries, there is financial aid of different sorts for those unemployed who are undergoing training. It is also important to note the role of the European Social Fund, which has been an important engine for increasing training for the unemployed in some European countries.

- *Training in the enterprise.* There are different models and levels of public financing across countries. In some countries there is no public funding of enterprise-based training; it is left to the market to be developed. In some cases the social partners, unions and enterprises have special arrangements but there is not public funding of learning. Other countries provide different types of incentives to individual learners to undergo training, such as regulations for paid leave of absence for employees or loans or grants. Individual learning accounts are also starting to be developed; these are not only supported by the government but also available to workers at the enterprise level. Some countries have tax exemptions for enterprises that provide training. Another model is a tax levy on workers or firms for training managed by the social partners. Subsidies for enterprises for training are also present in some countries. The funding of apprentices can also be included here. There are also other types of arrangements in collective bargaining agreements at sectorial level.

4.3. Features of policy design and implementation

Co-ordination and coherence of policies

Dedicated institutions may be the best way to co-ordinate activities and policy making to attain policy coherence.

This recent trend towards a holistic approach in adult learning has been followed by efforts to improve the existing lack of coherence and co-ordination that has prevailed among the different partners involved in the development and planning of related activities. In terms of policy coherence the approach implies joint efforts of different government departments and agencies to forge mutually reinforcing policy action towards defined objectives. With regards to co-ordination, it refers to institutional and management mechanisms by which policy coherence is exerted among the different entities involved. All countries have a broad variety of partners involved in adult learning, including ministries of education, ministries of labour, regional governments, local-level governments, educational institutions, special adult learning institutions and the social partners. Overall, there is no one good way to co-ordinate activities and policy making, as they depend on historical development and political, administrative and social frameworks. What counts is co-ordination across the board to attain policy coherence, and this may be best attained with the creation of specific institutions devoted to the endeavour. Country experiences reveal that there have been some efforts towards this end.

Collaboration across institutions

The degree of policy coherence can depend to a large extent on the degree to which the different institutions that participate in adult learning share their vision and co-ordinate their activities. In most countries, the ministries or responsible institutions for general education have the responsibility for adult education. However, their scope of activity has been focused on adult basic education, literacy programmes and other types of basic and vocational education. On the other hand, ministries of labour have focused their efforts on specific labour market training programmes for the unemployed or the working population. The degree of collaboration between the two ministries has been limited in most countries. Traditionally, each ministry has designed and provided its own training, without taking into consideration the existing supply from other institutions.

Coherence implies shared vision, and collaboration between ministries of education and of labour...

However, it is not only ministries of education and labour that design adult learning policies. Other institutions also participate in this process. Ministries and other institutions for regional development, ministries of industry and ministries of health and/or social services also carry on learning programmes and policies for diverse groups.

... not to mention the other ministries and institutions involved.

An example of the diversity of institutions that design adult education policy can be seen from two country examples. In Switzerland, the federal and cantonal levels have different competencies for adult education and training, with the Confederation, the Federal Office for Vocational Training and Technology (OFFT), the Federal Department of Interior, the Federal Department of Foreign Affairs, the Pro Helvetia Foundation and the regional governments in charge of a broad spectrum of learning policies. In Sweden, although adult education is comprehensive, policy design and evaluation is in the hands of a number of institutions: the National Agency for Education, the Swedish National Labour Market Administration, the National Agency for Higher Education or the Swedish National Council of Adult Education and the Ministry of Industry.

Not only across ministries but even within them, there is a large number of actors and institutions involved in defining and implementing adult learning policies. For example, in Norway there were three institutions under the ministry of education with particular responsibility for adult learning: the Norwegian Institute of Adult Education (NVI), the Norwegian State Institution

Even within ministries there are many actors and institutions involved.

for Distance Education (NFU) and the State Adult Education Centre (SRV). These have recently merged under one institution as a result of the Competence Reform. The new institution will cover provision of adult education, allocation of grants, R&D activities and international relations.

Structures have been created specifically...

Knowing that a more unified approach can facilitate policy coherence and consistency, governments have tried to create or improve mechanisms of co-operation among the different ministries or agencies involved.

... to improve co-ordination between ministries.

One way to do so has been through the creation of a new body or agency designed specifically for adult learning policy making. In its Adult Education Reform, Denmark defined three structures that have the specific aim of improving co-ordination between ministries (the Adult Education Council, the Council for General Adult Education at basic level and the Labour Market Institution for Financing of Education and Training); these will include the social partners. The creation of ANEFA in Portugal in 2000 responds partly to the need to co-ordinate the activities of the ministry of education and the ministry of labour and solidarity towards a common objective. The creation of the Learning and Skills Council (LSC) in England, which is supposed to deliver all post-compulsory education and training from April 2001, also falls within this category. In Finland, the T&E Centres house the combined regional units of the ministry of trade and industry, the ministry of labour and the ministry of agriculture and forestry. Their labour market departments have a crucial role in implementing labour market training for adults.

Also to that end, institutions have been merged.

Governments have also responded to this need through the mergers of different institutions in charge of education and/or training. Such is the case of Norway, with the merger of the NVI, the NFU and the SRV into VOX in January 2001.

Partnerships

Partnerships are another answer to co-operation and co-ordination problems.

Partnerships among different agents have appeared as a solution to problems of co-operation and co-ordination. Partnerships with the private sector in the form of semi-public bodies, such as the newly created Sector Skills Councils (SSCs) in the United Kingdom,[5] or the Regional Development Councils in partnership with local employers (such as the Autonomous Community of La Rioja) in Spain are examples. They have been viewed as a way to reach potential learners and use regional synergies in terms of funding, physical space and the optimisation of public and private resources. Regional industry councils have appeared in OECD countries. Functioning as semi-private bodies gives them flexibility for recognition of demand and for greater co-operation among the different agents that participate, but also raises issues of accountability.

Canada is a good example of the use of partnerships. The 1% employer tax in Quebec has created councils of the social partners to discuss the

---

5. SSCs have replaced Training and Enterprise Councils (TECs). Their objectives are to ensure that employer and workforce needs are met. They will work in partnership (in England) with organisations such as Regional Development Agencies, the Learning and Skills Council, the Employment Service and the Connexions Service to ensure a coherent analytical and practical approach to skills shortages.

training needs of individual firms, and union members in particular seem happy to play a greater role in such deliberations. Saskatchewan has created industry-education councils, and provides many examples where the brokering function of regional colleges creates programmes that could not be developed without such co-operation. The National Literacy Secretariat has developed productive partnerships with provinces to support research and information-sharing. There are a number of education-community partnerships; for example, in New Brunswick adult basic education is organised through community colleges, which provides assistance in developing curriculum materials for transition into the college, while the adult basic education programmes themselves are provided by community-based organisations. Throughout Canada there are many efforts to link educational institutions, particularly through articulation and transfer agreements linking colleges and universities.

The challenge of decentralisation

As mentioned previously, the trend towards a holistic approach has been accompanied by a trend towards decentralisation in the design and provision of adult education in different countries. This can be due to a number of reasons. Because national governments have not focused on adult education, regional and local governments have developed those policies. In states characterised by a federal structure, the local level has been quite active in adult education policy development. The trends also follow a general trend to bring decision making closer, to adapt to local needs and requirements.

Decentralisation, which has accompanied the trend towards a holistic approach...

Decentralisation has made co-operation among different partners easier because of the scale. At a local level it is easier to bring together education and labour market authorities, together with health and social services working towards the same objectives. It is often the case that adult learning centres are at the same place, and that social service orientation can gear people towards training programmes. Centring the focus on adults has developed systems that offer integral services to adults, whether for health, training or other services.

... has made co-operation easier because of the scale...

There is a certain risk with decentralisation that equity objectives can be lost, and that quality control is at risk. In fact, this has taken place in a number of countries. In Canada for example, quality control and standards depend on the provinces. Some allow for complete market provision, and there have been problems of adult education centres closing and leaving the students halfway during the school year.

... but it can also put equity objectives at risk.

Sweden has experienced a process of decentralisation in its adult education policy. The earlier central steering system was replaced in 1991 by a system of management by objectives with a large degree of local autonomy. Municipalities were given responsibility for the organisation, personnel and school resources. The Swedish Riksdag and the government draw up the national goals and guidelines for child care, the school and adult education in Sweden. In the School Act, the curriculum and different ordinances there are provisions that steer the contents of child care and guarantee equivalent education irrespective of where in the country it is provided. As part of achieving national equivalence, the National Agency for Education is responsible for drawing up national syllabi and grade criteria (OECD, 2001c).

Spain has also finished a decentralisation process in education as well as in training policies. The state reserves the rights to safeguard the homogeneity and unity of the educational system by guaranteeing conditions of basic equality for all Spanish citizens. Autonomous regional governments can develop national regulations, regulate non-basic aspects of the educational system and develop the executive-administrative responsibilities. In terms of training policies, the Public Employment Service (*Instituto Nacional de Empleo*) manages employment policies and the regional governments, in turn, exercise a series of responsibilities in the management of labour policies within their respective territories, in accordance with the guidelines of co-operation established with the PES.

The role of the social partners

Social partners play a multiplicity of useful roles in both policy development and programme delivery.

The social partners have a crucial role to play in both policy development and programme delivery. They can contribute to identifying educational requirements and the development and provision of relevant education and training programmes. They can also help bring about closer co-ordination between adult learning and the labour market, by ensuring that qualifications obtained are useful and are recognised in the labour market. They can have a multiplicity of roles to play in terms of design, promotion, provision, consumption and negotiation.

There are different mechanisms for their involvement.

The extent to which governments include social partners in policy planning and design varies across countries (OECD, 2002b). Mechanisms include:

- The establishment of tripartite agreements related to training. Portugal and Spain have signed tripartite agreements that cover increasing learning opportunities for all.

- No specific arrangements but forums for participation at different levels, with committees and councils in which the social partners are present. Such is the case with Denmark, where they take responsibilities at all levels (although participation of social partners in counselling as regards contents of education programmes is generally limited to vocational education and training as well as CVT). In Norway, there is also strong tripartite co-operation; the Competence Reform is the outcome of a tripartite effort to raise competencies of individuals with all employers, employees and governments as active contributors in the process.

- Special consultative agencies or bodies. The National Advisory Council for Education and Training Targets (NACETT) in the UK is an example of an employer-led body that advises government on education and training policies.

They can have also an impact on policies without government participation, through bipartite agreements.

The social partners can also play an important role without government participation. They can have an impact on education and training policies through bipartite agreements or co-operation in bipartite bodies, as is the case, for example, of sector councils in Canada. Sector councils bring together representatives from business, labour, education and other professional groups, and have proved highly effective in addressing human resource issues in key sectors of the Canadian economy. They have been active in developing voluntary occupational and skills standards; but they have also been active in training and school-to-work transitions. In Sweden as well, the social partners carry out considerable work with regard to outreach activities and orientation courses. This work has succeeded in motivating people that otherwise would not have taken on further studies.

4.4. Adult learning and policy making

Adult learning has become an important issue in policy making in recent years following the lifelong learning vision adopted by OECD countries. In fact, all reviewed countries have recently adopted some type of reform or have raised it as a policy issue. Some of the reforms are so recent that it is difficult to know how effective they may be. But most countries are indeed adopting a lifelong learning agenda for adults and are trying to broaden learning opportunities across the board. In this light, the development of coherent adult education policies is important for overall effectiveness.

Adopting a lifelong learning agenda for adults entails developing coherent adult education policies...

A coherent policy specifically focused on adults has to take the special needs of adults into consideration as the main objective. It has to take into consideration the fact that adults are most often working or have busy lifestyles, and they need time off from their employment or extra time. This implies flexibility in schedules, in provision and in the recognition of prior learning experiences, be it formal or non-formal. Supply should be available in evenings and weekends, or provide for time off from work, and the possibility of part-time studies should be allowed. Policy also has to take into consideration that enterprises offer a large proportion of training opportunities to adults, so it is important to strengthen public-private co-operation in this area. For those who are not working, it would mean providing the financial assistance to cover living expenses. If they have a family, it might require some support services for child care. It would also imply other complementary assistance to return to education, such as guidance and counselling and assistance with personal situations that might arise.

... that take their special needs into consideration as the main objective.

From a broader policy perspective, and keeping the special needs of adults in mind, it is really a matter of making the proper choices to attain effective results. Among the conditions that need to be met to have a coherent adult learning policy, one could include:

Different conditions for a coherent adult learning policy...

- The existence of a consensus on the need to invest in human resource development and especially on adult learning, from potential learners and the social partners to policy makers.
- Financial commitment to accompany the implementation of adult learning policies.

... such as a financial commitment...

- The existence of a structure that includes responsibilities for adult learning policy making and for effective provision of adult education, either centrally planned or decentralised. It is also important to include possibilities of co-operation for the different actors involved as well as formal channels of participation or consultation with partners that may be involved in other policies, such as employment, social, economic or health authorities.
- The establishment of priorities among the different kinds of adult learning, such as literacy, basic educational attainment or IT skills for example, and greater public funding channelled to them.

91

... the measurement of efficiency...

... or the integration in general education and training policies.

- The definition of the kinds of institutions that provide different types of adult learning and mechanisms to ensure their quality.
- Special provision and support, financial or other, for population groups with special needs.
- The inclusion of measurement of efficiency and outcomes and the evaluation of policies, as it is important for accountability of the system and for continued investment and support.
- The integration of adult learning in general education and training policies.

Table 4.2. **Different country approaches to adult learning**

CANADA

Objectives	Measure or reform	Main actors in policy design and implementation	Content or forms of adult education	Financing	Delivery methods	Evaluation measurement

• Make building a skilled workforce a national effort
• Focus on post-secondary policies, including adult education
• Focus on training for the unemployed and employed
• Focus on increasing literacy levels
	Learning and skills agenda at national level (2001) and *Knowledge Matters* (2002):
	• Plan to increase by 1 million the number of adult learners within 5 years
	• Help adults who have difficulty finding time or resources to improve their skills
	• Individual incentive mechanisms already assist those in need
	• Improve the loans available to part-time students, so more workers can learn while they earn
	• Give provinces a major role in providing post-secondary education (PSE) and delivery of Canada Student Loans Programme
		• Federal Government: Human Resource Development Canada
		• National Literacy Secretariat
		• CMEC (Council of Ministers of Education of Canada)
		• Provincial governments
			• Strong focus on post-secondary education
			• Employment-related training
			• Vocational training for the unemployed (Employment Insurance System)
			• Adult Basic Education, including literacy
			• Special Adult Basic Education
			  – for minorities
			  – for aboriginal people
				• Strong focus on individual initiative and choice mechanisms
				• Strong variation of levels of spending across provinces
				• Student loans for post-secondary education
				• Skills, loans and grants
				• Employment Insurance System (funding for short-term training)
				• Employer tax 1% of wage bill (in Quebec)
				• Public post-secondary institutions
				• Federal government has role in PSE in providing indirect investment, financial assistance (support for research and innovation, tax measures, block funding through Canada Health and Social Transfer, CHST)
					• Public and private post-secondary institutions (community and university colleges)
					• Community-based organisations
					• Partnerships of all types across public and private sector
					• Industry councils, etc.
					• Commercial institutions
						• Research

Table 4.2. **Different country approaches to adult learning** (*cont.*)

DENMARK

Objectives	Measure or reform	Main actors in policy design and implementation	Content or forms of adult education	Financing	Delivery methods	Evaluation measurement
• Provide vocational and personal qualifications • Provide adequate, relevant adult education and continuing training supply to all adults at all levels, from the low skilled to university graduates	*Denmark as a pioneer country* and *10-item plan* (1995): • Establish numerical objectives • Establish policy of free admission to training courses for all • Base provision on demand *Adult Education Reform* (2000): • Tie continuing training and further education programmes into a single, coherent, transparent adult education system • Hold each institution responsible for the quality of its education • Ensure that all have broad supply • Orient public funding to achieving formally recognised competencies for those with low levels of education	• Ministry of education • Ministry of Labour (AMU) • Social partners (tripartite agreements) • Decentralised administration of adult education for the unemployed • New interministerial council for advice to Ministry of Education, Labour and Trade and Industry • Shared responsibility between state and local government	• Formal recognition of competencies • Preparatory Adult Education (FVU): basic skills in reading, writing and numeracy • Adult Education System: including Basic Adult Education, qualifying vocational education for adults, and three advanced higher levels • Vocational education • Adult education for unemployed • Employment-based training • Teaching for the handicapped	• Taximeter funding for education institutions • Public financing of employee training leave • Financing for the unemployed by the Public Employment Service or the municipality • Public provision of training for employed persons, combined with user payment [except Continuing Vocational Training (CVT) or Vocational Education and Training (VET)]	• Folk high schools • Day folk high schools • AMU • General adult education centres (VUC) • Open education (vocational education schools and colleges) • University extension courses • Distance and e-learning	• Surveys • Taximeter system • New reform with set targets and effects analysed and measured at all levels

Table 4.2. **Different country approaches to adult learning** (*cont.*)

FINLAND

Objectives	Measure or reform	Main actors in policy design and implementation	Content or forms of adult education	Financing	Delivery methods	Evaluation measurement
• Provide learning content that supports the development of personality, consolidates democratic values, maintains social cohesion and promotes innovation and productivity • Target those who lack initial education or have a poor secondary education • Focus on constructing individual educational paths for adults	*The Joy of Learning* (1997): • Comprehensive reform of legislation on basic, secondary and adult education based on national regulation: – reinforcement of the foundations of learning – development of a broad spectrum of learning opportunities – public recognition of prior learning and experience – information and support for constructing learning paths – updating the skills of teachers and instructors – a comprehensive policy for the promotion of learning • Alternation and study leave • Increased powers of education providers applying equally to municipal, state and private education • Labour market training guided by the T&E Centres	• Ministry of Education: learning for change or general skills • Ministry of Labour: learning for jobs • Participation of social partners at different levels • Municipalities: the main maintainers of institutions • The labour market departments of the Employment and Economic Development Centres (T&E Centres) (combined regional units of the Ministry of Trade and Industry, the Ministry of Labour and the Ministry of Agriculture and Forestry) for labour market training	• Universal and free provision of adult certificate- or diploma-oriented education • Adults able to study in the same institutions as young people for same qualifications • Specific adult education structure for adult-oriented qualifications, upgrading of skills and competencies and leisure activities • Alternation leave: employee on leave from work covered by an unemployed job seeker • Study Leave Act enabling employees to take part in full-time studies • Informal learning recognition through competence-based examinations to obtain vocational qualifications	• Public funding of certificate- and diploma-oriented education • "Mixed model" financing in additional vocational training • State subsidy to major providers of additional vocational training (60% state budget for self-motivated additional vocational training) • State appropriations to higher and liberal education institutions for specific education and training (40%) • Education and training insurance scheme as financial aid to adults during their studies • Obligatory financial contribution by companies for individual educational leave managed by social partners	• Large variety of adult education and training institutions • Adults entitled to participate in the same initial vocational programmes leading to a qualification as young people • Special vocational adult education centres and national specialised institutions • For tertiary education: – continuing education centres – open university – open polytechnics • Liberal education institutions • Individual education leave	• Surveys used to plan the offer of education and training

Table 4.2. **Different country approaches to adult learning** (*cont.*)

NORWAY

Objectives	Measure or reform	Main actors in policy design and implementation	Content or forms of adult education	Financing	Delivery methods	Evaluation measurement
• Raise the education level of the entire adult population • Meet the needs of the labour market for skills and competencies • Satisfy the needs of individuals for personal and professional development	*Competence Reform* (1999) • Long-term initiative: – expand learning opportunities for all adults – produce highly skilled workforce – develop lifelong learning strategy – improve interaction between education and workplace – recognise the workplace as a place for learning – increase flexibility and use of ICT • Right to basic education • Right to upper-secondary education • Work on non-formal learning assessment • Right to study leave • Tax-free education • Reorganisation of the public education system • Motivation, guidance and information project	• Ministry of Education (KUF), responsible for educational system and national educational policy • Ministry of Labour and Government Administration (AAD), responsible for employment policy • Ministry of Trade and Industry (NHD), responsible for the tools of industrial policy • Municipalities and county municipalities, responsible for providing formal adult education • Social partners (strong role)	• Compulsory education, including primary and secondary education • Special needs education • Education for immigrants • Adult learning in NGOs • Labour market training for the unemployed, focusing on immigrants, young and older adults, long-term unemployed, individuals at risk and with low levels of educational attainment • Training in the enterprise	• Financial assistance (loans and grants) for most types of education and training, especially for primary up to upper secondary education • Free tuition for primary and secondary education, labour market training, for immigrants and higher education • Block grants to municipalities (central government) • Some grants to private institutions and associations in co-operation with public or NGOs • Tax exemption for employer-financed education • Study leave and employer-financed education	• Municipalities: compulsory education • County municipalities: upper secondary education • Folk high schools • Institutions of higher education (further and continuing education) • Private providers • Study associations: tradition of popular enlightenment	• Future policy based on analysis of the need for resources in the workplace and in society • Different research institutes

Table 4.2. **Different country approaches to adult learning** (*cont.*)

PORTUGAL

Objectives	Measure or reform	Main actors in policy design and implementation	Content or forms of adult education	Financing	Delivery methods	Evaluation measurement
• Improve competitiveness and social cohesion • Fight against low skills and educational attainment • Adopt active labour market policies and training to combat unemployment	*Strategy for the development of adult education* (1998) and *Recurrent education: Evaluation report* (1998) • Creation of ANEFA *Agreement on employment, labour, education and training policy* (2001): • Promote quality training • Consolidate a National System of Certification • Consolidate an adult learning system with informal and recurrent education • Develop enterprise training	• ANEFA: education and training (Ministry of Education and Ministry of Labour and Solidarity) • Community institutions • Social partners • IEFP: training for employment • Establishment of partnerships • Regional development plans • Social partners (strong role)	• EFA and initial vocational education for adults with low qualifications • Saber +: skills enhancement in specific sectors • Basic and secondary education • Literacy courses by EFA for LTU, handicapped, immigrants and those close to exclusion • Open University • IEFP: training for unemployment • Right of working individuals to a minimum of at least 20 certified hours of training • Vocational training: retraining	• Indirect tax levy for training: 4.2% of the social security budget, financed by a 33% tax on wages • Free provision • European Social Fund (ESF) (important role)	• Web of public provision: – adult education schools – vocational training centres • Regular schools for basic and secondary education • Arrangements with private institutions • Neighbourhood organisations and NGOs provide literacy and basic education programmes • System of recognition, validation and certification of competencies (CRVCC)	• INOFOR: diagnosis for training

Table 4.2. **Different country approaches to adult learning** (*cont.*)

SPAIN

Objectives	Measure or reform	Main actors in policy design and implementation	Content or forms of adult education	Financing	Delivery methods	Evaluation measurement
• Provide adults with access to education at all levels • Help them acquire or improve professional qualifications and the capacity to participate in the social, cultural, political, and economic areas of life • Establish their right to education, vocational training and self-advancement • In vocational training, place a greater emphasis on labour market insertion	LOGSE (1990): provision of primary and secondary education to the adult population *The National Vocational Training Programme* (1998-2002): • Articulates a comprehensive system for formal vocational training, for the unemployed and the employed • Creates a National Qualifications System with participation of the regional autonomies *New Vocational Training and Qualifications Bill* (2002) *III National Agreement for Continuous Training* (2000-2004): fund continuous training through a levy (tripartite agreement) • New Royal Decree Law to carry out open call exams for compulsory secondary education • Specific measures by regional governments	• Ministry of Education, Culture and Sports: basic adult education, secondary education certificate, vocational training, and social guarantee programmes, or official language classes • INEM, Ministry of Labour and Social Affairs: vocational training • Social partners (through the Tripartite Foundation for Training at Work, previously FORCEM) • Recently decentralised system: – regional autonomies – local governments	• Basic adult education. • Primary and secondary education degrees and personal development • Social guarantee programmes • Official language programmes • Spanish language for immigrants • Education in prisons • Vocational training programmes for the unemployed • Occupational training (craft school workshops, trade schools and employment workshops) • Continuing vocational training for employed workers	• Free provision of adult education for specific groups • Education dependent on the educational administrations financed through the state or regional government's general budgets and the ESF • Subsidies to private training centres • Training activities for the unemployed and employed financed primarily through the vocational training fee paid by the businesses and workers • Contributions from the European Social Fund and regional governments	• Specific adult education institutions for adult basic education and literacy programmes • Regular education centres cater to adults • Subsidies to private training centres (collaborative centres) • National vocational occupational training centres • "Aula Mentor", open, free training system carried out over the Internet • Education in Prison • National Distance University (UNED) • Catalonia Open University (UOC) • University extension education aimed at older individuals • Education TV • NGOs	• Education inspectorate at national level

Table 4.2. **Different country approaches to adult learning** (*cont.*)

SWEDEN

Objectives	Measure or reform	Main actors in policy design and implementation	Content or forms of adult education	Financing	Delivery methods	Evaluation measurement
• Support adult learning through redistribution and growth • Bridge educational gaps, promote economic growth, strengthen democracy and satisfy the wishes of individuals • Popular adult education: promote social well-being and strengthen democratic values and cultural life • Focus on the basis of individual needs	*The Adult Education Initiative* (1997-2002): raise the educational attainment of adults who lack knowledge on the secondary level with flexible provision of upper secondary education (90 000 places annually) *New parliament goals and strategies for adult learning* (2001): • Focus on more flexible support for individual learning, adjusting content and form to more individual needs • Develop competence in industry • Provide a broad range of financial assistance, including special grants for the unemployed and special study assistance for those who take a leave of absence from work • Advanced vocational education: since 2002, a regular part of the education and training system	• Ministry of Education • National Agency for Education • The Swedish Agency for Advanced Vocational Education • The Swedish Agency for Flexible Learning • The Swedish National Council of Adult Education • Municipalities (strong role in selection and delivery)	Strong public adult education and training system: • Adult basic education corresponding to compulsory and upper secondary level • Advanced vocational education • Popular adult education • Labour market training • In-service training	• Study allowances for university, university college or other post-secondary education, folk high schools, municipal adult education and other forms equivalent to compulsory and secondary school • New study grant (2003) for those with greatest needs and disabilities • Labour market policy financed by the state • Educational grants to support participants while studying • Part of in-service training and competence development in working life funded by EU structural funds • New state funding for municipal adult education and folk high schools for 2003-2005	• Municipal adult education (*Komvux*) • Adult education for those with functional disabilities (*Särvux*) • Swedish tuition for immigrants (Sfi) • Advanced vocational training (KY) • Folk high schools • Study circles • Labour market training carried out by private and public educational providers	• Follow-up and evaluation of publicly funded adult education • Different agencies responsible for the various forms of education

Table 4.2. **Different country approaches to adult learning** (*cont.*)

SWITZERLAND

Objectives	Measure or reform	Main actors in policy design and implementation	Content or forms of adult education	Financing	Delivery methods	Evaluation measurement

• Federal policy emphasis: develop skills for occupational purposes
• For the cantons: view adult learning as a whole, without distinguishing goals
• Vocational training: focus on qualifications for professional activity
• Efforts under way to develop a system conducive to occupational and personal development as well as social and occupational integration, to ensure equal opportunities to regions and genders
	• Federal structure and principle of subsidiarity in adult learning
	• Federal government to promote continuing and further training when cantons do not do so by law
	• Active labour market policies: training for the unemployed
	• Funding of infrastructure and teacher training at learning centres for the development of new technologies
	• "Learnfestival" to promote access and participation
	• EduQua: quality assurance scheme introduced
	• Modularisation of vocational courses, incentives for staff certification and amendments to legislation
	• Upcoming Law on vocational education (nLFP) to weaken the distinction between vocational education and general adult education
	• Cantons: a diversity of policies
		• Confederation in charge of vocational training
		• State Secretariat for Economic Affairs (Seco) in charge of training for the unemployed
		• Federal Office for Professional Education and Technology (OFFT) in charge of initial and continuing vocational training
		• General adult education attributed to the federal Office of Culture
		• Important role of the private sector and not-for-profit institutions of public utility
		• Cantons in charge of adult education have different approaches:
		  – encourage or support continuing training by subsidising groups, associations, or secondary and vocational schools catering to adult learners
		  – financial resources
			• New technologies
			• Languages
			• Diploma courses (*maturité* or higher education entrance examination for adults)
			• Federal certificates and diplomas
			• Secondary and upper-secondary education
			• Enterprise training
			• Leisure courses
				• Broad variety of arrangements
				• Financing by the enterprises and individuals
				• Public financing spread out across the confederation and cantons
				• Confederation funds the cantons for the distribution of grants to those who want to finish secondary or tertiary education with cantons, establishing their conditions
				• Subsidies to training firms for the unemployed
				• Financing of material and teacher training
				• Other financing to private institutions
					• Private training institutions or commercial schools
					• Privately run, state-approved institutions and (not-for-profit) associations
					• Denominational, trade union, political or ethical institutions
					• Local associations, community groups and third-sector enterprises
					• Popular universities
					• Private institutions with public objectives
					• Migros "club schools"
					• Secondary schools
					• Universities
					• Employers
						• Regular Surveys by Federal Statistical Office (OFS) on participation in adult education

Table 4.2. **Different country approaches to adult learning** (*cont.*)

UNITED KINGDOM

Objectives	Measure or reform	Main actors in policy design and implementation	Content or forms of adult education	Financing	Delivery methods	Outcomes measurement
Lifelong learning agenda: • Ensure that everyone of working age and beyond has the skills to meet needs of employment and to lead rewarding and fulfilling lives • Provide higher level skills needed for a successful innovative knowledge-based economy • Drive up standards of teaching and learning across education and training	The *Learning Age Green Paper* (1998): sets out the vision for lifelong learning • *White paper learning to succeed* (1999): sets out reforms to the delivery framework, including the establishment of Learning and Skills Council (LSC) for strategic planning for lifelong learning, to stimulate demand for and participation in learning • Joint White paper with DTI *Opportunity for All in a World of Change* (2001): provide people with skills to adapt to globalisation • *Skills for Life* (2001): national strategy to improve adult literacy and numeracy	• Department of Education and Skills (DfES): responsibilities in, *inter alia*, lifelong learning • Department for Work and Pensions (DWP): responsibility for, *inter alia*, helping unemployed • Learning and Skills Council (LSC) responsible for all post-16 education and training • Sector Skills Councils (SSCs) • Large array of players, such as the Campaign for learning and the Further Education Development Agency	• Lifelong learning • Literacy and basic skills • Flexible learning opportunities • Online learning in IT skills, business skills, basic skills and multimedia • Further education • Academic or vocational training • NVQs • IT literacy • Short training courses • Labour market training for the unemployed • Skills upgrading for those in work	Financial support mechanisms in process of reform: • Financial support to students through income contingent loans (ICL) • Individual Learning Accounts: grant given to the first million individuals opening a special bank account for vocational training (suspended) • Further education: system to reward colleges and other providers for taking students from poor neighbourhoods • Tuition-free remission • Loans and grants • Free provision	• Open University • Ufi/Learn Direct distance learning platform • Residential colleges • National Extension College (distance learning) • BBC Education • Further education colleges • Investors in People (standard for companies with active learning activities) • Local infrastructure for adult information, advice and guidance (IAG)	• Studies and evaluation of results of programmes

Note: For more information concerning specific country approaches please refer to Background Reports and Country Notes.
Source: Thematic Review on Adult Learning Country Background Reports and Country Notes (*www.oecd.org/edu/adultlearning*).

BIBLIOGRAPHY

BÉLANGER, P. and P. FEDERIGHI (2000),
Analyse transnationale des politiques d'éducation et de formation des adultes, UNESCO Institute for Education, Hamburg.

BJØRNÅVOLD, J. (2001),
"Assessment and Recognition of Non-formal Learning in Europe: Main Tendencies and Challenges", Communication prepared for the OECD-KRIVET International Conference on Adult Learning Policies, 5-7 December, Seoul, Korea.

BOYER, R. (2001),
"Promoting Learning in the Enterprise: The lessons of International Comparisons in the Light of Economic Theory", Communication prepared for the OECD-KRIVET International Conference on Adult Learning Policies, 5-7 December, Seoul, Korea.

EUROPEAN COMMISSION (2000),
A *Memorandum on Lifelong Learning*, Brussels.

EUROPEAN COMMISSION (2001),
Communication from the Commission: Making a European Area of Lifelong Learning a Reality, Brussels.

EUROPEAN UNION,
Grundtvig, *http://europa.eu.int/comm/education/socrates/adult/overview.html*

EUROSTAT (2001),
New Chronos Database, CVTS2, Brussels.

GRUBB, N. (2001),
"Formalising the Informal: Creating Effective Systems of Adult Education", Communication prepared for the OECD-KRIVET International Conference on Adult Learning Policies, 5-7 December, Seoul, Korea.

HECKMAN, J.J. (1999),
"Doing it Right: Job Training and Education", *The Public Interest*, Spring, pp. 86-107.

MARTIN, J. (2000),
"What Works among Active Labour Market Policies? Evidence from OECD Countries' Experiences", *Economic Studies No. 30*, OECD, Paris.

MARTIN, J. and D. GRUBB (2001),
"What Works and for Whom: A Review of OECD Countries' Experiences in Active Labour Market Policies", OECD, Paris.

NORD (2001),
Curious minds: Nordic Adult Education Compared, Copenhagen.

O'CONNELL, P. (1999),
"Adults in Training: An International Comparison of Continuing Education and Training", CERI/WD(99)1, OECD, Paris (*www.oecd.org/edu/adultlearning*).

OECD (1999a),
"Training of Adult Workers in OECD Countries: Measurement and Analysis", *Employment Outlook*, Paris.

OECD (2000a),
"The Role of National Qualification Systems in Promoting Lifelong Learning", DEELSA/ELSA/ED(2000)3.

OECD (2000b),
Where Are the Resources for Lifelong Learning?, Paris.

OECD (2001a),
Economics and Finance of Lifelong Learning, Paris.

OECD (2001b),
"Thematic Review on Adult Learning, Finland Background Report", Paris (*www.oecd.org/edu/adultlearning*).

OECD (2001c),
"Thematic Review on Adult Learning, Sweden Background Report", Paris (*www.oecd.org/edu/adultlearning*).

OECD (2001d),
   "Thematic Review on Adult Learning, Denmark Background Report", Paris (*www.oecd.org/edu/adultlearning*).

OECD (2001e),
   Knowledge and Skills for Life: First Results from PISA 2000, Paris.

OECD (2002a),
   "The Role of National Qualification Systems in Promoting Lifelong Learning: Progress Report", DEELSA/ED(2002)2.

OECD (2002b),
   "Supporting Economic Growth through Continuous Education and Training – Some Preliminary Results", ELS working paper, OECD, Paris.

OECD and STATISTICS CANADA (2000),
   Literacy in the Information Age: Final Report of the International Adult literacy Survey, Paris and Ottawa.

PONT, B. (2001),
   "Meeting Adult Learning Needs", Issues Paper prepared for the OECD-KRIVET International Conference on Adult Learning Policies, Seoul, 5-7 December, Korea.

Chapter 5

STRENGTHENING THE INCENTIVES AND MOTIVATION
FOR ADULTS TO LEARN

There is evidence that lack of motivation on the part of the individuals is one of the main reasons why participation is low. Clearly, sustainable incentive mechanisms have to be found if the situation is to improve. Findings suggest that adults who need to learn are often not aware of it or would deny it – even when it comes to basic literacy skills. Surveys also show that the most active learners are already highly qualified. In short, learners are in most cases already convinced of the value of learning.

Chapter 5 describes some of the barriers to work on removing and the incentives to be put in place to improve participation. The latter range from advertising the overall value of learning beyond the workplace (social value, citizenship, etc.) to making obvious the economic benefits of learning (increased productivity for the company and better employability of the worker). A range of good practices are described throughout the chapter; the most relevant of these concern the right to study leave, the scheduling of the learning activities, and financing schemes such as individual learning accounts. Special emphasis is also placed on groups at risk; those with obsolete qualifications or low educational attainment; workers in SMEs; and older workers or the unemployed. Professional promotion or immediate reward is not always the answer to improving incentives to learn. Better communication should be established around the value and the joy of learning, and greater attention paid to making individuals freer to resume learning.

5.1. Covering learning needs – the challenge

The initial reasons for learning – personal vs. professional – tend to blur over time

Although the initial motivations of learners are no doubt clear – they always know why they are embarking – once they have completed their education or training, it becomes increasingly difficult to distinguish those who underwent the training solely for personal or for employment-related reasons.[1] This is all the more true as time passes and individuals rationalise their past decisions in the light of more recent events. Training undertaken for personal reasons may well lead to a new job or to a change in professional orientation. Similarly, employers may need to train their staff in basic reading when introducing new machines that require workers to have adequate reading skills in their own language in order to follow instructions. However, since the needs of employers and of the labour market in general are more specific and often better defined, the incentives and motivations of learners with specifically employment-related aims will be addressed separately in Section 5.2. Finally, Section 5.3 discusses specific issues related to training for the unemployed.

Training inequalities are linked to lack of motivation

This section addresses those needs that are not *a priori* directly employment-related. It focuses on two findings. First, there are inequalities in training opportunities. Second, these inequalities are to some extent linked to a lack of motivation. Chapter 6 will look in depth at the other aspect of these inequalities: the absence of a pedagogical approach and practical training methods suited to adults.

Those in need of training do not know… or deny it

The basic skills of reading, writing and arithmetic, theoretically beyond motivation…

It might well seem that the logical starting point for discussing adults' learning needs would be to identify their aspirations in this regard. Part of the literature on education and andragogy[2] clearly explains the necessity of having adult learners create their own learning project, or at least the need to help them define the goal of their learning activity (project-based pedagogy – Chiousse, 2001). This section will start from an even more elementary premise about which there is a good deal of consensus, *i.e.* that there are certain basic needs, such as reading, writing and arithmetic, that are not necessarily connected with any personal or employment-related plans or specific project (unless "project" is defined in very broad terms). If it encompasses the ability to live in a modern society, to use all its services, then reading, writing and arithmetic are also projects. However, the situation is not as simple as that, because the very next question is: what needs have to be provided for by the community and, also perhaps, regulated centrally? In the case of a personal project, the need for public policy is more debatable – but that debate must take place. If the view is that every citizen has the right to be able to read, write and count, then there should be financial and other assistance provided.

---

1. For the sake of simplicity, the term "general education" is used for the former and "vocational training" for the latter.
2. Pedagogy for adults. Pierre Goguelin uses the term "andragogy" in his work published in Paris in 1970. The term is used especially in Canada in courses with the same name, and is defined as the "science and field of social practice whose specific objective is the link between educational assistance and adult learning" (*meq.gouv.gc.ca*). See also Chapter 6.

Individuals are not necessarily aware of these needs – in fact, it is rare that they are. One of the arguments that will be put forward here is that basic education needs have nothing to do with any kind of project in the normal sense – they are simply necessary to function in the countries covered by the thematic review (OECD and Statistics Canada, 2000). There are a wide variety of situations in which good reading skills or basic arithmetic skills are vital, such as reading the instructions on a fire extinguisher during a fire or the directions for the dosage of a drug to be administered to a small child. Apart from such drastic examples, many situations unconnected to any concrete project require adults to have basic skills.

... are necessary to survive in the countries studied.

Describing and analysing what motivates adults to learn is one of the hardest challenges for the thematic review. It is in fact a twofold task, for it also means understanding why some people with learning needs do not participate in learning. Information and data sources are relatively scarce on this point, precisely because the institutions in charge of adult learning have little contact with that public. In many cases they only see those who come to learn, rarely those who do not. It came as no surprise that relatively few opportunities arose to meet with adults who cannot or do not want to learn during visits to the nine countries covered by the thematic review.

Non-participation is, naturally enough, difficult to research.

The problem is partly one of observation (for lack of subjects), but it no doubt goes even deeper than that. The adults most in need of education and training are also those who refuse to acknowledge that need. For example, when an International Adult Literacy Survey (IALS) questioned persons with varying prose literacy levels – the criterion that most closely matches reading proficiency – those individuals with the lowest literacy levels (Levels 1 and 2) frequently did not think that they need training (Figure 5.1). At prose literacy Level 1, more of them replied that their reading skills are "excellent" (12.9%) than "poor" (10.6%). At Level 2, 80.8% stated that they have "good" or "excellent" reading ability. Consequently, it appears that many adults overestimate their real ability to understand a text and react appropriately or make adequate decisions on the basis of what they read. Similarly, of those who think that they have "excellent" reading skills, at least one of every four adults are at Level 1 or 2 on the prose scale, almost as many people as those actually at Level 4 or 5. Individuals' lack of objectivity about their reading level[3] is even more flagrant for those who say that they have good skills: about 50% at Level 1 or 2, as opposed to barely 13% at Level 4 or 5 (Figure 5.2).

Those persons most in need of education and training refuse to acknowledge that need...

The IALS makes it possible to take this part of the diagnosis of adult learning needs a step further. It appears that the individuals most in need of training and education do not believe that their lack of basic skills hinders their career advancement or their ability to find or change jobs. Of those adults who say that they are not at all limited in their opportunities for promotion or mobility at work, four out of ten are at Level 1 or 2, as opposed to only two out of ten at Level 4 or5 (Figure 5.3).

... nor do they believe that their lack of basic skills hinders job prospects.

---

3.   Further evidence shows that the situation is much the same for their writing and arithmetic skills.

Figure 5.1. **Self-assessment of reading skills by prose literacy level**

Percentage of population 25-64 years old at each self-assessment level by prose literacy level, 1994-98

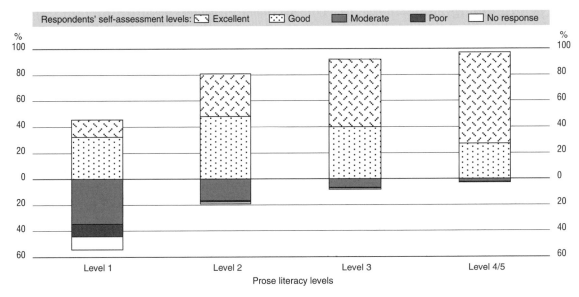

Source: International Adult Literacy Survey, 1994-98.

Figure 5.2. **Prose literacy level by self-assessment of reading skills**

Percentage of population 25-64 years old at each prose literacy level, 1994-98

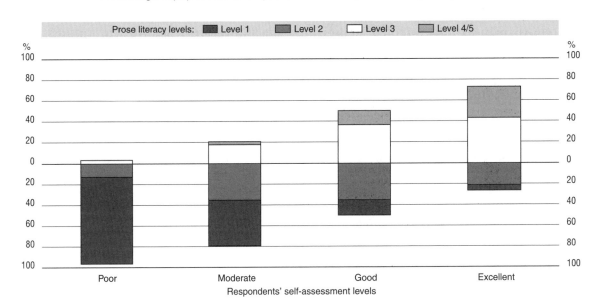

Source: International Adult Literacy Survey, 1994-98.

Figure 5.3.   **Prose literacy level by response to whether reading skills limit opportunities at work**
Percentage distribution of literacy levels within each response for population 25-64 years old, 1994-98

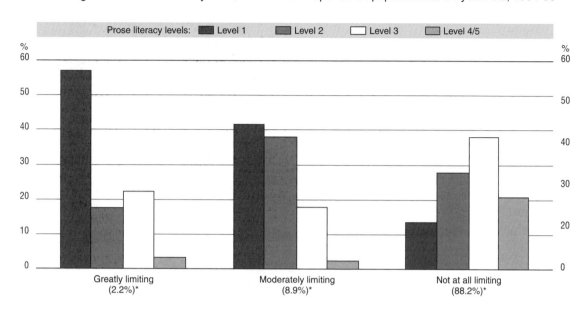

*   Distribution of all responses.
Source: International Adult Literacy Survey, 1994-98.

These results, although convergent, must clearly be treated with caution since they raise a number of complex issues, in particular regarding the literature on individuals' self-assessment of performance. For example, the fact that individuals do not think that their possibilities of being promoted or of finding a new job are limited by their poor reading skills is not necessarily due to a lack of self-knowledge. One-third of them recognise that their reading skills are poor, but still do not believe that they limit their opportunities at work. It is simply that the job they hold only requires a low level of basic skills, or that the individuals themselves have no career ambition. It is also clear that there are many explanations for the second set of results on employment opportunities (Figure 5.3), the most obvious of which concerns skill profiles. Naturally enough, the least skilled individuals are also those who hold jobs that require the fewest skills, and their lack of skills is not necessarily apparent. They are also, by extrapolation, the least likely to seek career advancement since many of them say that they do not suffer from any handicap in this respect. That could be dismissed as a tautology were it not for the fact that raising the skill level have an impact on economic growth, individual well-being and wider societal benefits such as citizenship or greater participation in society.

Those results may stem from complacency in low-skill jobs, but they are still cause for concern.

The first set of results (Figures 5.1 and 5.2) is interesting because it shows that there is no natural, spontaneous demand for government to raise skills such as basic literacy on the part of the natural target populations of such initiatives. This fact, which was established directly by the IALS, was also confirmed by a series of field observations conducted during the thematic review visits, and is widely referred to in the literature on this topic. During

Data indicate that these groups are not demanding any government initiatives to raise basic skills.

Figure 5.4. **Prose literacy level by self-assessment of reading skills in selected countries**

Percentage of population 25-64 years old at each prose literacy level by self-assessment level in selected countries, 1994-98

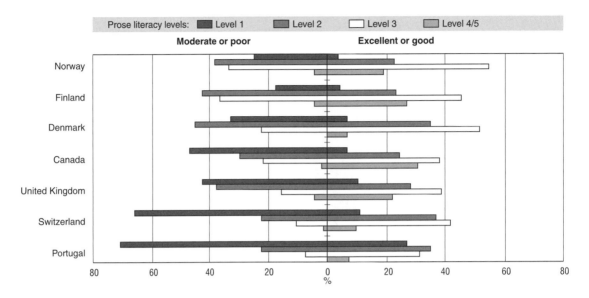

Note: The countries are ranked in ascending order in "Excellent or good" and "Level 1".
Source: International Adult Literacy Survey, 1994-98.

the interviews with the expert teams, many educators and field staff in all the countries visited said that people who are known to need remedial education in their own language are unwilling even to consider this possibility, for a series of reasons that the review was able to identify (outlined later in this section).

Country differences and time frames are important variables in addressing resistance.

These observations also highlight the necessity of explaining properly to adults in need of education the benefits that they can derive from improving their skills. It is also necessary to develop a sound system of incentives. Obviously, the number of adults convinced of the need to learn is very unevenly distributed and the idea of a cultural dimension to learning or wanting to learn is to some extent borne out when these results are broken down by country (Figure 5.4). The interesting question in this case is not so much how countries compare, but rather the degree of resistance to change in people's attitudes within countries. Although there can be no precise answer to this question without longitudinal data, it can be assumed that if the attitudes of the populations with the greatest adult learning needs can be changed in a reasonably short period of time – less than a decade, for example – then the policy to be implemented will certainly not be the same as it would be if one is talking about the long or very long term. Judging from the results of the research (with the IALS or the ALL[4] survey, for example), it is important to think in terms of the time-frame into which the initiatives must fit.

4. Adult Literacy and Lifeskills, a new international survey underway (*www.ets.org/all*).

The tradition of reading in Sweden, which arose from the fact that young people who wanted to get married had to be able to read the Bible, is very old. It is worth mentioning in passing that the tradition of writing in Sweden is not nearly as strong, which shows clearly that there is nothing predetermined or culturally *ex nihilo* about learning; rather, always, it is the outcome of a coherent and persuasive system of incentives. Another explanation regularly given for Sweden's strong performance on literacy tests (and the IALS in particular) is the fact that foreign films shown there are always in the original version with Swedish subtitles, which means that Swedes who want to understand the dialogue must be able to read the subtitles in their own language (not to mention the incentives for learning foreign languages in Sweden, even if only orally). These examples show the importance of historical and cultural background to understanding a given situation, for there are two parallel but unrelated explanations (the Bible, the cinema) that clearly contribute to a tradition of reading.

Neither the Bible nor the cinema, however, are the responsibilities of the Ministry of Education, and so public policy recommendations cannot be made based on these observations. On the other hand, there is room for reflection on the nature of a system of incentives. Understanding the fundamental reasons behind a culture of learning proves useful in terms of international comparisons. An interesting example from this point of view is Portugal, where there are subtitles in the cinema, but Portugal's performance on the IALS scale cannot compare with Sweden's. It turns out that in fact most of the productions televised in Portugal come from Brazil, where the language is also Portuguese.

In short, the idea that some countries have a learning culture while others do not is simplistic and probably false. Firstly, there is a gradation in people's desire to learn, and this continuum is clearly perceptible when one visits countries as different as those covered by the review. Learning opportunities must, therefore, be provided in harmony with the nature of the investment that individuals are prepared to make. Next, this continuum is also found within the same country just as between different countries; what changes are the relative volumes across countries. Lastly, nothing is predetermined in this regard, since individuals' motivations can be changed by their environment, in response to a persuasive set of arguments. If the case is not stated the task becomes enormous, because incentives that are not mere catalysts[5] only work if efforts are made to prepare the public well in advance of the learning. What learning involves has to be very precisely explained, and the best media for reaching target populations must be identified.

The notion that some countries have a learning culture while others do not is simplistic.

Adult learners are long-time converts

Although very difficult, it is nevertheless essential to attempt to describe and analyse what motivates learners and non-learners, since that is the key to improving adult participation in all kinds of learning activities.

Motivation, a key to participation, needs to be fuelled...

---

5. Some incentives in fact only act as catalysts, in that adults are already very inclined to learn. These already highly "educable", or "trainable" adults thus benefit from dead-weight effects, as it were: they would have learned in any case.

... by swift results
in the case of sceptics
tempted to walk out.

First, it should be pointed out that the distinction between adults who are convinced of the importance of learning – "converts" – and those who are not is no doubt one of the most pertinent distinctions in the study of adult learning. This approach raises issues in terms of pedagogical methods, financing, physical location and the kind of training provided. The reason those issues come into play is that there is a greater need to ensure that learning produces immediate results (when provided) to people who have been difficult to persuade of the benefits – or who, in any case, did not come to the training site on their own initiative. The interviews of the thematic review's expert teams have confirmed that these learners will often give up at the first pretext. The problem in fact is not so much to persuade adults to participate in education and training programmes, but to convince the few adults that have been persuaded to stay. That applies regardless of the motive for learning, whether professional or personal.

Financing and other
support is crucial
to those who may prove
hostile to learning.

Thus the method of financing is an important issue for the converted and probably even more crucial for the more sceptical, even though free provision is known to be a necessary rather than sufficient condition. It is essential to cover related costs (childcare, transport, etc.) for less motivated learners, since everything is much more complicated to organise for individuals who will quit a training programme at the first opportunity. These adults, who are not convinced of the benefits of learning, must also quickly be made to recognise the usefulness of what they are doing if they are not to complain and/or disappear. Therefore, the issues of usefulness, financing, motivation, consistency of policy and return on training are much more relevant for the populations initially hostile to learning. And "hostile" is not too strong a word, as is borne out by stories of certain encounters in learning centres. School dropouts have at times shown hostility towards the act of learning, towards the education system in general, and towards the traditional teaching format that gives centre stage to someone who possesses and transmits knowledge while others form an all too often passive audience assumed to know little or nothing.[6]

Throughout the rest of this analysis, the distinction between those who are convinced of the benefits of learning and those who are not[7] will be used in a cross-cutting approach, even though the breakdown of the sections does not directly reflect this dichotomy.

Adult basic education – the populations concerned

Make basic education
the foundation
of progress – a valid
approach.

Since it is often very difficult to differentiate between general education and vocational training, this section will just seek to define the needs of adults who are not well prepared to make their way in their own society, one that increasingly requires mastery of basic skills. Above all, it shows the validity of the approach that a number of countries have initiated: make basic education the foundation of all progress, even if it is undertaken specifically for employment-related purposes. Just as schools prepare pupils not only for the job market but also for life, adult learning has benefits that go well beyond employment alone. During

---

6. This argument is in fact somewhat more complex than it seems since passivity can sometimes be reassuring to adults who do not wish to be the focus of attention in a situation in which they are unsure of themselves.

7. To which a further distinction will sometimes be added – that between the "convertible" and those who are irremediably hostile.

the country visits, the expert teams observed a general but very full awareness that adult learning has an impact on the functioning of society as a whole (democracy, citizenship, etc.) and not only within firms.

Basic reading, writing and arithmetic skills are thus among the most important adult learning issues, as the IALS has shown. The orders of magnitude are open to discussion as are the ranking and absolute differences between countries, but the facts cannot be denied: a far from negligible portion of the population of the eight countries covered by the survey[8] have difficulties in using their own language. In most cases, this does not mean they are unable to read a text, but rather that they are unable to draw the correct conclusions from a document that may contain text, images and/or figures. On the basis of the IALS, it is estimated that at least one-fourth of the adult population may not be able to fully participate in the society in which they live (Figure 2.1).[9]

At least one-fourth of the adult population in IALS countries surveyed suffers from poor basic skills.

Although the various studies clearly do not measure the same thing, they all concur as to the magnitude of the problem. Consequently, basic education has become one of the priorities of government action.[10] It may be interesting to note that the population in need of basic education can be divided into those who never had access to it – described as "second chance" or remedial – and those who did go to school but have mostly forgotten what they learned because of lack of use or bad schooling experiences.

There are those who never had access to education, and those who did but have mostly forgotten what they learned.

A somewhat more ambitious objective could be to target the upper secondary education level. This level, which is reached at the age of 18 on average and which in most countries gives access to tertiary education, is an excellent reference point as well as a concrete objective. It is a level with an inherent value, since it opens the doors to further high-level lifelong learning, both general and vocational. In fact, all countries visited that are currently passing legislation in this regard are more or less explicitly targeting upper secondary education. Norway has tackled this objective with their Competence Reform and Sweden in their Adult Education Initiative (Box 5.1). This can be done by giving all adult learners the right – and in some cases access and financial resources – to start or resume their education to achieve this level. Chapter 4 offers an overview of the different country policies to this effect.

The upper secondary education level, which roughly corresponds to IALS Level 3...

It is worth noting that the level reached at the end of upper secondary education corresponds more or less to Level 3 on the IALS' literacy scale. In this survey, Level 3 is considered to be the appropriate minimum level for coping with the demands of daily life and work (OECD and Statistics Canada, 2000). The level thus represents a clear objective, about which there seems to be a consensus. It is a preparation for the knowledge-based society, since it opens the doors to tertiary education and training with high technological content.

... could serve as a benchmark goal...

---

8. Spain did not participate in the IALS.
9. These figures may vary depending on the definitions used and the institutions that calculate them. Another study, in the United Kingdom, shows that "approximately one adult in five has a low literacy level" (Moser, 1999).
10. For example, the "Skills for Life" project was launched in the United Kingdom in March 2001.

Box 5.1. **The Adult Education Initiative in Sweden**

Sweden has mainstreamed the Adult Education Initiative, a five-year programme established in 1997, into its adult education policy. The Initiative was mainly financed by reallocating funds earmarked for passive labour market measures to active education and training programmes. There was a consensus that unemployed persons who lacked upper secondary school competence needed education in order to acquire a stronger position on the labour market. For this reason they should have access to educational opportunities, and not unemployment benefits, in the first instance.

The aim was to achieve an overall boost in knowledge among adults at the national level in a short period, providing those with lower levels of education the opportunity to study and thereby achieving a more equitable distribution of knowledge and learning opportunities between generations. At the same time the Initiative aimed at contributing to the reform of adult education, in terms both of content and working methods. The intention for all education and training that takes place under the Adult Education Initiative is to be governed in form and content by the needs, wishes and capacity of the individual. On the other hand, the municipalities are to plan the supply of training in co-operation with the employment offices and the social partners. Approximately 800 000 adults, almost 20% of the workforce, will have conducted full time studies at upper secondary level for at least one year during the five-year period of the Initiative.

Source: OECD (2000).

... although for certain populations that goal is overly ambitious.

It also has drawbacks precisely because it is an ambitious objective. It is not attainable in the short or even medium term. It is going to be very costly in those countries where a very large fraction of the population has still not attained this level (Portugal[11]). In order to minimise the financial costs and loss of motivation on the part of adults studying on their own, a policy of prior learning recognition is also required (Chapter 6). Lastly and especially, for the populations with the illiteracy problems referred to above, the level of upper secondary schooling is neither a reasonable nor credible objective. It could be highly demotivating to set such an objective given the all too obvious gap between the level from which they start and the level sought. It is well known from the research on andragogy that adults have to believe in the objectives they set themselves.

"Leisure learning", though not represented in basic adult education, can also contribute to well-being.

There are also a vast number of learning needs that are useful, pleasant or necessary for adults to study, but which are not represented in adult basic education. Because these types of learning are difficult to define, they will be discussed in the context of the numerous themes that follow. They can include language classes before going on holiday, golf lessons, or subjects that are difficult to identify up front and thus to classify with certainty. An example may illustrate this: many observers and those involved may find it

---

11. It is absolutely essential to distinguish between the number of years of schooling adults may have, and the level of vocational qualification they have attained. Portugal is a perfect example of this. Although an appreciable proportion of adults have no more than six years of schooling, many of them have acquired a very high level of vocational skills. The debate on the recognition of prior learning is thus absolutely central.

difficult to accept that diving lessons be financed out of public funds or as part of vocational training. And yet, it could seem that, given individuals' new consumption patterns, leisure can become a significant component in an individual's well-being. Learning how to dive can therefore open up future employment opportunities in this sector.

A general approach focused on adults' learning needs could be complemented by an approach focusing on specific population groups. The visits to the nine countries covered by the thematic review revealed the existence of several such groups. As a general rule, highly qualified individuals were deliberately excluded from the review (OECD, 2000). Some countries like Portugal boldly decided to concentrate on individuals with low qualifications, even if it meant presenting their national situation in a less favourable light than is actually the case. It is not within the scope of the review to define all population categories in terms of their level of qualifications. Nevertheless, it is worth pointing out in this chapter on motivation that the learning needs of qualified individuals are usually well provided for, either by their firm or through mixed systems of assistance. Quite often, the most deprived are also provided for to a certain extent by the community (the state or voluntary or charitable organisations). On the other hand, what struck the experts in countries like Canada or Finland for example[12] was that the group immediately above the most deprived was not the core concern. And yet this group is very important: it comprises people who work but are on a low or minimum wage, and a large proportion of the unemployed covered by unemployment insurance or solidarity schemes. Their learning needs may not necessarily be urgent from the standpoint of the usual criteria, but a good number are mildly illiterate and need training in, *e.g.*, the basics of information and communication technologies (ICTs). These population categories should therefore probably be taken into account in the current debate on reserves of labour, since they can help reduce bottlenecks and limit potential shortages of skilled workers. This issue will be addressed in Section 5.2.

The needs of specific population groups should be recognised.

A description of the characteristics of learners and non-learners, and the analysis of the solutions that work in the countries visited, is given in the next section. It will be recalled that, while vocational training is explicitly dealt with in Section 5.2, the descriptions and analysis of learners' motives presented here – and of the manner in which they can be encouraged to learn – sometimes have a cross-cutting relevance and often apply to the whole population and all the possible forms of learning. Again, it is very difficult to draw a clear dividing line between basic education and vocational training.

Motivation cannot always be seen as relating exclusively to basic education or vocational training.

---

12. A particular difficulty – one due to the fact that the exercise consists of a field visit – is to know whether the opinions the experts arrive at following their visit are the outcome of adequate observation of the situation in the country, or whether there is an inherent bias stemming from the fact that they inevitably see only a tiny fraction of adult learning activities and those taking part. While the host countries did their best and even surpassed themselves to facilitate the experts' task, it is clear that choices have to be made when a programme is being drawn up, and it cannot be exhaustive. What is at issue, therefore, is the nature of the bias introduced.

Learners and non-learners

Non-learners can be divided into those who cannot learn and those who do not wish to.

In any discussion of learners and their characteristics, it is just as important to describe those who do not learn. A further breakdown of the non-learner group into those who cannot learn and those who do not want to learn has proved fascinating. It should also give food for thought to those implementing policies to encourage adults to learn.

Lack of "trainability" can stem from personal experience or an unconducive environment.

The reason is probably simpler than it looks. Those who cannot learn are prevented, it can be assumed as a working hypothesis, by material constraints. Those who do not want to learn do not do so (also a hypothesis) for cultural reasons.[13] As suggested earlier, here as elsewhere, the diagnosis has a direct impact on the remedy or remedies, since one clearly does not treat a material constraint in the same way as a cultural block. In the former case, people are probable "trainable" – *i.e.* they are willing to be educated, or at least they are not hostile to the idea of starting or resuming learning if the barriers that prevented their access to education are lifted. In the second case, the "trainability" of individuals is largely impaired by personal experience or an environment that is not conducive to education.

Policies need to take account of extreme reluctance and even hostility.

The discussion that follows, therefore, attempts to distinguish between learners, the trainable and the non-trainable. The first learn in one way or another in a formal or a non-formal setting, or deliberately in an informal setting. The second group does not learn but could imagine doing so if they were helped to overcome their constraints. The third group does not learn either and, furthermore, tends to be hostile to the very idea of learning. This does not of course mean that a suitable incentive scheme could not convince them. It is just that they are the hardest to convince and thus the most reluctant group. It thus makes sense to identify them as such in terms of the policies adopted.

The Matthew effect and the dead-weight effects

The least disputed result is the one clearly shown in Figure 5.5: adults with low levels of qualification participate less in learning activities than those with a high level. The ratio is the exact inverse with a distribution pattern of 15/85[14] for individuals at ISCED[15] Level 1 and 70/30 at ISCED 6 or 7. The pivotal point is the central level: 51/49 – virtual equality – at ISCED Level 3. This has been called the Matthew effect, referring to the Bible: "Unto everyone that hath shall be given, and he shall have abundance". Applied to learning, it is those who have higher educational attainment levels that learn more. Two issues arise, which are treated very differently in different countries.

Qualification levels could be made the criterion for financial assistance.

The debate on dead-weight effects again surfaces. It can be argued that if individuals who learn would do so regardless of public support, then public assistance for them should be reduced. It should, however, be clearly understood that there are no obvious ways of distinguishing "opportunists"[16]

---

13. To simplify the argument, the word "cultural" is used here in a very broad sense. It includes, for example, a psychological block resulting from a disastrous schooling.
14. 15% learn and 85% do not.
15. International Standard Classification of Education.
16. In terms of dead-weight effects.

Figure 5.5. **Learners and non-learners by educational attainment**

Percentage of population 25-64 years old by educational attainment who is learning or not, 1994-98

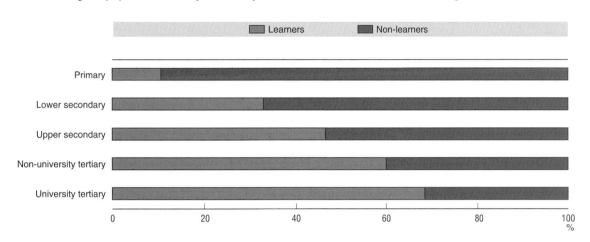

Source: International Adult Literacy Survey, 1994-98.

– the convinced who receive financial assistance – from those who would not learn without such financial assistance. One way may therefore be to go by level of qualification: there would be no assistance, at least financial, for people above a certain level. This is how it is viewed in Denmark, Norway and Sweden, for instance, where free education is provided to everyone who has not reached a certain education level. This approach nevertheless causes problems – especially in terms of equality, as two individuals with different levels of qualification receive different coverage.

The approach also places the debate on vocational training and higher vocational training at the top of the agenda. Linking learning to its immediate purpose and the degree of personal motivation is an interesting approach to financing it. However, this solution has not yet been put forth, and approaching it in the terms depicted in Figure 5.6 is only a starting point.

There are at least two reasons for suggesting that the level of literacy of an individual, for example,[17] should be positively linked with the level of individual financial assistance (Figure 5.6). The first is the fact that there is a high risk when one tries to persuade individuals known to be little motivated. Employers and others concerned have little inclination to take that risk. By investing a small amount, and suggesting that employers invest a small amount, it may be hoped to convince them that the potential gains in return for a small financial risk are considerable. The second reason is that learning to read and write is less demanding in terms of teachers and teaching materials than training highly skilled technicians on high performance machines or blue-collar high-skilled workers. Moreover, from the viewpoint of

There are two arguments for positively linking financial assistance with levels of literacy.

17. Or any other clear evidence of an individual's level: level of qualification is among the most obvious.

Figure 5.6. **Linking individual financial assistance and individual level of qualification**

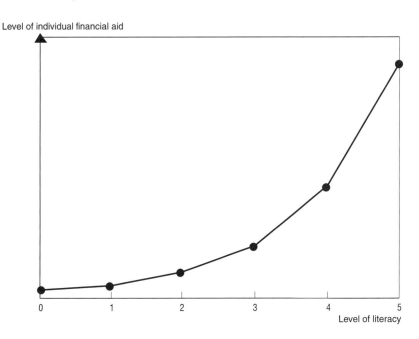

the firm's and potential productivity gains, the returns must justify their investment.

In cost distribution the figures may well prove the same for the low and highly qualified.

It is worth noting that overall spending might well be the same for the low-qualified group and for the highly qualified group: spending one currency unit on 100 individuals costs the same as spending 100 units on one individual. Again, this is just a very normative model; some examples of good practice are given in Section 5.2.

Willingness to learn, failure to enrol

Many who finally receive education or training have experienced at least one failed attempt.

Some further evidence from the IALS is worth putting into perspective in a chapter on motivation to learn. Apparently there is an unsatisfied demand for learning, as Figure 5.7 shows: some people have tried to undertake education or training but have not been able to in the past 12 months. This does not mean that they have not learned at all,[18] but they have not been able to at least during one attempt. Associated with the variable showing those who actually did gain access to learning, Figure 5.7 shows that among those who finally received some education or training, a quite large fraction found it difficult to do so: about a third (30% for vocational reasons and 28.2% for non-vocational ones). In addition, of those who did not receive education or training, a fair fraction tried (20% and 19.5%, respectively). In short, not all the individuals willing to learn are able to do so, whatever the reasons for learning.

───────────

18. The IALS may identify up to three periods of education or training over the past 12 months.

Figure 5.7. **Unsatisfied demand for learning**

Percentage of population 25-64 years old who could not participate in at least one learning session, by type of training, whether it finally took place or not, 1994-98

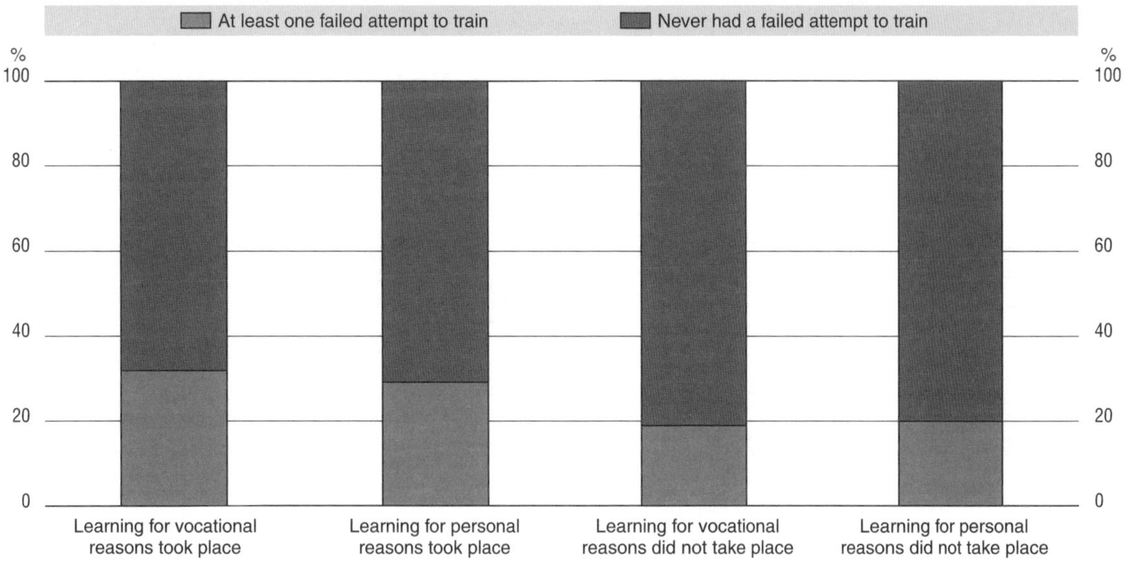

| At least one failed attempt to train | Never had a failed attempt to train |

Learning for vocational reasons took place — Learning for personal reasons took place — Learning for vocational reasons did not take place — Learning for personal reasons did not take place

Source: International Adult Literacy Survey, 1994-98.

When one considers the unsatisfied demand for learning by level of qualification (Figure 5.8), it is clearly primarily the highly qualified adults who are frustrated in their ambition (33.4% at ISCED Level 6 or 7); less than 10% of those with a low level of qualification had their plans frustrated (10% at ISCED Level 1). Here too, the progression between the two extremes is perfectly even and the results are the same for both vocational and other training (albeit with a small inversion in the ranking for vocational training between ISCED Level 5 and Level 6 or 7). In short, the higher the level of qualification, the harder it is to satisfy the demand for learning.

Highly qualified adults are more frustrated in their learning attempts than those with low qualifications.

Existing or prospective incentives or barriers

This section, before coming to any recommendations that might result from the observations and analysis, mixes incentives and barriers because they are intrinsically linked. Creating the former often means getting rid of the latter and *vice versa*. This section also mixes existing incentives and those to be created, as well as existing barriers and those that might arise.

Place and form of training

There has been little innovation in how knowledge is transmitted. Teaching and learning is always based on more or less the same model: a teacher who transmits and learners who receive. Yet it is known that many adults have been turned off by the traditional school system. It is therefore hard to imagine that they would agree to learn in a setting that they fled when

Reaching those who earlier rejected learning means breaking with familiar patterns...

119

Figure 5.8. **Unsatisfied demand for training by educational attainment**

Percentage of population 25-64 years old who could not participate in at least one training session, by type of training and educational attainment, whether training finally took place or not, 1994-98

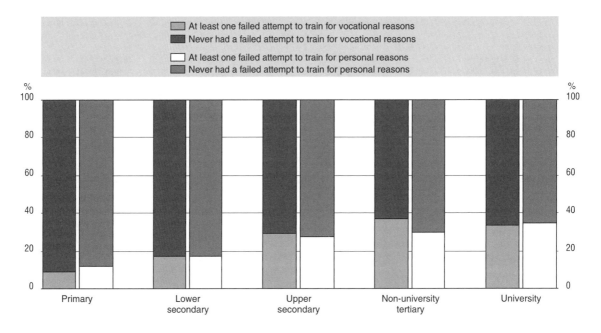

Source: International Adult Literacy Survey, 1994-98.

they left school. In that light, most efforts to break with lecture-type teaching methods are welcome.

... such as desynchronising the teacher-learner relationship in space and time.

There have been several attempts in that direction. Probably the most innovative is the one that involves desynchronising the relationship between the teacher and learner, both in space and time. Naturally it uses information and communication technologies and allows everyone to work at their own pace, in their own context. It is a major step forward precisely because it no longer demands a teacher and a group of learners to assemble in the same more or less confined space. It is a crucial venue for the future but it cannot be and probably can never be a universal solution because of the costs involved and the obvious cultural barriers for populations still very unfamiliar with advanced technology. Some benefits and drawbacks of these methods are covered in Chapter 6.

But technological barriers continue to pose problems, in spite of the computer revolution.

Before electronic communication media were developed so intensively, distance learning methods relied essentially on the post, radio, television and sometimes the telephone. Since the 1970s, computer-aided learning has been presented a solution for the future. The availability of interactive devices (CDs, interactive television, personal computers, etc.) has made this solution even more attractive. However, it runs into the same kind of problems mentioned in the case of ICT, cultural barriers to the technology and entry cost. The Open University in England made a deliberate decision to operate by exchange of documents through the post in order not to force students to buy or even arrange access to personal computers. The National

Distance University (UNED) in Spain has also chosen to increase virtual provision more and more, but still offers personal tutorials in their associated centres.

One interesting experiment is a network set up in New Brunswick, Canada, to allow access by everyone to computer equipment suited to modern needs and reasonably close to home. The McDonald Community Access Centre in Moncton operates as one of 230 resource centres in schools or community centres[19] which allow four or five students at a time to be taught the basics of personal computing, the Internet and other applications or programmes. The interesting point, apart from the small size of the groups and the very good distribution of these centres across the province, is the idea of Internet access as a source of information. In this case, ICTs are both the goal of training and a tool, typically to take learning activities further or to look for a job.

In Canada, there are resource centres where small groups learn how to use the Internet to further learning and seek jobs.

Another way of dissociating teaching from the negative image it may have is to take it out of the normal classroom situation. Many initiatives can be cited: in Portugal, it was seen how facilities that existed already in the community – sports centres, associations, etc. – were used to promote and dispense learning in a familiar context (the "cuckoo" strategy). The cost savings remain a key argument. Folk high schools, like Örebro, in Sweden typically provide training that has little in common with a school timetables (training time is personalised) or a classroom (teaching is outside, in small buildings, etc.).

Teaching's image can also be freshened by having it take place in novel settings.

Bearing in mind the geographical aspect, critical in at least four of the nine countries visited (Canada, Finland, Norway and Sweden), distance learning – especially through ICTs – also allows the traditional drawbacks of lecture-type teaching, which is not very appealing, to be bypassed.

Distance learning is an attractive alternative made possible through ICTs.

The benefits of learning

Encouraging adults to start learning again or start relearning, and showing them the potential return on the investment they have made, are making or are going to make is a top priority. Unless adults can be convinced that learning will give them something back – given that learning can be very demanding in time and effort – they will probably not invest in education or training.

Adults must be made to see the value of learning.

On the vocational training side, the most obvious benefits are professional mobility, a better job, promotion, more responsibility, initiative or independence, and the recognition of a skill. During the country visits, expressions of self-confidence came up quite often in the discussion.

Among the many benefits of vocational training, self-confidence was often mentioned.

In slightly more general terms, a wide range of reasons may be given why adults are encouraged to learn. Acquiring basic skills (reading, writing, arithmetic) will open up a great many opportunities. Those responsible for delivering basic skills must concentrate on the task of convincing them. Many incentives can and must be suggested: the ability to read newspapers, to have access to information of all kinds (health, job advertisements), to use the broad range of services available in the society in which the individual

Those delivering basic skills must convey to the sceptical adult how those skills can open the door to their world.

---

19. The one visited was in a residential centre for the disabled.

lives and, of course, ultimately, to use e-mail and other Internet services. One of the key reasons commonly found why adults learn is the idea of helping their (grand-)children in school. Acquiring status in the community in which one lives, having access to a form of social acceptance are also elements often mentioned by the people concerned and practitioners.

Creating incentives

Learning should be presented as a project with a clear goal.

To convince adults that learning is worthwhile, education and training must be offered in the context of a project, in the broadest sense, with a clear goal. The educational approach and the entire learning scheme must be suited to adults' needs, the pace at which they work and the many kinds of constraints they face.

Its particulars and cost must be tailored to fit the needs of the learner.

Cost should not be a hindrance. There are examples of free learning that has not been received with great enthusiasm, but there are also many instances where adults cannot obtain learning because they cannot afford it or because they cannot meet their other needs simultaneously (Figure 5.7). Whatever the case, the cost of learning must be consistent with the amount the individual is prepared to invest and the expected outcomes.

The ability to demonstrate the benefits of learning will always be a major plus for practitioners on the ground. In all the countries visited, it was mentioned time and again that word of mouth is by far the best method of circulating information about the value of learning. Clearly identifying the direct and indirect effects of learning is, of course, a challenge for those involved: successfully encouraging adults to come to learning sessions stems in part from meeting that challenge.

Barriers to avoid

Those whose desire for learning had been frustrated most often cited lack of time as the reason.

Barriers to be lifted to some extent echo the incentives to put in place – two sides of the same coin. The IALS highlighted the main barriers encountered by those whose desire for learning had been frustrated at least once during the past 12 months (Figure 5.9). It is quite clear that lack of time is the argument most commonly advanced. And so for populations convinced of the value of learning, and especially for purposes other than professional, enabling them to find the time is a crucial factor. This argument is very tricky because it also often leads to a sense of time-wasting for people learning, especially if they are not helped to manage some of their most pressing time-related needs. In the particular case of "lack of time", the IALS results also show the value of distinguishing between vocational and other training.

Lack of financing was the second major reason.

The second major argument used by people who could not satisfy their desire to learn is lack of financing. Overall, time and money are the two scarcest commodities. This is not really surprising, but the orders of magnitude teach an interesting lesson: finding time for adults and, to a lesser extent, subsidising them could solve much of the participation problem.

Practitioners of learning in general cite the psychological barriers.

In interviews, practitioners of basic (non-vocational) education said they thought the psychological barriers seemed large. In their view these were the main reason why those who do not undertake training do not do so. There is much talk of shame and fear of being the laughing-stock of the neighbourhood – proof that it is absolutely essential to dissociate adult

Figure 5.9. **Reasons for not participating in adult learning activities**

Percentage of population 25-64 years old, by reasons for not participating and type of training, 1994-98

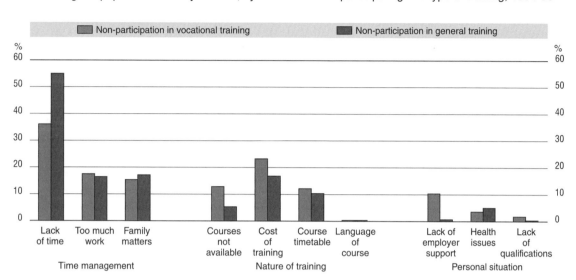

Source: International Adult Literacy Survey, 1994-98.

learning from the notion of school or classroom. One also finds that those who do not go in for training at all often complain of the lack of support from those close to them (relatives and friends) or their employer.

It also has to be said that many adults who have given up learning see little value in it. Some are satisfied with their situation, from a family and financial point of view. Others attach more importance to leisure or voluntary activities of benefit to the community. Indeed many, not having a structured project or an ambition of some kind, see no point in "wasting their time".

For others, learning simply is not one of life's priorities.

For those most at the margins of learning, there is another form of psychological barrier: fear of assessment. In a work environment, it can extend to fear of losing one's job. In other cases, it is fear of the consequences of possible failure (in front of the family, the neighbours, the children, other learners). For people who have very little desire for it at the outset, learning for fun, stripped of any form of assessment, seems the only possible springboard. Later, when it has been demonstrated that learning does not have to be a grind and is quite painless, more formal training plans can probably be introduced.

Then there is the prospect of assessment, which for many is indeed daunting.

Motivating potential learners

To conclude this section on motivation in general and individual incentives to learn, it is worth recalling the main messages, more or less explicit, gathered in the countries covered by the thematic review or that flow from the experiences and constraints identified during visits. They represent avenues to explore rather than general rules. They are not universally applicable but could represent interesting alternatives in some of the countries covered. Lastly, they are not arranged in any specific order because no one idea necessarily works better than another, let alone all others:

- Establish and distil a clear political message which makes upper secondary education compulsory or, at the very least, strongly recommended as a base for future learning: that learning, like voting, is a duty as much as a right.

- Give everyone the means to undergo adult training or some form of lifelong learning. That is the aim of the laws that are being prepared in countries like Norway or Sweden on access to upper secondary education for all.

- Ensure that the end of compulsory schooling is determined by level rather than age. Although hard to achieve, this measure would give all young people the minimum needed to return to learning later. It would also be a strong incentive to finish school for those who wanted to leave early.

- Reach those most in need of training; use the media they themselves use, know and understand: television is a means of reaching some sections of the population that newspapers, magazines or brochures cannot reach, if only because some of them cannot read well enough. This would be especially useful in restoring the image of training as well as explaining its role and to play down the ins and outs (training for fun).

- Develop training without high stakes, training that is fun, to reconcile adults who dropped out of school and the system with the idea of learning. Show that learning does not have to mean compulsion, exams and evaluation, and possibly failure. Show, too, that learning does not have to lead directly to a review of the employee's position in the firm. Dissociate, for the unconvinced, the act of learning from any possible penalties for failure.

- Recognise all kinds of previous experience, at least if justified. Recognition could re-motivate adults, allowing them to pick up without having to demonstrate all over again what they know or can do. It also has an external value, in the labour market for example. This dichotomy must be better explained and incorporated in programmes and targeting of population groups.

- Set up pilot schemes to assess the speed with which the "culture" of individuals changes in relation to learning. The potential for convincing individuals of the value of training must be measurable at a lower, local level. It would be a valuable lesson for decision makers and those who design adult learning programmes. However, it must also be possible to convert pilot schemes into large-scale universal schemes.

- Build the scheme around the principle that people's motives for staying in training are not the same as those that made them come in the first place. That can call into question certain measures that do not distinguish between starting training and staying, but it should not overturn the entire panoply of intervention.

- Find optimal conditions for the transmission of knowledge, be they theoretical or practical (knowing and doing). Action should be built around the fact that the optimal way of teaching and getting people to learn is not the same for everyone and can change over time for a particular person.

- Set reasonable objectives that are achievable in terms of basic skills (reading, writing and arithmetic), and at the same time institute ways of achieving them.
- Create observatories on how basic skills are acquired (self-taught or through the system) and how they are lost: longitudinal data.
- Carefully state the conditions under which e-learning works, bearing in mind local conditions; availability of personal computers, connection, form of invoicing of connection, etc. The conditions for success are numerous and certainly do not all apply everywhere.
- In firms, consider forms of time management that leave time for training. For people who are not in employment, take account of their time constraints.
- Construct a gradient of government intervention based on observable characteristics.

The two main messages which should come out of this section are that learning cannot, and must not, be just for vocational purposes. It also attempts to show that satisfying a need for non-vocational learning may have beneficial effects for the firm and, moreover, for subsequent investment in actual vocational and/or focused training. The second message is perhaps a cause for some concern. Those adults who most need to learn are the least motivated. And there is no way of escaping a fundamental debate on the system of incentives needed. It is much more than a simple question of culture.

In conclusion, there has been little innovation since the concept of the classroom with one or more teachers on one side and learners on the other. In the absence of such innovation, all the solutions proposed to educate or train adults are often no more than reproductions of the same model in a less strict and less formal framework (open air courses, smaller groups, more teachers, etc.). Attracting adults to learn thus involves efforts in other directions rather than challenging the school model. There are many solutions for captivating rather than capturing adults. All the countries in the thematic review are taking this line and there are areas where doing so is extremely necessary. Vocational training, the subject of the next section, is one.

5.2. Employment-related training

There are, as far as is known, no exhaustive quantitative or qualitative studies of what works and what does not work in vocational training schemes for workers. The objective of this section is thus to evaluate certain aspects. Employment-related training may be regarded as an investment in which the interests of companies and employees converge to make the former competitive and the latter employable. Companies have an interest in having well-trained workers with broad, flexible skills meeting the challenge of flexible specialisation. However, this interest may not be strong enough to ensure adequate investment in training by companies and workers. Training by companies involves costs to the employer because workers are not contributing to production while they are in training, or to the direct costs of training. Companies then tend to choose only investments from which they expect a high return. This state of affairs clearly leads to major inequalities for

Workers do not have equal access to training.

workers in access to training. One finds a chain of cumulative advantage for workers who are already qualified in relatively high professional status in large companies and a chain of cumulative disadvantage for low-skilled or older workers, those in small companies or on temporary contracts. Even in the case of highly skilled workers, the return on investment for companies is risky and, bearing in mind the possibility of "poaching" skilled labour in imperfect labour markets, companies often prefer to "buy in" skilled labour rather than invest in training.

Linking continuing vocational training, productivity and employability at the micro level

The direct value of continuing vocational training is still not sufficiently clear.

Promoting continuing vocational training raises the question of the returns it generates.[20] The lack of visibility of the favourable training outcomes in terms of benefits to companies as well as workers is a recurrent theme in meetings with researchers in this field, trade unions, human resources managers in companies or even trainees themselves. Yet these training actions appear to have a positive impact on both companies and workers.

One such value is improved productivity.

It would appear that by providing continuing training, company managers can expect to improve productivity. The little information available suggests that training does indeed increase company profits and those of the sectors concerned. A study of companies in the United States (Barron, Black and Loewenstein, 1989) shows that a 10% increase in training activities is accompanied by a 3% increase in labour productivity with only a 1½% increase in wages. A specific study recently carried out in the United Kingdom (Dearden, Reed and van Reenen, 2000) also shows that productivity gains are perceptibly greater than wage increases, which means a half point reduction in unit labour costs for a one point increase in training activities.

The economic context can sometimes force the hand.

It is also often the economic context that forces companies to restructure the skills of their workforce. This approach may be preventive in the context of skills auditing management or caring driven by a crisis. Dismissals may be accompanied by assistance with external retraining, in conversion courses for example. The case of a large enterprise like the post office is interesting as a halfway house between the two approaches. In Switzerland, the privatisation of post office activities led to the launch of a campaign to train workers to allow them to leave voluntarily. On the other hand, internal qualifying training for newcomers tends to be reduced. As the post office was traditionally the only enterprise in the field, it provided vocational training for its workers in the form of initial training; however, with the introduction of competition, a federal preparatory post office diploma became necessary. In

20. This subject has been analysed in other OECD publications (1999, 2001c). It will also be reviewed in the new activity launched in the Autumn of 2001 by the ELSA Committee on the subject of vocational training and its impact on economic growth. It has a dual objective: to provide Member countries with *a)* an empirical analysis of the contribution of vocational training to human capital formation and economic growth and *b)* a set of recommendations on policies largely initiated by the social partners which could result in more adequate investment by companies and workers in training.

Denmark, the post office is one of the country's largest enterprises with some 32 000 employees. A quality management budgeting exercise has led in recent years to numerous training measures. Under the Total Involvement in Quality (TIQ) programme, all permanent employees received qualifying training in an external training institution that led to a diploma. The aim was to motivate the workers and involve them as much as possible in the pursuit of quality.

For trade unions, the issue of continuing vocational training for adult workers primarily serves to enhance the employability of those trained. As few collective agreements include a clause linking training to wage rises, the main benefit of training for workers is not that it improves wages but that it makes it easier to keep a job or increases mobility in the external labour market.

Trade unions are aware of training's role in promoting workers' employability.

Thus in Finland vocational training has been seen by individuals, especially during the high unemployment period of the 1990s, as a guarantee of being personally able to cope in the case of mass redundancies and find another job, if possible at a higher level. In Portugal, on the other hand, low-skilled men generally give priority to overtime that yields additional real and immediate income – unlike investment in training, where it is hard to see a return. The country note of Portugal emphasises that this factor seems to play a crucial role in the low-skills trap in which workers over the age of 35 seem to be caught.

Even if the return on investment in continuing training is uncertain, some individuals find it easier than others to make training a part of their qualification (and their wages). This is often true of those with the highest qualifications – who, as a rule, have the greatest access to training. There are also gradations between training measures which can inherently accentuate inequity. The best qualified and best equipped in socioeconomic terms are those found to be over-represented in training provision leading to a qualification appreciated by employers.

Training for benefits comes most easily to the most highly qualified...

Even then, highly qualified workers are not all equal when it comes to training. They may have other characteristics that can offset their comparative advantage. Having seniority in a company may be a handicap in obtaining training, since training only pays back if it takes place in the early years of work. This is what is suggested by Brunello (2001), who carried out research in 13 European countries based on the European Community Household Panel (ECHP) as to how far initial education and continuing training are complementary. He shows that continuing training results in higher returns, measured as wage increases, for people who have taken higher studies and have less than 15 years' seniority than for those who have the same professional experience but are less well educated. Conversely, highly educated people with longer professional experience (over 15 years) obtain a lower return from a training activity than less well qualified workers with the same professional experience. The value is thus highest for people with a higher diploma and relatively short experience in the world of work. One of the reasons, perhaps, is that highly specialised initial training becomes increasingly obsolete over time. For less well-educated workers, the return derived from continuing

... but even the most highly qualified are not all equal.

127

training does not appear to vary, irrespective of their professional experience.

Synchronising macroeconomic policy and the training environment

The extensive model of investment in training is more conducive than the intensive model.

Two situations appear to coexist in the nine countries that participated in the review. On the one hand, in some countries, mainly the Nordic countries, there is a productive environment where continuing training tends to be extended to all workers in companies, especially as adult education has traditionally been valued by society. The investment in training model is extensive and the main problem is not to neglect certain groups of workers and companies that may be excluded from training, such as unskilled workers, older workers or those working in SMEs. The task, then, is primarily to develop measures targeting these groups at risk. On the other hand, in other countries, there is little systematic access to vocational training in companies; it depends very much on local, random initiatives by company directors and workers. The investment-in-training model is intensive and the priority is to establish a voluntary framework more conducive to promoting vocational training among all adult workers. From the outset, promoting an effective and equitable model is crucial, as the groups at risk are particularly liable to stay away from training measures in this unpropitious environment and efforts aimed at them must be supported by a strong political will.

Apart from cultural explanations a low-skills/low-quality equilibrium could persist.

The existence or otherwise of an environment conducive to adult education is rooted in the culture and traditions of each country, but it also depends on the country's level of specialisation and economic performance. Assuming the existence of an equilibrium between low skills and low quality, Finegold and Soskice (1988) showed that employers respond rationally to a whole range of institutional incentives and attitudes they have inherited. Supply and demand of intermediate qualifications are limited, because company managements focus their attention on quick returns and compete on the basis of low costs and low prices. Those among them who invest in enhancing skills will not necessarily use new skills, given that competition in the market is driven more by price than by quality. If these arguments prove to be true, a policy based solely on the supply of skilled personnel might not be very effective. People who raise their skills would continue, despite everything, to perform the same tasks as before. Their new skills would procure them only limited advantages and the incentives to invest in the acquisition of new qualifications would be reduced in the sense that it would be difficult to obtain sufficient benefits from that investment. This would lead to a low-skills trap, a vicious circle in which the supply of jobs that required little skill would encourage under-investment in education and training.

A high-skills route demands changes in the educational and skill formation systems.

In this context, Ashton and Green (1997) argue that a high-skills route demands simultaneous change of the educational system and the skill formation system (Box 5.2). This implies the involvement of the main stakeholders: individuals, practitioners, social partners and policy makers. Any perceptible improvement in workers' skills requires attention both to the demand for skilled personnel by companies and the supply of skilled labour by workers.

Box 5.2. **Five institutional requirements for following a high-skill route**

1. The ruling political elites should be firmly committed to the high-skill route, and effect this commitment both in their general management of the economy and in their support of the education system.

2. A sufficient majority of employers should also be committed to both demanding high skills from their workforces and providing the means for acquisition of workplace skills on the job.

3. There should be an adequate regulatory system to control both the quality and the quantity of workplace training.

4. There should be sufficiently comprehensive incentives for virtually all young people and workers to acquire and to continue to acquire skills.

5. The education and training system should be sufficiently developed to allow workers to achieve a mix of on-the-job and off-the-job training.

Source: Ashton and Green (1997, p. 6).

Ways of escaping a low-skills trap are analysed in particular in the country note of Portugal. Apart from improving the initial education of young people, the key tool is programming an increase in the amount of working time devoted to continuing vocational training, until the economy tips from a low to a high equilibrium. The analysis, it is true, is theoretical, but observation of the countries of Southeast Asia in the 1980s, or Ireland in the 1990s, shows that this transition is possible even if it probably requires a high degree of co-ordination and cohesion among the various elements of economic policy. The problem is to synchronise training with industrial and economic policy on the one hand, and the evolution of industrial relations on the other.

The shift entails synchronising training with industrial and economic policy and industrial relations.

In the case of Portugal, industrial and economic policy as a whole is based on four kinds of training and qualification strategy. For the sector exposed to international competition, the stress is on the national policy of innovation, creation of higher technical education in information and communication, and the development of co-operation between businesses and universities. In the main, it is the under-35s who provide the thrust of this sector, which calls for adjustment in universities and professional institutions and the creation of short courses leading to specialist technical diplomas. A second pillar of the strategy concerns development of sectors linked to infrastructure and the environment, which require fairly diversified intermediate qualifications. There is also the question of restructuring the traditional sectors of clothing, furniture and agro-food industries as the result of competition from developing countries, which calls for enhanced average skills. Finally, the personal services market offers extensive employment opportunities in areas such as services to the family, day-care centres, help for the elderly, and areas where the public sector has a major role. Training is thus likely to be somewhat diverse, a fact which should be accepted but if possible offset by government financing. Such a strategy cannot be implemented without the co-operation of all the parties concerned. It is in

Portugal has devised a four-pillar strategy.

129

this context that the February 2001 agreement between the social partners and the government, within the Economic and Social Council, is so important. The objective is to develop an integrated approach to education, training and employment. First, existing measures are incorporated and structured, for example the establishment of a national certification system. Then the agreement sets out the arrangements for continuing training, granting new rights and instituting a minimum volume of training (individual right to 20 hours per year for all workers and an annual training provision of at least 10% of all workers). It is true that access to 20 hours of training per worker per year from 2003, increasing to 35 hours by 2006, is fairly modest – but it has the advantage that it also applies to SMEs. It will be essential to closely monitor the practical outcomes of this agreement, which is as yet too recent for any firm judgement to be given concerning its long-term impact.

General financing arrangements to promote employment-related training

Many countries have employed a variety of methods to support training.

Faced with shortcomings in the training market, many countries mobilise a variety of resources to support and sustain the development of training for workers in companies through legislation, financial incentives and contractual agreements. These mainly involve compulsory financing and financial penalties for companies that do not spend a minimum amount on training determined by the government. There are also promotional measures that may take the form of an award of a quality label for companies that provide the most and the best training, or subsidies for training. Another approach adopted in the past decade is to target measures directly at workers to overcome the main barriers to training, which are time and cost. Finally, and this is probably the most novel aspect, the visit to each country with its own peculiarities revealed numerous innovative strategies to promote vocational training among groups at risk. While it is important to draw them to the attention of groups with comparable problems, the central issue is to reproduce good practice in other places.

Compulsory training levy schemes are not often among them.

Among the countries participating in the thematic review, only Spain has instituted a compulsory levy at national level to finance training in companies. Within the OECD countries, this financing obligation has existed only in France since 1971, Korea and Australia having abolished it in the late 1990s. There are certain regions of the countries visited, such as the Canadian province of Quebec or the Swiss Canton of Geneva, where such an obligation exists (Box 5.3).

Systems of compulsory levies from companies to finance specific measures can also be found. In Finland there is a compulsory company levy for a fund managed by the social partners to finance, with state support, individual study leave.

Some countries do provide financial contributions based on intersectoral or sectoral agreements.

Furthermore, some of the countries of the thematic review have financial contributions based on intersectoral or sectoral agreements.[21] In some cases, these are participating funds for the development of qualifications established under company or branch agreements. In Spain, there is a compulsory but indirect company contribution instituted in 1992 under an intersectoral

---

21. Further information will be compiled through the new activity launched by the ELSA Committee on vocational training as an extension to the project on growth.

Box 5.3. **Compulsory training levy schemes in Quebec, Geneva and Spain**

The Development of Labour Promotion Act in Quebec Province, Canada

The Development of Labour Promotion Act, passed in 1995, seeks to boost workers' qualifications, skills and performance through continuing training. It is a government measure of the "train or pay" kind: the Act requires every employer whose wage bill is over CAD 250 000 to invest the equivalent of at least 1% of his/her company's payroll costs in training the workforce. Companies which do not reach this threshold must pay contributions to the national workers' training fund (*Fonds national de formation de la main-d'œuvre*, FNFMO). The plan of allocation of the FNFMO's resources is drawn up by a committee of labour market partners (*Commission des partenaires du marché du travail*, CPMT) and approved by the minister of labour and employment.

This Act replaces the single reimbursable tax credit for training (CRIF) introduced in 1990, the results of which were disappointing: only 2.5% of employers used it with declared training expenses of 0.3% of payroll.

It is too early to judge the impact of the progressive application of the Act, from January 1996 to January 1998,[1] on training levels provided by employers. The Five-Year Report 1995-2000 on the application of the Act highlights the following points (Emploi-Québec, 2000):

- In 1998, training expenses accounted for 1.53% of payroll. Some three-quarters of employers spend at least 1% on training; 26% were required to pay 1% of their payroll costs to the FNFMO. Compared with 1996, as a result of small companies coming within the scope, training costs as a proportion of total payroll declined, and the number of employers that did not reached the statutory level of training expenditure rose.

- It is precisely these small companies that do not submit projects under the FNFMO resource allocation plan, but employers and the public and parastatal sector. In 1998, with contributions of 2.8% of sums paid to the FNFMO, they obtained 17.2% of the subsidies granted by the FNFMO.

- According to a survey by the Canadian Federation of Independent Enterprises, the main reservations expressed by employers concern the "red tape" involved in claiming eligible expenses. The survey also showed the extensive ignorance among employers concerning the FNFMO.

Source: Emploi-Québec (2000).

The Fund for basic and advanced vocational training, Canton of Geneva, Switzerland

The Fund for basic and advanced vocational training (*Fonds en faveur de la formation et du perfectionnement professionnels*, FFPP) is the Canton of Geneva's own measure, introduced in 1985 and managed on a tripartite basis by employers' associations, trade unions and the state. It was introduced as a result of a trade union initiative.

The Fund is financed by a state subsidy and contributions from companies (including the state of Geneva but excluding international organisations) which pay CHF 20 per employee. The amount of FFPP resources must not exceed 0.5% of the total payroll of the Canton.

Only organisations providing advanced vocational training can apply to the FFPP for a subsidy for expenses not covered by the Canton and the Confederation. Individual applications are not considered, nor are courses in basic education, health, sociology, arts or sciences. Obtaining access is seen as difficult because the organisation must obtain approval from both the Fund's Board and the Central Interprofessional Board which limits its use. In 1998, the FFPP paid out CHF 1.9 million for adults.

Source: Office d'orientation et de formation professionnelle (2000).

The Tripartite Foundation for Training for Employment in Spain

Enterprises or individuals can request training funds through the Tripartite Foundation for Training for Employment (previously FORCEM) in Spain. Funding comes from a vocational training levy on workers

---

Box 5.3. **Compulsory training levy schemes in Quebec, Geneva and Spain** (*cont.*)

and enterprises (of 0.7% of the wage bill directed to training for the unemployed and employed) and the European Social Fund. Organisations (business, business and/or labour organisations, bipartite foundations covered by sectoral collective bargaining at a national level, co-operatives or worker-owned companies) may request financial assistance. There are also so-called Complementary and Supplementary Training Measures. Individuals can request Individual Training Permits. According to the FORCEM data, more than 30 000 Spanish companies requested funding for Training Plans in 2000 for more than 77 000 training programmes, covering more than 4.7 million workers. Computer training was the most frequently requested. There were 2.5 million participants.

---

1. In January 1996, only employers whose payroll totalled one million dollars or over were subject. In January 1997 and January 1998, it was extended to employers whose payroll exceeded CAD 500 000 and CAD 250 000 dollars, respectively.

Source: OECD (2002).

---

agreement subsequently ratified by a tripartite agreement (Box 5.3). Half the levy for training of 0.7% of the wage bill is spent on continuing training. In Denmark, various sectoral agreements establishing funds to promote vocational training are under tripartite management. Over a million employees are covered: 780 000 in the public sector and 330 000 in the private sector.

In the United Kingdom, a compulsory levy on companies is included in the statutes of industrial training boards in construction (CITB and ECITB). The Sea Fish Authority (SFIA) collects a statutory levy from processors based on the weight of fish both landed and imported into the United Kingdom, and part of this levy is used to support training in the industry. Other sectors have introduced a levy on a voluntary basis, such as Skillset, the National Training Organisation (NTO) for recording, film, video and multimedia. The policy commitment of the government is: "a regulatory framework for training will be established where the social partners are in agreement". The idea is that any training levy introduced by a voluntary agreement between the social partners will have the government's support.

The United Kingdom notably has voluntary employer-led sector arrangements through its Sector Skill Councils.

Concerning specific actions from the social partners in the United Kingdom, it is important to emphasise the voluntary employer-led sector arrangements through the Sector Skill Councils. The Councils are nation-wide bodies that give responsibility to employers to provide leadership for strategic targeted action to meet their sector's skills and business needs. In return they receive substantial publicly funded support, greater dialogue with government departments about the impact of policies on skills and productivity, and increased influence with education and training partners. Trade unions also take the initiative by encouraging employers to invest in training of their workforce through a specific fund, the Union Learning Fund (ULF). This fund, established in 1998, resulted in the implementation of 220 projects promoted by 66 trade union branches in 1 000 workplaces. The government has provided subsidies of GBP 27 million for 2001-2004. Since the launch of the fund, over 2 000 Union Learning Representatives have been active on the ground, and the government is considering proposals to recognise their work by giving them paid time to perform their role of adviser on training at work and access to every kind of learning opportunity.

The French-style training levy is known to have both positive and negative effects [Conseil d'analyse économique (CAE), 2000]. The positive effects of the legal obligation to finance training in France are as follows:

Should companies be legally obliged to finance training?

- A spectacular increase in training by companies which allocated an average of 3.5% of payroll to training in 1998, well above the statutory 1.5% and almost twice as high as the late 1970s (2%).
- Only a small proportion (30%) of companies pay a balancing charge for insufficient expenditure on training.
- The minimal obligation to mutualise financing is justified by the risk of "poaching": the training from which an employee who changes companies benefits is of value to society as a whole even if not for the company that paid for it.
- The big winners in the system are training organisations in a rapidly expanding training market.

On the downside, the persistence of considerable inequality of access to training in the course of a career depending on gender, age or qualification of workers, or even the size of company, is often stressed. Equally unfortunate is the lack of involvement of those concerned in an increasingly complex system, in contrast to the scale of the financial input: "on the employee side, they do not pay much or expect much; on the company side, they pay but generally do not get involved" (Didier, 2000).

The pros and cons of a compulsory training levy on employers are the subject of an extensive literature (OECD, 1999). Among recent analyses, Greenhalgh (2001) is highly illuminating. The author ponders the pertinence of introducing a "train or pay"-type measure along French lines for companies in other countries.

Both pros and cons have been observed.

The introduction of such a measure would be doubly advantageous to large companies which already train compared to SMEs which often do not train. The latter would first have to bear the additional cost of the levy and secondly would be ill-equipped to operate in a labour market which had reached a high level of equilibrium in training. Nevertheless, the introduction of a "tailored" compulsory levy in companies would be preferable to promoting an increase in private investment by workers.

The advantages would go to larger companies rather than SMEs.

Several approaches to tailoring a potential levy are suggested in Greenhalgh (2001):

A "tailored" compulsory levy appears preferable to an increase in private investment by workers.

- The levy should be linked to profits and not payroll.[22]

---

22. Stevens (2001) developed a model which shows that if, because of imperfections in the labour market, training allows companies to make significant profits through their skilled workers, it is appropriate to make those companies bear higher training costs by a levy on their profits.

- The levy should be graded so as to avoid penalising new companies and SMEs.

- To make its effects less inegalitarian, priority access should be reserved to less-skilled workers rather than leaving the employer free to choose whom to train.

- To tackle the risk of "poaching", a sufficiently progressive taxation of wages would be needed so that those who achieved wage increases would redistribute part of their wage gains to public funds which partially finance public training expenditure.

- More fundamentally, an increase in investment in training could only generate productive use of resources with strict quality control of training organisations and monitoring of the level achieved by those in receipt of training.

Acting on several levels to overcome barriers to training

Three difficulties in implementing training are...

Companies may encounter difficulties in implementing training. Three spring to mind: arranging and financing training; reconciling production time and training time; and putting the gains from training to profitable use.

... arranging the plan in the first place...

Companies, especially the smallest among them, often find it hard to develop skills-based training plans. The reasons given are primarily their inexperience in setting up a training plan, the lack of clarity in the provision of training and their ignorance of public measures. To introduce training and successfully carry out competence development projects, it is preferable to avoid an overly formal and "bureaucratic" approach to a training plan, especially in SMEs. Drawing up terms of reference is a way of setting out the means of achieving previously defined objectives.

... reconciling production time and training time...

As to the reconciliation of production time and training time, if the training takes place during working time, on-the-job training is by definition more compatible with the demands of production than external training. Case studies in France on training practices in SMEs for low-skilled workers clearly show that on-the-job training is one of the factors in favour of training and professional development of such workers, who are often faced with inhibitions about traditional theoretical learning methods and thrown off balance by any questioning of their professional identity (Guiraudie and Terrenoire, 2000). It would appear that for this type of employee, training in the context of work involving supervisors and peers can gradually overcome anxiety, resistance and worry by encouraging involvement in a joint project and demystifying training. Recognition of skills as they are put to use can create a process which will facilitate subsequent access to diplomas by avoiding the discouraging effect of a "ladder" that is too high to begin with. On the other hand, encouraging training in an unproductive time (breakdowns, maintenance, temporary layoffs, etc.) often obstructs the preparation time needed to ensure proper training conditions. Otherwise there is the risk that training is seen as a stopgap.

Another possibility for continuing normal production, especially when the employee has to go for training outside, is based on worker rotation schemes. In Norway, Elkem Aluminium has organised production into six teams where traditionally only five were needed. This releases ten training days per worker per year in a training system where teamwork is at a premium (Box 5.4).

In Denmark, the use of rotation schemes in employment and of training leave can improve both planning of training activities in companies and individual training needs. This rotation normally relies on replacing workers on training leave with unemployed people. In a tight labour market, however, where the unemployment rate does not exceed 5%, unemployed workers are often too far from employment to adapt quickly to a new job. The system has had to be modified through increased collaboration between companies in networked training partnerships and worker exchanges.

When it comes to putting what they have learned to good use, individuals are often at a loss as to their ability to put their investment in training into effect and profit from it, because of the imperfections in the labour market. They may therefore be unconvinced of the value of the training provided to them. The expected returns are reduced by these uncertainties and the training desired by individuals is lower. The introduction in a chemicals firm in Norway of an internal wage scale for seven levels of skill perceptibly increased workers' motivation, except those over 40 years old and with over 15 years' seniority (Box 5.5). The question of evaluation and recognition of

... and putting the gains from training to profitable use.

Box 5.4. Elkem Aluminium: A team-based training system in Norway

A subsidiary of the world-wide Alcoa Aluminium Company, Elkem has three sites in Norway. The Mosjøen plant, founded in 1957, has many long-time employees. It has downsized from over 1 000 workers ten years ago to currently half that number. There were no layoffs in the interim, due in large measure to a plan whereby workers at age 60 continue part-time and at age 62 can receive half of their pay as retirement.

Since 1981, the company has adopted a variety of initiatives to promote continuous improvement. Taking an example from Toyota, they now centre on customer satisfaction as the key driver in improving their business systems, ensure quality at a low cost and shorten the lead-time in all of their systems. All this work is done through teams. Personality analysis is being used to organise the teams, but the company is convinced that the key is in identifying the competencies required for each. A Competence Toolbox has been developed that includes requirements for developing a team; the professional, technical and leadership skills needed; stability requirements; improvement techniques focused on technical problem-solving and maintenance; and business knowledge. A pool of 25 multi-skilled workers assists the teams and helps to promote structured on-the-job training.

An important change Elkem made was moving from five shifts to six in order to "make room for training" in the work schedule. While most of the training continues to be on-the-job, it was determined that more was needed. Individuals have a "tree plan" for training. This is included in a required ten days of training per year that each of the six shifts must undertake.

The firm has no internal education department and uses a mix of service providers for the different types of training. A resource centre serves as the technical trainer for the firm and helps brokering other training resources for them. As Elkem knows it will be hiring in about three years, they are now developing an apprenticeship programme in concert with the school.

Source: Meeting with the human resource manager, Mosjøen, March 2000.

Box 5.5. **Pay incentive scheme in Norway**

Orkla is a tree-based organic chemical company with 22 000 employees across the world. Borregaard is their subsidiary in Sarpsborg, with 2 800 employees. The subsidiary has launched an ambitious human resources reorganisation that includes a wage structure based on seven levels of competency. Approximately 2 000 tasks for all jobs have been reviewed, sometimes reordered, and placed within the seven levels of competency. The company believes this method has allowed them to pinpoint the differences between formal and real competencies.

The first three levels do not require a craft certificate. The fourth requires a certificate, the fifth level one additional competency, the sixth two additional ones, and the seventh at least one more. Each craft worker is to develop an individual training plan in order to move up the Competence Ladder. This new scheme has required a substantial reorganisation of the way the human resource department conducts its own work. A Secretariat has been established to support a central committee composed of management and union representatives. One of the key roles of this committee is to ensure fairness for both the worker and the front-line manager, because it was recognised that there is often a "familiarity bias" close to the job. There will be local competence assessment committees centred on approximately ten trades to "certify" workers' abilities.

The union is in cautious agreement with the plan. However, they do have concerns about workers who have been in their jobs for over 15 years and are over 40 years of age who are hesitant about the required training. Their motivation could be increased if training is organised only during working hours and if their work experience is more adequately taken into account.

Borregaard has taken several lessons in building this plan from their active participation in the recently restructured apprenticeship programme for upper secondary students.

Source: Meeting with Human Resource Management and Unions, Sarpsborg, March 2000.

training results must also be matched by the new measures to validate professional experience now being promoted in all the countries visited.

Subsidies and loans encourage training.

Subsidies could be introduced to encourage individuals, companies and employees to attain an appropriate level of continuing vocational training through worthwhile compensation for part of the opportunity cost and removing the uncertainty surrounding the investment in training. For companies, it may be a case of relief for provisions or amortisation of training costs so as to develop investment in training. These instruments will only affect companies that already spend on training without encouraging those who do not provide training to do so. Training loans are also offered. In the United Kingdom these loans, for companies with less than 50 employees, are provided through a partnership between the Department for Education and Skills (DfES) and commercial banks. They are offered at a preferential rate of interest and the government pays the interest for between 6 and 12 months, depending on the size of the loan. The allowable training costs are a maximum average of GBP 5 000 for each trainee included in the training plan. It is also important to mention the Small Firm Development Account, which is currently being piloted. This aims at firms of 5-49 employees; it offers financial help, advice and guidance to encourage small firms to develop their workforce.

Box 5.6.   The Investors in People (IiP) label in the United Kingdom

The Investors in People (IiP) label celebrates its tenth birthday in 2001. It was established by a working group, the National Training Task Force, in collaboration with the principal organisations concerned, such as the Confederation of British Industry, the Trades Union Congress and the Institute of Personnel and Development, to encourage companies to invest in training. It was built on good practice throughout the country. The label provides a national reference framework for improving company performance and competitiveness through skills objectives achieved through training. The label is based on four key principles: 1) commitment; 2) planning; 3) action; 4) evaluation. Company performance is measured against a set of 12 indicators before being awarded the label. A quarter of employees in the United Kingdom work in companies which have this label. Eighty per cent of them say that they are satisfied with their work, while that is the case for only 37% working in companies that have not been awarded the label. Over 70% of IiP companies say that they have gained in terms of customer satisfaction and productivity. The label is administered by a company, Investors in People UK, whose principal shareholder is the Department for Education and Skills (DfES). In April 2001, the network of partners responsible for delivering it changed. In England, it is now the regional branches of the Learning and Skills Council (LSC) and the Small Business Service (SBS).

Source: www.investorsinpeople.co.uk

In the United Kingdom, actions are envisaged in favour of companies that are particularly innovative in training. The Investors in People (IiP) label is awarded to (mainly large) companies that make a recognised training effort (Box 5.6). In the Learning and Training at Work 2000 survey, 16% of employers in England said that their company had been awarded the IiP label, the proportion ranging from 13% for companies with 1 to 4 employees to 48% for companies with 500 or more.

Some companies offer innovative training.

Good practice for workers

Arrangements exist which can help to remove some barriers to training for workers. Chief among these are the lack of time for training and the problem of the cost – not just the direct cost of training but also the derivative costs, such as the opportunity cost of taking up training again and the loss of earnings if wages are not maintained. In addition, if adults are truly to benefit from the opportunities on offer, adequate support services (transport, child-caring, etc.) are essential.

Arrangements are needed to address the problems of time and cost.

To reconcile training time, working time, family and leisure, training hours must be made compatible with working hours and children's school hours. This means favouring flexible time management such as the possibility of a temporarily part-time contract to allow resumption of complementary studies and flexible hours during the day, week, month or even year. Local support services and training can also allow rapid movement from one place to another.

To extend access to training, some countries have introduced an individual training right. It may take the form of paid training leave under certain conditions. Under this arrangement, it is up to the individual, not the company, to decide whether or not he or she wants to receive training and to

Some countries have established individual rights to training in the form of leave.

137

---

choose the type of training. Since 1974, there has been an ILO Convention on Paid Educational Leave (Convention No. 140). To date, this Convention has been ratified by 32 countries, including Finland, Spain, Sweden and the United Kingdom[23] of the nine countries of the thematic review.

In Norway, in November 1999, Parliament adopted a law giving universal statutory entitlement to leave for educational purposes. It is essentially a codification of previous collective agreements between the social partners. The law provides that persons who have been engaged in a professional activity for more than three years, and in the same company for the last two years, are entitled to full- or part-time leave for a maximum of three years to enrol in an educational programme. The law came into force on 1 January 2001. It does not deal with the issue of wages or subsistence during the period of leave, the financing of which has not been decided.

Collective agreements in both the public and private sector, under certain circumstances, contain the right of an employee to be absent for educational purposes. When this absence is related to the employee's personal wishes and needs the right becomes a mere possibility, and it is generally unpaid leave. When the training is part of a skills development plan envisaged by the company, the leave may include continued payment of wages.

In Finland, the third phase of the training guarantee scheme was approved by a working group of the social partners. While the first two phases were focused on the long-term unemployed in 1997 and all unemployed in 1998, the third phase, starting in August 2001, primarily involves employees with 10 or more years' seniority in their company. Training leave includes the possibility of replacement in the job.

These rights too can lead to inequities. In France, in order to involve those concerned with training more closely, Gauron (2000) suggests that the nature of the obligation to training should be changed from an obligation to pay to an obligation to train. However, Guiraudie and Terrenoire (2000) do not think that the individual right to training can offer more equal access to vocational training for different categories of employee. The least-skilled workers are, indeed, ill-equipped to take advantage of the opportunity. They might even use up their individual right without that being part of a structured professional development project. The authors therefore envisage that training should be a joint project between the employee and the company.

It is a fact that individual training leave is taken in the majority of cases by highly motivated people able to draw up a professional or personal project, validate the qualifications acquired and choose training activities appropriate to their project. The same goes for training vouchers, which presuppose that the beneficiary can make a justifiable choice based on an individual project.

Financing of training relies primarily on co-financing, loans and tax credits. In principle, employees can contribute personally to the financing of training by accepting a temporary drop in wages and/or agreeing to work outside normal hours to make up the time spent in training. On the other hand, an allowance can be paid to the employees undergoing employment-

---

23. The other OECD countries that have ratified Convention No. 140 are Belgium, the Czech Republic, France, Germany, Hungary, Mexico, the Netherlands and Poland.

related training outside working hours in their own leisure time. In practice, it does not appear that workers co-finance their training by reductions in wages, and it is not known to what extent other mechanisms are used for that purpose. The mechanisms highlighted in the various countries of the thematic review tend rather towards co-investment by the company and the employee through a training savings account or individual training accounts. There are also loan schemes, but these are not at all widespread. Thus in the United Kingdom there are loans for workers (Career Development Loans, CDLs) to lift the financial barrier. They are bank loans repaid in instalments supported by the participation of four high street banks. The beneficiaries do not have to repay the loans until they have finished their course, or not for 18 months if they are unemployed or in receipt of social security. The DfES pays the interest during this period. Tax relief on income after qualification, in the form of training tax credits, can also be a way of enhancing the private return on the training of workers, even if that only affects workers who pay a certain level of taxes.

The principle of individual learning accounts (ILAs) has been developed and applied recently in a few OECD countries, including Sweden and the United Kingdom. Their aim is to encourage adults to learn and increase the effectiveness of training. Like training vouchers, these accounts start from the principle that *a*) the individual is the best placed to choose what he/she wants to learn and how he/she wants to enhance his/her skills and *b*) the investment cost is shared. Aid from the government or the company consists of contributions to match those of the individual. These accounts are generally not tied to a company but follow the individual. ILA holders have access to a whole range of financial incentives to plan and pay for their training. Tax incentives can be used to encourage employers to invest jointly with their employees. That should be beneficial both to companies and employees (especially, it is hoped, in small companies), since it reduces the cost of their contributions to training. More generally, it is hoped that ILAs could encourage personal responsibility for obtaining training and career development.

Individual learning accounts have yet to make their mark.

To ensure maximum participation in the arrangement, it is important that it is simple from an administrative point of view and not overburdened with rules. ILAs are still at the development stage and have yet to make their mark (Box 5.7). The scheme was suspended in December 2001 in England, mainly because of the poor quality of the training provided to workers. In Sweden, it is emphasised that the funds allocated belong to the individual and it is up to them to decide how to use them. The basic idea is that the whole subsidy is paid to them. However, the possibility of subsidising employers to encourage them to contribute to their employees' accounts is also under active consideration at the present time. The Skandia initiative, a pilot in this field, is being followed with interest by other Swedish companies.

A fundamental question in the long-term evaluation of ILAs is how far they really generate new investment in training. The dead-weight and substitution effects must be taken into account. Will subsidies not be sought largely by those who would, in any event, have invested in their own training? Will some individuals not transfer funds from their existing accounts to ILAs in order to benefit from the higher return (substitution effect)? Will some companies not try to obtain provisions for tax relief through ILAs by substituting training or courses recognised as ILAs for their own in-house training?

Box 5.7. **Individual learning accounts: an innovative scheme to finance training yet to make its mark in Sweden and the United Kingdom**

The aim of individual learning accounts (ILAs) is to make training more accessible to all by increasing the volume of low-cost training which those concerned can finance themselves. Individuals benefit in terms of productivity and wages, as well as better protection from unemployment, while for the company, the advantage is lower training costs, higher workforce productivity and the reputation of "good" employer. For the government, the cost depends on the volume of subsidies granted.

In Sweden, ILAs are at present at an experimental and final development stage, to be introduced from July 2003. Under the latest government proposal, individuals will be able to set aside a maximum of 25% of a base amount (approximately SEK 9 500) per year, including a tax reduction, to an ILA. Employers that deposit funds in an employee's learning account will receive a tax deduction. To enable the rapid introduction of the system, savings will initially be made in accounts administered by a government agency, with the consideration later on of saving with different financial institutions. The full premium will be paid on one-year full time study. When a lower number of study days is used, the maximum premium will be proportionally reduced.

The Skandia company, a national and international insurance and banking consortium, has since 1999 offered a development account to its employees. Thirty-five per cent of them decided to participate in the project. The company pays an amount to match that saved by the employee, who can save up to 5% of his/her wages in an insurance scheme that will compensate the loss of wages when he/she takes training leave. The wage supplement is tripled for employees over 45 years old who do not have a higher secondary diploma. Seven years of joint saving will finance about six months of full-time education and training. Everyone is free to choose his training. "In-house" training is provided in any case and is not replaced by this new scheme. Participants have access to a website where they can find information on the level of their savings, training opportunities and advice on writing a CV. For the company, the aim of the scheme is to provide bridges between work and training, and create an arrangement to encourage employees to continually update their knowledge.

In England, ILAs were designed to provide government funding for a wide range of learning to people aged 19 and over. Similar arrangements existed in Scotland, Wales and Northern Ireland. The 1997 Labour manifesto committed the government to introducing ILAs, with a re-start for up to a million people alongside individuals making small investments of their own. The overall aim of ILAs was to widen participation in learning and to help overcome financial barriers to learning faced by individuals.

The package of ILA incentives were:

- £150 government contribution on a wide range of learning for the first million ILA holders, provided the individual made a contribution of £25.

- 20% discount on a wide range of learning, up to a limit of GBP 100 per year.

- 80% discount on a narrowly targeted range of learning, introductory-level ICT and basic maths up to GBP 200 per year.

The target of one million ILA holders was reached in May 2001. However, regrettably, over the Summer of 2001 the DfES received growing volumes of complaints from individuals and Trading Standards Officers about mis-selling, aggressive marketing, poor learning, poor value for money, and alleged fraud. In response, the DfES took action against some learning providers.

On 24 October 2001, the Secretary of State announced the decision to suspend the scheme from 7 December. The ILA programme was closed on 23 November 2001. There will be a successor ILA-style programme building on the best of the original: "one that attracts non-traditional learners, one that balances measures to protect the public purse, provides simplicity for the learner, and avoids bureaucracy for providers".

Source: Arnal, Ok and Torres (2001), OECD (2001c), Didier (2000) and *www.dfes.gov.uk/ila*

The public authorities can try to overcome the problem of dead-weight effects by targeting their publicity (and possibly the entitlement to benefits) on low "human capital" groups and those least likely to invest to increase it. In practice, that means targeting low-skilled and low-paid employees in small companies, as well as individuals who have suffered a break in their career and are now trying to re-enter the labour market.

Some actions in favour of groups at risk

There are innovative strategies that favour groups at risk...

The aim of this subsection is to focus on some innovative strategies favouring groups at risk implemented in the countries of the thematic review. The difficulty one faces in trying to draw conclusions from a presentation of this kind comes precisely from the novelty of these initiatives and their unique character. The question that arises, therefore, is whether they can be reproduced elsewhere.

... and so reduce the marginalisation of...

The central issue is how to involve in an education and training scheme a whole series of individuals who are the hard core of adult workers. They may be older workers, low-paid workers (working poor), or those working in traditional or endangered sectors and/or SMEs. The challenge is not to widen the gulf between these adult workers at risk and the others, with the former confined to marginal jobs without any chance of developing and with a prospect of loss of skills and accelerating exclusion for those who cannot access continuing training.

... workers who are victims of restructuring...

One of the crucial tasks in a restructuring for workers dismissed after many years in the same company is for them to have access to a skills assessment so that they know their "market value" and what they should do to find the best possible new job. Conversion leave often forms part of the period of advance notice in the framework of a social plan.

Early intervention in favour of qualification of adult workers is necessary, certainly before they are made redundant after a restructuring. Wolter and Weber (1999) provide a critical analysis of policy in Switzerland during the prolonged period of unemployment that had an enormous impact on unskilled workers in the 1990s. They highlight especially the inadequate provision of continuing training for the labour force due to insufficient financial incentives. Private returns from continuing training are, indeed, insignificant in inducing adults to learn. In a mainly private adult education market, public training programmes are only provided for workers when they are unemployed. The labour market authorities are then faced with an insurmountable difficulty in making up for the ten, twenty or sometimes more years when skills have not been developed. The authors envisage that intervention must occur at an earlier stage if it is to be effective. Companies should constantly promote qualification of their employees and reward training with wage rises, which are too often linked only to length of service. For low-paid workers, a government financial incentive would be needed to avoid facing them with a prohibitive financial sacrifice.

... older workers...

As has been observed, older workers in particular are denied access to continuing training and its rewards. In the first place, investing in training of workers over the age of 50 requires a much more rapid return than for younger workers. Secondly, companies have been accustomed for decades to managing their need to renew skills essentially by preferential recruitment of newly qualified young people, and early retirement of employees whose skills are considered obsolete. Often, early retirement of experienced workers is done in haste, without a real period of transmission of their know-how to their replacements. The system of on-the-job training for new recruits by tutors, often older workers whose experience is little formalised, has been tried, for example in the Randers Reb company in Denmark (Box 5.8).

When it is harder for companies to recruit externally for demographic reasons or because it involves manual trades in heavy industry often geographically remote, older workers offer the chance to satisfy new skills needs. If companies do not acknowledge this problem, they will have to manage their modernisation and the organisational changes involved using a stock of low-skilled or insufficiently experienced adult workers.

A scheme to promote training and certification in the second half of working life for adult workers can encourage them to stay on in the job as they get older. The example of the Skandia company (Box 5.7), which supplements

---

Box 5.8. **Randers Reb – the enterprise as a learning place in Denmark**

Randers Reb, an enterprise founded in 1840, produces all kind of ropes, and exports to many parts of the world. It has undergone a dramatic technological change in recent years: it has invested in high-tech machinery, a change that would not be possible without also investing in personnel. One could call this "human resource investment", which was part of an overall enterprise development plan – a joint venture with the local Adult Vocational Training (AMU) Centre – to organise the continual skill upgrading of their employees. Employees were told it was practically unavoidable for them to take up the offer of training if they wanted to continue to work for the company. The offer comprised not only all of the teaching – of which the AMU Centre delivered the major part – but also the provision of flexible arrangements which made it possible for the employees to participate without cutting ties with the company.

At the time of recruitment, a young unskilled worker will be trained on-the-job for 3 to 5 months with a tutor and will then follow various "modules" in more or less technical domains. Internal and external training, especially that offered by AMU, is used. The enterprise explained that around 10% of wages go to a fund devoted to education and training. The company now is one of the best-performing producers in this industry world-wide.

Important parts of the internal training processes started in Randers Reb through the ISO norms. The emphasis is on training both inside and outside the enterprise. From the lowest level (7 years in school) to tutors and managers, training is extensively used. The ISO is seen as a way to help the enterprise better focus its education and training efforts, mainly balancing cost and time devoted to internal and external training in order to increase the competencies of employees. On average, a person spends three weeks a year in training. New machines are very expensive investments: employees are required to be capable of using updated and new technology, to rely on communication and teamwork, and to be able to monitor quality control.

In addition to and as a result of the training, an annual test for skills and competencies was introduced which permits the employee to gain points on the salary scale. The UK programme "Investors in People" was adapted to the enterprise. The enterprise created a "learning room" in which all employees can exchange and propose ideas and innovations, which will eventually be tested and experimented with. The enterprise provides a home computer for its employees, and they are required to demonstrate, after one year, that they can take the European Computer Driving Licence.

Source: Meeting with Human Resource Managers, Randers, November 2000.

the older and less qualified workers' savings more than those of other workers, is worth noting. Taking account of experience acquired in the course of a career can be a powerful incentive to any adult to develop their skills throughout their career and add to their knowledge through continuing training.

In Finland, the national older worker programme launched in 1998, covering a five-year period, is intended to encourage workers over 50 to retire later. Its main objective was to push back the actual age of leaving the labour market by two to three years between now and 2010. The programme includes a monitoring committee consisting of the social partners and an independent evaluation system. It contains 40 measures, key among them vocational training for employees aged 45 or over. Training is considered to be crucial in maintaining the employability of older workers. The Finnish authorities are aware that it will take at least ten to fifteen years to fill the training age-gap and eliminate employment problems among the older group. A vast information campaign was launched, on the theme "experience is the nation's wealth". Training and information programmes on age management were arranged for employers and company managers. Training sessions were held on how to use and pass on older workers' experience and how to motivate older workers. Some 4 000 company directors participated in seminars on organisation of work. The labour inspectorate was given the task of advising on age management in companies. Already, it can be reported that the process of early retirement has begun to be reversed. The experience in the public sector is revealing (Box 5.9).

In the case of graduate workers, employment-related training is justified by the concern to keep knowledge up to date. For a large number of people who did not have a proper initial education during their youth, getting a second chance to acquire and catch up on the skills and qualifications they

... poorly educated workers...

Box 5.9. **Developing older workers' skills in the public sector in Finland**

Employees in the public sector in Finland number 125 000 – 33% of them with a university degree, much higher than in other sectors. One of the greatest challenges for the state as employer is the ageing of these employees, whose average age was 42 in 1999. The largest age group is 45-49 and one-third of today's staff will retire between now and 2010.

The state wants both to attract young graduates and to maintain and develop the level of skills of the oldest up to the end of their careers. For the oldest, individual skills development plans are prepared that will result in wage gains.

As to recruitment policy, special training programmes to meet the needs of the public sector are being negotiated in the initial education system and in secondary and higher education.

More generally, an ambitious programme to encourage learning is being developed through paid and unpaid training leave, temporary reassignments, the use of university centres and secondary institutions, and new pay schemes which recognise training achievements.

Source: Interviews with the Finnish authorities, Helsinki, February 2001.

need to work better and participate in social life is essential. The idea that continuing vocational training could take the place of initial education is currently the subject of impassioned debate. On one side, there are those who hold that investing in training people who are poorly qualified is not economically justifiable. As Heckman (1999) says, "the lack of interest of private firms in training disadvantaged workers indicates the difficulty of the task and the likely low rates of return of this activity" (p. 105). On the other hand, as Figure 5.10 shows, training activities procure high wage gains for less-educated workers. Yet they are the category that have the least access, it seems, to these activities. Training policies aimed primarily at poorly qualified workers could therefore have a dual effect of reducing social inequalities and improving company performance (Boyer, 2000).

The country note of Portugal draws attention to a variety of approaches of value in raising the probability of success in training people with low levels of education. They all have in common that they complement training with simultaneous actions involving improvements in company management methods and incorporation in a local development strategy, using civic motivation to underpin the value of education and training, as well as the explicit link between training, enhancement of skills, higher pay and promotion in the company. These approaches, very different in their methods, their target group and ultimately their effects, also have in common that they encourage motivation and demand for acquisition of knowledge and/or development of skills, by heeding people's concerns and involving them in their own learning. Success depends on the trainers' ability to embed their input in a broader vision of the role and objectives of education and training. In contrast to a standardised and uniform approach, it requires a certain degree of autonomy and ability to innovate.

Figure 5.10. **Return to training by initial educational attainment**

Proportional mean wage differences[1] for workers trained, by initial educational attainment, 1990s

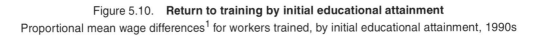

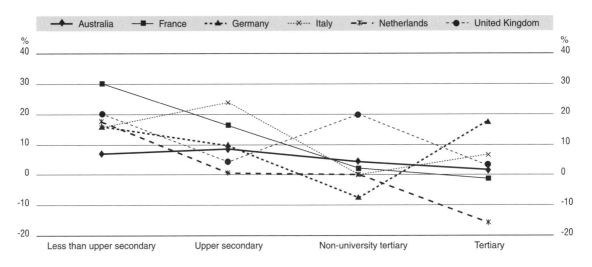

1. Mean earnings of workers trained minus mean earnings of workers not trained, divided by mean earnings of workers not trained.
Source: OECD (1999).

At company level, it is increasingly recognised that training only yields the desired results if it fits within the objectives of the company in respect of quality, productivity, innovation or rapid response and adaptation to the market (Crouch, Finegold, Sako, 2001). Training providers must offer an integrated service that meets companies' expectations, especially SMEs. The strategy set out by the Minho industrial association in Braga takes this lesson on board (Box 5.10). Unlike a strategy aimed only at the individual independent of any contact with the company where they work or intend to work, the central idea involves incorporating the individual training action within an overall company strategy. Thus, in the case of a small or medium-sized enterprise, those concerned must convince the entrepreneur to undergo training or update their basic knowledge. Once convinced and reassured that they will not be shown up by more competent colleagues, the entrepreneur will be the best proponent of training actions for their employees. This industrial association adopts a similar strategy for the largest companies. On the one hand, the training is preceded by a diagnostic analysis concerning improvement of the management system, and on the other the human resources management is brought in to prepare a training plan which is then passed on to the employees. This guarantees a synergy between training and the company's general strategy which aims at improving productivity and quality.

... and workers in SMEs and companies with low productivity.

Box 5.10. **The Minho Industrial Association, Braga, Portugal: Advice to companies on training plans for the head of the company and their employees**

The main activity of this industrial association is to provide advice to companies. To this end, it performs an overall analysis of economic trends in the region, strengths and weaknesses in terms of competitiveness. The diagnosis tries to reduce the danger of specialisation in low-productivity industries. The aim is thus to raise the quality of this specialisation through an approach based on improving the organisation of firms and their ability to master the necessary technologies. A particular feature of the Minho Industrial Association is that it stresses the integration of training within overall strategy to improve the quality of management in firms. Finding that of 100 training actions and 1 400 course participants, 75% of participants attended classes individually without any connection with the company that employed them, managers decided to tackle this separation between individual training decisions and management of the company. That led to a series of measures whose common feature was integration of training in the management of the company:

- Developing diagnostic analysis in companies of their organisational and technological capacity.
- Convincing heads of SMEs or human resource managers in the largest companies to decide their training programmes in line with this strategic objective of developing competitiveness. Drawing up training plans for the selected employees, such that their new skills have a place in the company's development.
- Administering a CRVC (Centre of Recognition, Validation and Certification of Competences), in collaboration with the IEFP, ANEFA and all public authorities involved in training. The aim is to ensure cumulative enhancement of skills in line with benchmarks demanded by various occupations.

Source: Interviews with training managers, Braga, March 2001.

145

5.3. Public training programmes

In most OECD countries, it was the rise and subsequent persistence of unemployment – mostly among unskilled workers – and recognition that a degree and/or vocational training were the best protection against underemployment and job insecurity that brought the issue of training to the top of the agenda. With this in mind, the labour market authorities established a panoply of public training programmes to improve adults' ability to obtain employment. Three aspects will be discussed in this section: the role of the public employment service (PES) in training; the potential conflict between different objectives; and the contrasting results shown up by evaluation studies.

The PES and training for unemployed and employed adults

Training activities for the unemployed are normally regarded as active rather than passive measures.

Public training programmes are rooted in the activities of the PES. In countries with a low unemployment rate, the PES has an important role to play in training employed adults. This is particularly the case with the Institute for Employment and Vocational Training (IEFP) in Portugal. In most countries, the PES provides or buys training places for the unemployed to improve their chances of finding a job, preferably in higher-skilled positions. Training activities for the unemployed are part of an activation measure: the programmes are normally regarded as active rather than passive (in other words, designed to help the unemployed person find a job rather than pay him unemployment benefit), even if this distinction is blurred in practice. In fact, as noted by Robinson (2000), one of the essential characteristics of active programmes is that participation or non-participation in such programmes increasingly plays a role in access to benefit payments.

Exemplary practices can be seen in Denmark (Box 5.11). Training programmes available to employers to improve the qualifications of their employees and prevent labour shortages are now also open to jobseekers, under an essentially remedial approach. Two features are worthy of mention:

- Public financing of training programmes is reserved for generic skills, while skills specific to a company are the responsibility of companies as clients of public centres. Special financing for training planning in SMEs is provided under a new institution managed by the social partners.

- Effective preventive measures exist to avoid shortages of skilled workers.

Shares of participation and of active public expenditure in these programmes vary considerably between countries.

On average, in 2001, the nine countries examined spent 0.23% of GDP on public training programmes (Table 5.1). Training expenditure tends to fall when unemployment falls (OECD, 2001a), except in Denmark, Spain and, to a lesser extent, Portugal and Switzerland. Training activities normally form an important part of expenditure on active measures – on average, the nine countries concerned allocated around 26% of their active public expenditure to them. The situation varies considerably between countries: in 2001, it ranged from 7% in Norway to 54% in Denmark.

The number of participants in training programmes in relation to the labour force averaged 5% in 2001 in the nine countries considered. While training expenditure did slightly decrease as a proportion of GDP, the number of new participants has risen. In 2001, the number of adults enrolling in a training programme was more than three times higher than in 1985, and had increased by more than 50% since 1993. These figures most probably reflect

Box 5.11. **In Denmark, the system of adult vocational training is faced with new challenges in a changing PES**

Since the 1960s, adult vocational training in Denmark has been considered a state responsibility. That is still the case in March 2001, as the 16 vocational training centres (AMU) come under the Ministry of Labour through the national labour market authority (AMS). These centres, however, are increasingly managed along commercial lines.

The main clients of AMU centres are local PES employment agencies (AF) and local authorities which send the unemployed and those on social security for training, as well as private and public sector companies and their employees. Unemployed people under individual mobilisation plans keep their unemployment benefit during training. Employees are trained free of charge and may receive an allowance to cover the cost of travel and accommodation.

Since 1 January 2001, the financial aspects of training the unemployed and beneficiaries of social security have been made more transparent. In the case of the unemployed, the AF agencies buy training courses from the AMU centres or other training organisations and thus pay the institutions according to the same general principle of the taximeter that is the basis of public financing of adult education and training in Denmark. The same goes for the local authorities who finance training of beneficiaries of social security. Employees are only sure to receive a full training allowance for courses involving "generic formal skills". For specific recognised and more specialist skills, their allowance may be progressively reduced. Companies which could previously train their employees free of charge can only do so for generic transferable skills and not specific skills that only apply to their own specialist area. Customised courses for companies can be arranged, subject to financial participation or external financing, notably through European programmes. A new institution managed by the social partners (AUF) is responsible, among other things, for arranging financing for training planning in SMEs.

The integration of the actors concerned in training also occurs at regional level in the 14 regional labour market councils with representatives of the social partners and local authorities. Their role is to control the budget and decide policies to improve the local labour market in the short and long term. The skills profile required at regional level is determined twice a year through reports which allow monitoring of the pattern of regional demand, and setting measures to prevent shortages of skilled labour.

Thus, in Åarhus, the objectives of the regional labour market council for 2000 are to seek to overcome bottlenecks, prevent marginalisation of vulnerable groups, raise the level of education of the unemployed, develop an effective job placement system, ensure a close link between active measures and demand for labour, and promote employment growth. Few courses are envisaged to meet skills shortages since the preventive measures are effective. On the other hand, groups at risk, such as older workers, immigrants and the uneducated, face real difficulty in obtaining jobs, even in a tight labour market. Individual action plans are prepared with and for them applying the "step-by-step" concept of progressive learning from motivational courses to in-depth learning.

Source: Interviews with managers, Åarhus, November 2000.

greater use of shorter training courses and the diminishing value attached to costly programmes such as long training courses leading to a qualification. The number of participants varies significantly from country to country, ranging in 2001 from 0.5% of the labour force in the United Kingdom to 15.9% in Denmark.

In the nine countries of the thematic review, participants are more often employed rather than unemployed adults. Figure 5.11 shows that on average 5.5% of the labour force participated in public training programmes in late 1990s/early 2000s, 3.6% of them employed and 1.9% unemployed. However, there are only three countries where there are relatively more

Public training programme participants are more often employed rather than unemployed adults.

147

Table 5.1. **Public training programmes**

Spending as a percentage of GDP on active measures and inflows of participants, 1985, 1993 and 2001

	Spending on public training (% of GDP)			Spending on public training (% of active measures)			New participants (% of labour force)		
	1985	1993	2001	1985	1993	2001	1985	1993	2001
Canada[1]	0.35	0.31	0.17	54.6	47.0	42.0	1.7	2.8	1.6
Denmark[2]	0.43	0.47	0.84	38.9	26.9	54.3	5.6	11.2	15.9
Finland	0.26	0.47	0.29	29.3	27.5	30.4	1.2	2.8	2.8
Norway	0.10	0.33	0.06	16.3	28.6	7.3	0.8	3.5	0.9
Portugal[3]	0.18	0.25	0.15	51.4	29.9	25.1	0.2	1.3	9.9
Spain	0.02	0.11	0.14	6.7	21.0	19.4	0.5	2.9	14.6
Sweden	0.50	0.75	0.30	23.7	25.6	27.6	1.9	4.2	2.3
Switzerland	0.01	0.06	0.08	6.5	16.2	17.7	0.3	1.0	1.3
United Kingdom[4]	0.07	0.15	0.05	9.2	26.4	13.0	..	1.3	0.5
Unweighted average	0.22	0.32	0.23	26.3	27.7	26.3	1.5	3.4	5.5

.. Data not available.

Note: Canada, Denmark, Finland, Norway and Sweden: 1986 instead of 1985; Portugal: 1987 instead of 1985.
1. Fiscal years starting on 1 April. Last update for data on new participants in 1997-98.
2. Last update in 2000.
3. Last update in 2000 for data on spending and 1998 for data on new participants.
4. Fiscal years starting on 1 April. Last update in 1999-2000.
Source: OECD database on labour market programmes.

Figure 5.11. **New participants in public training programmes**

Percentage of the labour force, 1998-2001

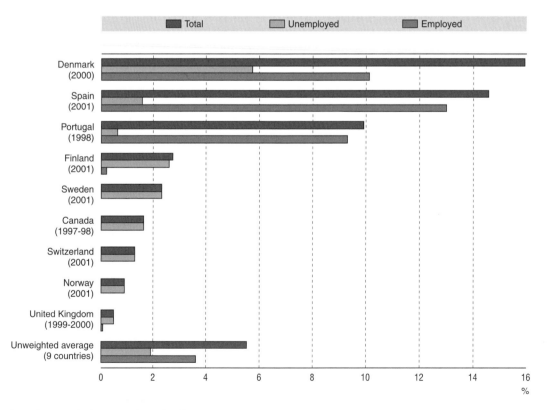

Note: Countries are ranked in descending order of the total participation rate.
Source: OECD database on labour market programmes.

workers in training, Denmark, Spain and Portugal. In the other six the opposite is true; there are even four countries where only the unemployed have access to public training programmes: Canada, Norway, Switzerland and Sweden.

Potential conflicts between different objectives

The objectives of public training programmes include enhancing participants' prospects of getting a job and giving them the means to improve their qualifications. The PES subsidises training to prevent insufficient investment, especially in technical training, and to achieve greater equality of opportunity. Public training programmes can be regarded as seeking three distinct global objectives at the same time: 1) reduction in unemployment; 2) reduction or prevention of skilled labour shortages; 3) raising levels of education or skills. These objectives may conflict. Programmes seeking to quickly end unemployment benefits do not allow the beneficiaries to undergo full training and thus to raise their level of skills. The problem becomes more acute when the economy is growing rapidly and there is a shortage of labour, as trainees are often forced to give up their training programme because they have found a job. Some argue that in the long term, this means a loss of skills to society.

The objectives driving these programmes can conflict.

While in a tight market the unemployment rate declines, the limited group without employment is increasingly made up of people who are very far from being job-ready. Often, they lack initial education and have only a very low level of basic knowledge. At the same time, fewer resources are allocated to training by the PES since the number of unemployed is shrinking. The challenge then, with less resources, is to effectively enhance the employability of the long-term unemployed knowing that these persons have a particular need for progressive and intensive training using appropriate teaching methods to overcome serious learning difficulties.

In times of low unemployment, those without work should be recognised as those most needing training.

According to analyses by the Danish Ministry of Labour (Maerkedahl, 2000) activation measures based on the principle of the beneficiaries' rights and obligations can have three main effects at the individual level: the upgrading of qualifications effect, the motivation effect and the retention effect. The first two encourage people to get out of the unemployment benefit system, by increasing and promoting the employability of the beneficiary and motivating the unemployed person to explore all employment opportunities, including before the beginning of an offer of activation. The retention effect, on the contrary, means a reduction in the unemployed person's jobseeking activities during the activation period. The application of these different effects to public training programmes shows that upgrading of qualifications requires a period of retention in a training programme before becoming effective. It should be recognised, however, that most public training programmes are of fairly short duration.

For groups of unemployed who have the best chance of rapidly finding employment, the retention effect on activation measures is sometimes comparable to the dead-weight effect if the benefit during the activation measure is relatively high in relation to wages. It is then recommended that training be targeted at the long-term unemployed and that workers who are easily employable not be encouraged to participate in public training programmes at the beginning of the period of unemployment. This is the opposite of the creaming-off effect which results from quantitative objectives imposed on local employment agencies in evaluating the implementation of training programmes. PES staff then tend to select for programmes those individuals who have the best chance of quickly finding a job at the end of their training.

In some cases, upgrading qualifications might require more intensive courses.

In some cases, the effect of upgrading qualifications cannot be attained in programmes that are too short and not sufficiently intensive. Thus it is shown in the country note of Canada that upgrading courses for adults with reading and writing difficulties who want to reach literacy Level 3 require in the best cases six to twelve months of full-time study, whereas the programmes established in Canada provide one or two three-hour sessions a week. At that rate, it is observed, it would take three to six years to reach that level of competency, whereas few adults can be motivated to participate in programmes lasting that long. Yet there is a long waiting list for such courses.

The implementation of public training courses must take account of the combination of these individual effects. In Norway, some local employment agencies apply a new model for the implementation of public training programmes (Box 5.12). This flexible model, where the key words are

---

Box 5.12.   **A new model of public training programmes in Norway**

The new model of public training programmes is constructed on a system of modules, personalised individual training, continuous admission to modules and award of certificates on completion of each module, and a formal qualification on completion of about five modules.

The example of the welding course at Mosjøen, traditionally lasting two years, is illuminating. In the past, the maximum capacity of programmes was 12 trainees over two years; now there are 80. The new system has made it possible to reduce the training period to 15 weeks, with five modules that can be taken at the same time or one after the other. There are no more dropouts in the middle of a module and a break between two modules is not a problem: the trainee can therefore train mainly in winter, when he/she is temporarily laid off. Theory and practice are combined in the learning process. Each trainee has a personal training programme and the trainer must monitor everyone's progress as a group or individually. Trainees are motivated to take charge of their own learning.

The successful implementation of this new model relies on close local co-operation between the employment agency, the skills resource centre (MRK) and employers. The practical part of the training takes place in companies which produce a course report with a view to improving the training programme.

The employment agency and the MRK co-operate in determining the level of each trainee. A standard procedure is followed:

- The employment agency sends each trainee's CV to the MRK.
- The MRK discusses the CV directly with the trainee to determine which modules should be included in the personal programme.
- The MRK sends the personal programme to the employment agency.
- The employment agency decides whether or not the trainee will take the course.

The employment agency and the MRK hold weekly meetings to follow trainees' progress, discuss all kinds of possible improvements or problems that arise, and co-ordinate continuous admissions.

Source: Interviews with managers, Mosjøen, March 2000.

modules, tailor-made programmes, continuous admission and certification, was developed to overcome the weaknesses and problems that are found in more traditional and rigid organisations, such as:

- Admission at a fixed date, which rules out those who become unemployed afterward.

- Long courses that must be taken without a break in order to obtain a certificate.

- The impossibility of replacing people who leave the programme, which leads to high costs per trainee.

- Non-recognition by a certificate for partial completion of a course.

- Content that is not adaptable to individual needs or to the practical experience of people with reading and writing difficulties.

Contrasting effects revealed by the evaluations

Evaluations of public training programmes in OECD countries suggest a very mixed track record (Martin, 2000 and Martin and Grubb, 2001 for an overview of the evidence from recent OECD countries' experience). It has been estimated that some programmes have a low or even negative return for participants if the effects on wages or employment are compared with the cost of achieving those effects. However, there are some public training programmes that work, more in terms of increased employment opportunities than significant effects on wages. In the case of adults, it is observed that the results are almost always positive in the case of women and less favourable for men. Some public training programmes seem to be effective for certain target groups and not for others. Martin and Grubb (2001) highlighted four critical features in the design of public training programmes: *i*) the participants must be strictly targeted; *ii*) the scale of programmes must be fairly small; *iii*) the programme must be lead to a certificate that is recognised and valued by the market; and *iv*) the programme must have a significant on-the-job training component, thus establishing strong links with local employers. It will be shown here whether other important factors were identified in the countries examined in terms of good practice, especially for long-term unemployed.

Public training programmes have produced very different results.

A recent evaluation of the effect of government-sponsored training programmes in Canada on the transition to the labour market of disadvantaged young adults shows that their participation in training activities while on unemployment insurance results in a better success rate in finding employment (Gilbert *et al.*, 2001). On the other hand, for poorly educated men participating in welfare training activities, the effects are not as good as for those who do not participate in these activities, even taking into account the diverse nature of the population in question. In Norway, Aakvik (1999) finds that the unemployment insurance system influences the selection of participants in training programmes. It is the low-paid workers who do not have a strong link to the labour market prior to training who are over-represented. Yet the effects of training in terms of jobs are positive and significant, especially for women.

Switzerland, also faced with a rapid rise in unemployment in the 1990s, developed an ambitious policy to activate the unemployed, which included training programmes. Gerfin and Lechner (2000) were able to draw on a huge wealth of data in an administrative database on management of unemployment and social security. They distinguished five fairly homogeneous categories among the 16 different kinds of courses: 1) basic courses to enhance jobseeking and self-confidence; 2) language courses; 3) continuing vocational training courses; 4) computer courses; and 5) other courses (mainly for specific occupations). They evaluated the effects of participating in these courses on the likelihood of employment in the short term. The effects are somewhat contrasting and inconclusive based on type of course, the best results coming from continuing vocational training courses, other courses and computer courses, and the least good from language and basic courses.

They have proved less effective when unemployment is high.

Hämäläinen (2001) also explores the hypothesis of the negative correlation between effectiveness of training programmes and unemployment levels in Finland. The unemployment in that country rose abruptly between 1990 and 1994, by 15 percentage points from 3.4% to 18.4%. The government responded to this rise in unemployment by increasing active measures, especially training programmes (Table 5.1). The author highlights the following results based on micro-data for participants in training programmes (the trial group) and other unemployed (the control group) by comparing a peak period (1988-89), a period of rising unemployment (1991-92) and a period of persistent high unemployment (1993-94):

• The effects in terms of employment of public training programmes are positive and statistically significant. They declined considerably over the period but only three years after unemployment began to rise and especially for participants who did have good employment prospects (high level of education, short-term unemployment, etc.).

• Between 1989 and 1994, the impact became more effective for categories at risk, which suggests that in a period of high unemployment, training programmes yield better results when they are targeted at individuals whose initial employability is low. In a period of low unemployment, the opposite seems to be true.

• The loss of effectiveness in a context of high unemployment is attributed not only to traditional factors such as discouragement, declining scale returns of over-large programmes and the reduced role of training as a signal, but also to non-observable factors. The author suggests two elements which in the early 1990s affected the selection process for training programmes and acted as an incentive only to keep job-ready participants in programmes. In the first place, there was the introduction of management by results, first in three districts in 1990 and then throughout the country in 1991. This in turn introduced specific targets both for the number of new places in programmes and the proportion of trainees who must find a job on completion of the training. The second change was the loss of the monopoly of public vocational training centres, which allowed the PES to buy training courses from other organisations. The result was a 60% fall in the proportion of training days provided by public vocational training centres.

The longer-term effects are positive and rise with the length of the training.

Calmfors, Forslund and Hemström (2001) recently presented a report on Sweden's experience of active labour market policies. With respect to public training programmes, the authors observe that:

• The estimated effects of training linked to the labour market in the 1980s differ from those in the 1990s. The estimates in the 1980s show significant positive effects on employment and the wages of participants, while the effects of training in the 1990s are either insignificant or negative. They attribute that to the high unemployment in the 1990s, the introduction of large-scale programmes, the use of these programmes to requalify participants for unemployment benefits, and the considerable fall in demand for labour.

• The short-term effects are generally not significant or even negative, while taken over a longer period the results are markedly better. Their hypothesis is that training increases participants' reservation wages.

• The long-term effects on incomes and employment tend to rise with the length of training.

In the majority of OECD countries, only a non-experimental evaluation of training programmes is possible due to lack of suitable data, to the extent that there is no question of implementing arbitrary social programmes as one does to test the impact of medicines (Baslé, 2000). In the countries that participated in the thematic review, there are few "experimental" evaluation studies of training programmes based on a strictly random distribution between trial groups in order to eliminate the bias involved in self-selection and to determine the real average impact of training. Ham and Lalonde (1996) hold that even if this method could provide an adequate short-term mean programme impact, it does not guarantee that long-term impact would be void of any systematic biases. Certain evaluations reconstruct a control group from administrative files but such a group is hard to follow longitudinally because it is subject to a phenomenon of attrition for reasons not necessarily related to the programme. In the United Kingdom, Payne (2000) advocates allowing social experiments, but as long as there is no political will to do so it is better to try to understand the process of selection for programmes. Some new administrative files, such as the *New Deal* evaluation database, allow evaluations that can better help to decide the policy to adopt.

There are few experimental evaluation studies.

The results of social experimentation on public vocational training programmes in the AMU in Denmark clearly illustrate the difficulties in conducting such experimentation. This method of experimental evaluation was applied in 1994 to determine the effects on employment of the participation of unskilled adults in training courses lasting an average of two weeks (Rosholm, 2001). The problem is how to determine and maintain the experimental character of the trial and control groups' composition because of people who do not turn up (no-shows) and unemployed excluded from courses who somehow still manage to follow them (cross-overs). The unemployed in 1994 who enrolled for specific courses beginning in May or June 1994 were randomly distributed between a trial group (425 individuals) and a control group (387 individuals). Only the individuals in the trial group received confirmation of their enrolment but just over half (219 individuals) actually came to the course; the others did not turn up. In the control group, one-fifth (86 individuals) managed despite everything to follow the course and the actual control group thus contained only 78% of the original group.

The results of this experimental study show that, for all unemployed, participating in a training course increases the probability of being unemployed six months after participating compared with not participating. One of the reasons is that jobseeking takes time and that training reduces the intensity of the search. Another reason is that unemployed non-participants had the benefit of other more effective measures such as assistance with jobseeking, other types of training or job creation schemes. Finally, the objective evaluated, leaving unemployment, is perhaps not relevant to this specific training which is primarily aimed at adults in employment to increase their productivity, with the unemployed having the lowest priority in access to this type of course.

A reasonable balance should be struck between efficiency and equity.

Even if some programmes are evaluated on paper as cost-effective, the implementation process is crucial. Some schemes can dissuade certain groups from participating. As an example, Gray (2000) lists serious disincentives arising from a too-narrowly defined output-related funding system for training organisations leading to creaming and the curtailment of skills training in order to secure an immediate job. Short-term success rates, for example 60% of participants finding a job within two months after completing the training, may prevent any disadvantaged unemployed person being selected for a training course. Employability is clearly a key outcome of any successful training activity, but a reasonable balance should be struck between efficiency and equity, such as social inclusion. High-performing training programmes should be specifically targeted at low-skilled and socially excluded people.

For Nicaise (2000), there is no inherent equity-efficiency dilemma in training for disadvantaged groups. The added value of training programmes should be measured not merely in terms of raw placement rates that measure the possible effects of training but also in terms of the impact of participants' entire previous history (initial education, work experience, etc.), which has nothing to do with the training programme itself. Differential placement rates for participants with comparable characteristics show that participation in training is more efficient for those whose position in the labour market is weaker. He advocates redirecting resources towards deprived groups by removing a series of legal, administrative, material, financial, psychological and especially educational barriers so as really to be able to respond to the needs of the target groups. The beneficiaries of social assistance and other unemployed people not eligible for unemployment benefits are particularly vulnerable because they are often not eligible to participate in traditional training programmes.

Grubb and Ryan (1999) also try to isolate the critical elements that make public adult training programmes work. They think that many of them offer cheap, short-term catch-up courses and fail to get their beneficiaries into worthwhile permanent employment. To achieve the latter, these public training programmes would have to prepare people for qualifications in demand in the labour market and provide quality training valued in the market – that would also reduce the displacement effects. However, the objectives of this kind of programme should not be limited to the efficiency criteria to which the evaluation is often confined. Above all, they should tackle issues of equity, especially giving a chance to disadvantaged people. It is in this sense that Grubb and Ryan put forward nine recommendations to allow a pragmatic evaluation of vocational training (Box 5.13).

Good practice in public training programmes

A number of good practices can be found in the countries examined in terms of funding and of effectiveness of training for the unemployed:

Box 5.13.   **Towards a pragmatic perspective on evaluating vocational education and training (VET) programmes**

Evaluation should be pragmatic rather than orthodox and based on a wider variety of approaches and measurements of results, more closely matching the programmes' initial objectives and the results achieved. Two considerations are central: evaluation generates new and better information about the programmes, and evaluation is best used to understand how programmes work and have evolved.

1. Evaluations of VET programmes should never lose sight of labour market outcomes and should be more concerned by the processes leading to those results.

2. The analysis of VET programmes should try to use a variety of evaluation methods, given that each is imperfect and incomplete.

3. VET evaluations should consider a broader range of outcome measure.

4. Evaluations should consider long-run as well as short-run effects of VET programmes.

5. Evaluations of VET programmes should examine results not only in terms of efficiency but also in terms of equity.

6. Although publicly sponsored training appears to succeed less often than does privately sponsored training, governments should approach with caution any harnessing of private provision to public goals.

7. Countries and international agencies should seek to incorporate evaluation into tripartite discussions and other political forums, recognising that the use of evaluation evidence depends on political factors.

8. Countries and international agencies should view the evaluation enterprise as a long-term activity, one that requires stability and longevity to become more influential and more sophisticated over time.

9. Rather than continuing with conventional programme evaluation, countries should incorporate systems' perspectives into evaluation.

Source: Grubb and Ryan (1999).

• Public financing of training programmes is usually reserved for general skills, while skills specific to a company are the responsibility of companies as clients of public centres. Special financing for SMEs is envisaged.

• Training organisations are not financed solely on the basis of quantitative results achieved in the short term, which leads to creaming and the curtailment of skills training, since the objective is immediate placement. Quality criteria must also be included in the call for tender.

• The process of implementing the training programmes involves co-operation among all those concerned with training at all stages of the training scheme.

• The PES operates a flexible model for implementing public training programmes where the key words are modules, tailor-made programmes, continuous admission and certification.

• Public training programmes prepare people for qualifications in demand in the labour market and provide quality training valued by that market.

- Preventive actions are implemented to avoid shortages of skilled workers.

There are also good practices to reach the long-term unemployed or disadvantaged persons:

- When unemployment is high, training should be targeted at the long-term unemployed, and workers who are easily employable should not be encouraged to participate in public training programmes at the beginning of the period of unemployment.

- It is necessary to avoid the creaming-off effect which results from too-narrow quantitative objectives imposed on local employment agencies in evaluating the implementation of training programmes, because it could prevent any disadvantaged unemployed person from being selected for a training course.

- Employability is an essential outcome of any successful training activity, but efforts must be made to strike a reasonable balance between efficiency and equity, taking account of social inclusion by giving disadvantaged people a chance.

- Programmes of training opportunities for the unemployed are extended to cover the needs of the most marginalised using progressive and intensive training with appropriate teaching methods to overcome serious learning difficulties.

- To redirect resources towards deprived groups, a series of legal, administrative, material, financial, psychological and especially educational barriers must be removed so as really to be able to respond to the needs of the target groups. The beneficiaries of social assistance and other unemployed people not eligible for unemployment benefits are particularly vulnerable because they are often not eligible to participate in traditional training programmes.

BIBLIOGRAPHY

AAKVIK, A. (1999),
"Assessing the Effects of Labour Market Training in Norway", document presented at the Zentrum für Europaïsche Wirtschaftsforschung (ZEW) Conference, "Econometric Evaluation of Active Labour Market Policies in Europe", Mannheim, 24-25 June.

ARNAL, E., W. OK and R. TORRES (2001),
"Knowledge, Work Organisation and Economic Growth", Labour Market and Social Policy Occasional Papers No. 50, OECD.

ASHTON, D. and F. GREEN (1997),
Education, Training and the Global Economy, Cheltenham, Edward Elgar, United Kingdom.

AUTOR, D.H. (2000),
"Why Do Temporary Help Firms Provide Free General Skills Training?", NBER Working Paper No. 7637, Cambridge.

BARRON, J.M., D.A. BLACK and M.A. LOEWENSTEIN (1989),
"Job Matching and On-the-job Training", *Journal of Labour Economics*, Vol. 7.

BASLÉ, M. (2000),
"Comparative Analysis of Quantitative and Qualitative Methods in French Non-experimental Evaluation of Regional and Local Policies: Three Cases of Training Programmes for Unemployed Adults", *Evaluation*, Vol. 6, Part 3, pp. 323-334.

BOYER, R. (2000),
"La formation professionnelle au cours de la vie: Analyse macroéconomique et comparaisons internationales", Conseil d'analyse économique, pp. 89-122.

BRUNELLO, G. (2001),
"On the Complementarity between Education and Training in Europe", Discussion Paper No. 309, Institute for the Study of Labour (IZA), Bonn, June.

CALMFORS, L., A. FORSLUND and M. HEMSTRÖM (2001),
"Does Active Labour Market Policy Work? Lessons from the Swedish Experiences", document presented at the Conference "What are the Effects of Active Labour Market Policy?", October, Office of Labour, Market Policy Evaluation, IFAU, Stockholm.

CHIOUSSE, S. (2001),
"Pédagogie et apprentissage des adultes, An 2001: État des lieux et recommandations", document prepared for the Thematic Review on Adult Learning (*www.oecd.org/edu/adultlearning*).

CONSEIL D'ANALYSE ÉCONOMIQUE (CAE) (2000),
Formation tout au long de la vie, Conseil d'analyse économique auprès du Premier Ministre, La Documentation Française, Paris.

CROUCH, C., D. FINEGOLD and M. SAKO (2001),
Are Skills the Answer? The Political Economy of Skill Creation in Advanced Industrial Countries, Oxford University Press, first published in 1999.

DEARDEN, L., H. REED and J. VAN REENEN (2000),
"Who Gains when Workers Train? Training and Corporate Productivity in a Panel of British Industries", Centre for Economic Policy Research, Discussion Paper Series, No. 2486.

DIDIER, M. (2000),
"Commentaires", Conseil d'analyse économique, pp. 77-83.

EGLOFF, M. (2000),
"Stagnation de la formation continue dans les années 90", *La Vie économique*, No. 4, pp. 56-59, Bern.

EMPLOI-QUÉBEC (2000),
Loi favorisant le développement de la formation de la main d'œuvre (Law promoting the development of vocational training), rapport quinquennal sur la mise en œuvre 1995-2000, Québec.

FINEGOLD, D. and D. SOSKICE (1988),
"The Failure of Training in Britain: Analysis and Prescription", *Oxford Review of Economic Policy*, pp. 21-53.

GAURON, A. (2000),
"Formation tout au long de la vie. Une prospective économique", Conseil d'analyse économique, pp. 11-76.

GERFIN, M. and M. LECHNER (2000),
"Microeconometric Evaluation in the Active Labour Market Policy in Switzerland", mimeo.

GILBERT, L., T. KAMIONKA and G. LACROIX (2001),
"The Impact of Government-Sponsored Training Programs on the Labour Market Transitions of Disadvantaged Men", National Institute of Statistics and Economic Studies (CREST), No. 2001-15.

GRAY, A. (2000),
"The Comparative Effectiveness of Different Delivery Frameworks for Training of the Unemployed", *Journal of Education and Work*, Vol. 13, No. 3.

GREENHALGH, C. (2001),
"Does an Employer Training Levy Work? The Incidence of and Returns to Adult Vocational Training in France and Britain", Skills, Knowledge and Organisational Performance (SKOPE) Research Paper No. 14, Spring 2001.

GRUBB, W.N. and P. RYAN (1999),
"The Roles of Evaluation for Vocational Education and Training, Plain Talk on the Field of Dreams, ILO", Geneva.

GUIRAUDIE, I. and J. TERRENOIRE (2000),
"L'avenir des emplois peu qualifiés : que peut la formation ?", Cahiers du Groupe Bernard Bruhnes, No. 5, June, Paris.

HÄMÄLÄINEN, K. (2001),
"The Effectiveness of Labour Market Training in Different Eras of Unemployment", in E. Koskela and S. Ilmakunnas (eds.), *Labour Market Institutions and Employment*, VATT Publications 32.

HAM, J.C. and R.J. LALONDE (1996),
"The Effect of Sample Selection and Initial Conditions in Duration Models: Evidence from Experimental Data on Training", *Econometrica*, 64(1), pp. 175-205.

HECKMAN, J.J. (1999),
"Doing It Right: Job Training and Education", *The Public Interest*, pp. 86-107.

MÆRKEDAHL, I. (2000),
"Active Labour Market Policies in Denmark", *Labour Market Policies and the Public Employment Service*, OECD, Paris, pp. 291-301.

MARTIN, J. (2000),
"What Works among Active Labour Market Policies? Evidence from OECD Countries' Experiences", *Economic Studies*, No. 30, OECD, Paris.

MARTIN, J.P and D. GRUBB (2001),
"What Works and for Whom: A Review of OECD Countries' Experiences with Active Labour Market Policies", document presented at the conference "What Are the Effects of Active Labour Market Policy?", 8 October, Office of Labour Market Policy Evaluation, IFAU, Stockholm.

MOSER, C. (1999),
"Improving Literacy and Numeracy: A Fresch Start", the report of the working group chaired by Sir Claus Moser, Department for Education and Employment, London.

NICAISE, I. (2000),
"Formation des groupes défavorisés: Dilemme équité-efficacité ?", in V. Vandenberghe (ed.), *La formation professionnelle continue. Transformations, contraintes et enjeux*, Bruylant-Academia, Louvain-la-Neuve.

OECD (1999),
"Training of Adult Workers in OECD Countries: Measurement and Analysis", *Employment Outlook*, Paris.

OECD (2000),
"Thematic Review on Adult Learning: Sweden Background Report", July (*www.oecd.org/els/education/adultlearning*).

OECD (2001a),
Employment Outlook. Paris.

OECD (2001b),
"Education Policy Review – Lifelong Learning in Norway", Background Report, DEELSA/ED(2001)7.

OECD (2001c),
"Investment in Human Capital through Post Compulsory Education and Training", *Economic Outlook*, Paris.

OECD (2002),
"Thematic Review on Adult Learning: Spain Background Report" (*www.oecd.org/els/education/adultlearning*).

OECD and STATISTICS CANADA (2000),
  Literacy in the Information Age, Paris and Ottawa.

OFFICE D'ORIENTATION ET DE FORMATION PROFESSIONNELLE (2000),
  Le paysage de la formation continue à Genève, Département de l'instruction publique, République et Canton de Genève, June.

PAYNE, J. (2000),
  "Evaluating Training Programmes for the Long-term Unemployed. An illustration of the Matched Comparison Group Methodology", Policy Studies Institute Research Discussion Paper No. 1, Oxford.

ROBINSON, P. (2000),
  "Active Labour-Market Policies: A Case of Evidence-Based Policy-Making?", *Oxford Review of Economic Policy*, Vol. 16, No. 1, pp. 13-26.

ROSHOLM, M. (2001),
  "Is Labour Market Training a Curse for the Unemployed? More Evidence from a Social Experiment", Working Paper No. 4, The Danish National Institute for Social Research, p. 31.

SPILLSBURY, D. (2001),
  "Learning and Training at Work 2000", Research Report, April, No. 269, Department for Education and Employment (DfEE), London.

STEVENS, M. (2001),
  "Should Firms Be Required to Pay for Vocational Training?", *The Economic Journal*, 111, July.

WOLTER, S.C. and B.A. WEBER (1999),
  "Skilling the Unskilled – A Question of Incentives?", *International Journal of Manpower*, 20, No. 3/4, pp. 254-269.

Chapter 6

IMPROVING THE DELIVERY OF LEARNING TO ADULTS

There is a degree of overlap between the question of the pedagogy and delivery of adult learning and that of adults' motivation to learn. If adults feel at ease in the learning setting, do not have external constraints (transport, child caring), feel that what they are learning is accessible and worthwhile, and realise that what they already know is valued and taken into consideration, then the incentive to enrol in a course and to follow it through is much greater.

This chapter sets out different dimensions of delivery that are key to the well-being of the learner and the smooth functioning of the adult learning system. All the components of the system, including the enterprise and the teacher, should be included in a comprehensive approach that produces an environment conducive to learning. Pedagogical methods should be focused on the learner, informed about their personality, expectations and motives, whether professional or personal, and availability. The cognitive style of potential learners should also be kept in mind when setting new programmes in motion. Interactivity between the learners and the system (through teachers or counsellors) should be encouraged in order to adjust the learning activities to all the components of the system.

Certain delivery mechanisms have proved efficient in increasing participation. Recognition of prior learning, distance and e-learning, flexible organisation such as modularisation, and certification of current learning are certainly issues to deal with urgently in order to best suit the adults willing to learn or already engaged in learning activities. Another element vital to the health and longevity of the system is routine assessment of its different components (programmes, learners, teachers).[1]

---

1. This chapter owes much to a document expressly prepared for the Thematic Review (Chiousse, 2001 – *www.oecd.org/edu/adultlearning*

6.1. Learning methods specific to adults

Adults can make education decisions if the learning supply is integrated, transparent and coherent.

The need to establish a general framework for adult learning and to provide an integrated learning plan with collateral support services is recognised and taken seriously in all the countries involved in the thematic review. At the same time, the idea of making adults responsible, free to come to their own decisions about education and training, was also widespread in most of the countries visited. There is something to be said for that attitude, though one of the underlying assumptions of this report is precisely that the ball is initially in the court of those offering learning, and it will be easier and fairer to make adults responsible once learning supply is integrated, transparent and coherent. This is true for all adults, whether they believe in the value of learning or not, although these issues are that much more important when the sections of the population targeted are not convinced or are difficult to convince.

Suppliers must recognise the factors that differentiate adult learning from children's education.

Pedagogy is by definition the science that studies the way in which children are taught. In the case of adults, we speak rather of andragogy, even though this distinction is not always pertinent and may not be generally acknowledged.[2] It seems more important simply to recognise that child learning and adult learning are bound to have points in common. In both cases the object is the acquisition of new skills and competencies. An adult nevertheless exhibits special qualities in terms of willingness, maturity, motivation or interest, and it is essential that they are taken into account. The object of this section is to identify the conditions that are favourable to the acquisition of competencies by adults.

An appropriate type of pedagogy

The rationale and mechanisms behind adult learning are multidisciplinary issues

The question why adults learn (Courtney, 1992) or how they learn (OECD and US Department of Education, 1999) has long been a major part of the work conducted in many disciplines concerned with adult learning. Chapters 2 and 3 have already reviewed part of the reasons why adults undertake learning. A large number of disciplines are mobilised in this task, though it must be recognised that psychology and, to a lesser extent, physiology, sociology and ergonomics often provide the theoretical basis; educational science only comes in much later (Chiousse, 2001).

The economic arguments are not enough

Economic advantages are insufficient incentive.

The point of departure here is the frequently established fact that the economic argument does not always win everybody over. Individuals will not be attracted to just any form of learning merely because it is free. Nor is it enough to justify learning in terms of the economic advantages it will confer when successfully concluded. As Chapter 5 has shown, it is only those individuals who are convinced of the value of learning who are receptive to a cost-benefit analysis in the broad sense. The fact is that a system has to be established, in which learner, teacher, course content and learning

---

2. The term "adult pedagogy" is sometimes used and therefore, unless otherwise indicated, the terms will be assumed to be synonymous.

environment are properly matched. It is necessary to take account of a series of factors, which are all the more difficult to determine since they vary from one type of learner to another. This is where the arguments about pedagogy and those about participation in learning activities converge: if people are to be persuaded to participate, the first step must be to take all the necessary measures to ensure that the instruction or training provided are appropriate.

What is learning?

In areas where children's and adults' teaching methods overlap, it is particularly apparent that the "cognitive" has long been given increasing priority over the "transmissive"; in other words, the teacher tends to encourage the learner to think rather than impart knowledge to her/him directly. Moreover, in both cases, it would seem that even the tripartite system "school, classroom and lesson" has suffered a fall from grace in the current conception of the teaching chain, even though it remains the dominant model. The teacher's role remains central, though even this point needs to be qualified: sometimes they are eclipsed by the machine (computer-aided learning – CAL) or they become one among many (experiments with several teachers). These points are taken up in this chapter; however, for the purposes of the exercise, the comparison between children and adults ends here – and the rest of the chapter concentrates on measures to be applied for the benefit of adults.

Adults and children have gone from being knowledge receptors to learning how to learn, and are shifting away from the standard school setting.

Macro-social and statistical studies on inequality and its manifestations (notably in work, social life and access to culture, education and health care) are increasingly giving way to studies that analyse individual behaviour and put forward strategies, including learning strategies. Equally, pedagogy is no longer really concerned with questions of classroom authority, direction or lack thereof. From a sociological point of view, for example, the critical, quantitative outlook is now being superseded by a micro-sociology of educational measures and practices. Pedagogical questions now encompass everything the individual "actually" learns, over and above the formal requirements of the programme.

Pedagogical questions now focus more on what the individual "actually" learns than on formal requirements...

In so far as they concern young adults who left the educational system early, the long-term unemployed, immigrants, people starting work again, or indeed people heading for retirement (Vimont, 2001), the objectives of training institutions have altered (Parmentier and Arfaoui, 2001). Modern training places more emphasis on the complete transformation of individuals and enhancement of their well-being and not simply their ability to regurgitate information. Questions therefore focus more directly on ways of transforming professional and social identities, and the task of preparing people for society turns out to be almost as important as that of teaching: there is a shift from the notion of instruction to that of learning.

... and on the transformation and well-being of individuals rather than their ability to regurgitate information.

Providing for a comprehensive approach to learning

If there is to be a move towards an overall conception of learning, which goes beyond mere teaching, it is now agreed that several references, considerations, and practices must be given priority:
- A redefinition of knowledge.
- A learner-centred approach.

Shifting from "mere teaching" to an overall conception of learning entails a number of considerations.

163

- Work on behaviour.
- An appropriate learning context.
- A differentiated pedagogy.
- A completion of training.

It involves a quest for genuinely new knowledge.

Considering the options for improving the life of the individual, it would appear preferable, in a changing world, to have the means to acquire new knowledge rather than be restricted to the same old knowledge, acquired during the initial stage of education (Berbaum, 1996; Commissariat général du plan, 2001). Knowledge quickly becomes obsolete, which often places its holder in a position of inferiority – or perceived inferiority – whether in professional circles or in the social or family environment.

But the very notion of a comprehensive approach may not be realistic given country differences.

Even if a comprehensive approach to adult learning should probably be sought, differences remain between and within countries, and it is difficult to envisage the possibility of harmonising the various approaches.

Having addressed the first question, namely "what is learning?", the next question is whether "learning" can be learned,[3] and if so how the individual can do so. The problem is once again of knowing how best to apply the most suitable approaches identified.

Learning to learn

Pedagogical theories may have changed over time...

All of the different pedagogical and andragogical theories have introduced new elements or reinforced existing ones. But although the theories have changed over the past century, the pedagogical practices derived from them have changed little and are still very like those put forward earlier by the representatives of the *Éducation nouvelle*. Houssaye (1994), defining what he calls "the pedagogical triangle", gives a fairly accurate summary of the current situation and the different concepts adopted over time and still prevalent today, together with their merits and demerits. If adapted to the andragogical situation, the pedagogical triangle takes the form shown in Figure 6.1.

... but pedagogical practices, reflected in the three relationships of the andragogical triangle, have not.

Learner, teacher and knowledge (in the broad sense as before, and thus comprising both theoretical and practical knowledge) are located at the three corners of the triangle. The sides of the triangle show how these three elements are related. The approach to the pedagogical or andragogical method differs depending on the particular relationship chosen.

The best approach would be to give all three sides equal weight.

Each of the theories considered seems to give priority to one of these relationships, stressing one of the three angles (knowledge, learner and teacher) and the method best suited to it. The most effective andragogical method would certainly be one that could encompass all three elements and all three relationships at the same time, stimulating the learner while ensuring that the right learning context was established.

---

3. The theory and practice of cognitive educability in this connection indicate it can be (Chiousse, 2001).

Figure 6.1. **The pedagogical triangle**

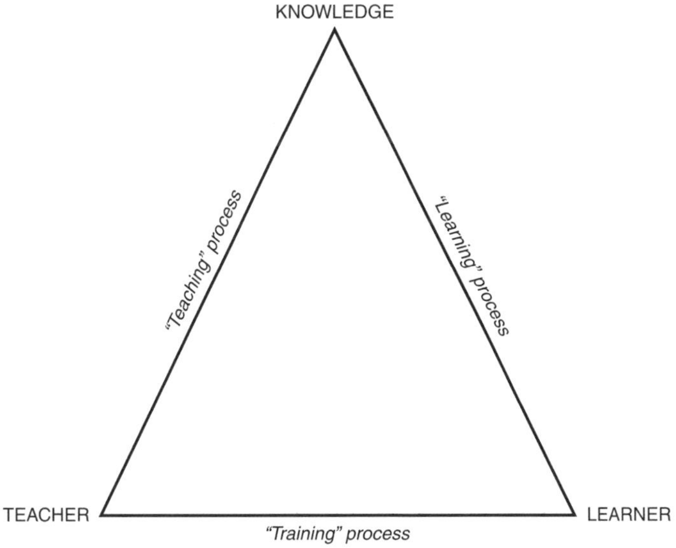

KNOWLEDGE

"Teaching" process

"Learning" process

TEACHER

"Training" process

LEARNER

Source: Chiousse (2001).

Putting the learner at the centre of the learning process

There are a number of "active variables" in the learning process. They have been examined in many studies and each of the different pedagogical and andragogical movements has stressed one or another of them; they are seen as variables "providing leverage", and likely to have a positive impact on learning (interest in learning, quality of personal relationship, importance of social interaction, etc.) as well as negative barrier variables (such as the weight of social determinism).

A number of "active variables" could have a positive impact on learning...

If training is to be effective and reasonably successful, it must at the very least:

• Be motivating, *i.e.* its objectives must be precise.

• Set goals that can actually be attained by individuals, providing a challenge though not an impossible one.

• Require the individual to draw upon knowledge s/he has already acquired – so that s/he does not feel lost – while at the same time enhancing it so that s/he has the sense of being able to reuse his/her knowledge in everyday life.

• Give the individual the opportunity to choose – so that s/he can exercise his/her new-found autonomy.

• Take place over a sufficient period of time, so that the learner's other occupations and obligations can be catered for.

• Lead to a final achievement, *i.e.* meet the goals initially set.

We must then consider what criteria, operators and operations must necessarily be in place if all these options are to be observed and satisfied. It should be borne in mind that such measures are necessary but not sufficient; in addition to factors specific to the learner, it is necessary to take account of variables that are external to the learner and also to appreciate the influence

... but external variables and the overall learning context must also be considered.

of the overall learning context – which complicates still further the search for the appropriate methods and techniques that will guarantee effective learning.

There is no universal method

Decisions must always be taken in a given context.

Bearing all these elements in mind, and given the range of methods that have been described and analysed, it becomes increasingly apparent that there is no ready-made pedagogical/andragogical method applicable in all cases. Pedagogical and andragogical methods fall within the field of "action theory", where it is acknowledged that accurate modelling is never possible. The main point to emerge from the study is that decisions must always be taken in a given context, and regulations are a permanent factor in pedagogical action.

No one policy can be the answer given differences between and even within countries...

In addition, the choices made in the learning field and the resulting systems are first determined by the history, the culture and the geographical, economic, social and political conditions in each country. Although they face similar problems (restructuring, globalisation, unemployment and exclusion *inter alia*), each country employs different training models and techniques, which are diversified still further at local level and from one training provider to another. With different demographic and socioeconomic histories and circumstances in each country, it is by no means easy to say which adult learning model is to be preferred or to identify the specific policy options that determine or should inspire the choice.

... but a number of recommendations remain valid regardless of setting.

It is nevertheless possible to make a certain number of recommendations with a view to ensuring that training is properly conducted and the learning process is successful. These recommendations are often based on examples of good practice or on good initiatives and will have as much to do with variables external to the learning process – though active – as with the elements inherent in the process itself. Precisely because they apply at different levels, some recommendations are valid across the board. Evaluation, for example, is applicable to learners and teachers, and also to the courses and policies in place.

A conducive general environment

Some preliminary conditions

The chief requirements are a favourable environment...

Any learning initiative requires a favourable environment, one that is conducive in its socio-historical, economic, political and cultural aspects. This preliminary recommendation is certainly the most obvious one, implicit in all cases and independent of time or place. It concerns society as a whole, the state, and the nation in which a policy of promoting adult learning is contemplated. The nine countries involved in the thematic review are remarkably stable ones, in which the question does not really arise. Nevertheless, for the purpose of sustaining the argument, it might be noted that during the visit to Portugal, experts observed that the Portuguese revolution (May 1974) in a sense provided a reference point for all actors.

All laws, actions and programmes adopted there are considered – not surprisingly – in relation to that event.

Other indispensable preconditions are that structures and infrastructures are adequate and that decision makers are convinced of the benefits of adult learning, policy issues reviewed in Chapter 4. They call for development of a national policy geared to adult learning, the provision of public funding to encourage the introduction of learning schemes, and co-ordination and co-operation among the different partners involved.

... adequate infrastructures and convinced decision makers.

Countries have developed different financial arrangements for learning, also reviewed in Chapter 4. In Denmark for example, a system of funding for training people in the labour market (*Arbejdsmarkedets Uddannelsesfinansiering* – AUF) has been introduced, in addition to the existing system for the reimbursement of employers (AER) (CEDEFOP, 2000). The Scandinavian countries provide special benefit for the unemployed – followed by supplementary training grants – to enable individuals to take a new direction during their active lives.

Where there is a general national policy to promote adult learning, it is admittedly necessary for actors and decision makers at other levels of political and public life to be able to adapt the general policy of the country to more local requirements, taking account of the labour market, the companies established, the population and the levels of affluence. This is the principle underlying the operation of the new Learning and Skills Council (LSC) in England.

Adult learning policy must be adapted to local requirements.

Employers aware of the benefits of learning

On a still more localised scale, enterprises must be involved in this adult learning policy and review a certain number of points, such as the organisation of working time and the number of working hours set aside for the training of its staff. Generally speaking, there are many advantages to viewing staff training as a benefit, one that extends beyond the strict limits of the company itself and its financial capital. Training of staff should be seen as an investment with numerous repercussions: financial, cultural, social, individual and collective.

Enterprises should be involved...

This may involve proposals for training made to entrepreneurs or decision makers that explain – perhaps not for the first time – the merits of learning and what might be expected of it, both in general and in the particular case of the company or its sector of activity. It has to be said that one of the problems most often encountered in the world of work is that a departmental head, or even a managing director if the company is a small one, is often reluctant to send subordinates or employees on training courses for fear of their coming back better trained than earlier and possibly supplanting her/him. This raises the thorny question of who makes the decision to send a worker on a training course: the individual employee (and this eventuality can be catered for by, *e.g.*, training leave), the senior management or the human resources department, or someone at an intermediate level. Here again there are no optimal solutions, but it is important to guarantee that the decision-making process is fair.

... although the question of who decides to send the employee on a training course is tricky.

A targeted approach

Training also needs to accommodate not just the most favoured individuals, or those most disadvantaged…

A targeted approach, aimed at calling upon the main partner (the company for example) to give the "weakest"[4] individuals the best possible incentive to embark upon a course, is certainly most suitable for delivery purposes. A certain number of appropriate target groups are generally recognised: those with poor qualifications, immigrants, handicapped people. To this end it is necessary to offer training that is suited to their level and allows them to develop.

… but all those who seek it.

Even if training is offered and initiated by the company, it should not be restricted to those who are most favoured (hi-tech or management programmes, for example) or most disadvantaged (literacy programmes). The company must be able to offer training to all those who ask for it, whether such training is given internally or by a specific outside organisation, and whatever the current or required level of attainment of the staff.

Indeed it is the group at the middle of the achievement ladder which is most often left out.

Attention should be drawn to an impression that formed over many of the nine visits organised in the countries participating in the thematic review. It would seem that those most in need of training – according to the definition of target groups for public action, at any rate – are very often provided for. The corresponding action will include, for example, general literacy programmes.[5] At the other end of the achievement ladder, we find that many companies also take great care of their most qualified workers. But there is a group that falls between the two that rarely receives any attention, either from the company or from the authorities. This group is in employment; it is fully integrated into the company and is all too often paid something in the region of the statutory minimum wage. It is sometimes referred to as the "working poor". The term is not necessarily appropriate in all cases, though it must be admitted that the workers in question represent a fringe group in society that could well benefit from more systematic learning. It must also be said, however, that they are not always very willing to learn (Chapter 5).

Portugal's EFA programme is a response to this problem.

The Portuguese EFA programme (*Ensigno y Formação por Adultos* – a teaching/training programme for adults with a low level of school attainment), jointly established by the ministry of education and the ministry of employment and solidarity, is another response to this particular need. It offers education and training to "citizens aged 18 or more, who are without qualifications or without sufficient qualifications to make any headway in the labour market and who have not completed the four, six or nine years of basic education. Priority is given to those either in work or unemployed who are registered with the IEFP (Institute for Employment and Professional Training), those earning the statutory minimum wage, those undergoing vocational retraining and SME employees" (Cedefop, 2001). At the end of the training programme, the individual receives a certificate of adult basic education (FB) and/or professional training (FP). The latter will have entailed practical training in a real work situation.

---

4. For example (in the context of the company), those poorly qualified who are likely to be disadvantaged (risk of unemployment and/or lack of career prospects).
5. Or even action in favour of the unemployed.

Individuals motivated to learn

Potential learners must be enthusiastic and won over to the cause if learning conditions are to be optimal. They must have a sense of being able to acquire something useful (in terms of knowledge, know-how, knowing how to behave) and not see learning as a constraint that offers no advantage (personal, professional and/or financial). The time spent on the course must not be regarded as time that might have been better spent on other activities but as something that will bring a particular bonus in their personal and social life (including working relationships and relationships with colleagues as well as professional status). Motivating individuals to learn is one of the key issues to address in the near future. The experience of United Kingdom suggests that focusing on incentives, improving the quality of provision and promotional activity, and encouraging individuals to take greater responsibility for their own learning can be effective strategies that serve to raise investment in human resources by individuals and employers.

Co-ordinating research and action, researchers and practitioners

If the goals and objectives set are to be attained, it is increasingly important that organisers, course planners and teachers have access to research on questions of adult learning and are able to make use of it in practice. As those who plan learning processes become increasingly concerned with understanding the "human factor", they are required from the outset to draw upon psychological research to gain an adequate picture of the individuals for whom courses are intended. In the context of company training provision, more advanced analyses of working methods and the strategies and goals of the players might involve contributions from the fields of ergonomics and the sociology of organisations, for example. If the practical realities in the field are taken into account and more scientific approaches are adopted, it should be possible to appreciate all the variables relevant to the planning of training programmes and identify those most closely suited to the needs and expectations of each individual.

During the review visits, a frequently heard complaint was the apparent lack of research. In most cases however, the sense of frustration among practitioners clearly owes more to a lack of communication between researchers and practitioners than to an actual lack of top-level research. Similarly, researchers must be in a position to take account of tried and tested practice and pilot projects conducted with a view to stimulating thinking so that educational, pedagogical and andragogical ideas might be further refined. There is thus a growing sense that researchers should direct their work more towards the problems teachers and trainers have actually experienced and then give some feedback in order to create a virtuous circle. The latter, for their part, should acquire the habit of studying research into pedagogy to find answers to their questions (Viau, 1996).

In the United Kingdom, for example, all new Department for Education and Skills (DfES) research reports are now available in full and free of charge on the Internet. DfES has also supported the development of the Current Educational Research (CERUK) that produces a database available free via the Internet. The National Educational Research Forum website also provides a number of links for practitioners aiming to find out about research.

Motivation on the part of potential learners is key and must be earned.

Organisers, course planners and teachers need to keep abreast with research on adult learning...

... although the communication between researchers and practitioners is evidently less than ideal.

In the United Kingdom, research reports are now available free of charge on the Internet.

169

Routine assessment

Assessment is imperative.

Assessment is imperative, the *sine qua non* of a genuine national drive to promote learning. It is essential that bodies and instruments are devised for the purpose of evaluating the arrangements introduced, so that policies implemented may be changed or adjusted if necessary. It should be possible to conduct assessments at the institutional and national levels and also through groups of independent organisations.

It must be performed at all levels and at different times.

Assessment of what has been, is being or will be done is certainly crucial in the construction of a coherent adult learning system. Routine assessment must be encouraged at all levels of the training and learning processes and rank among the top transversal priorities. It must be possible to assess learning at different times – before it is finished, for example, especially if a course is long or if other courses of the same kind are starting up and stand to benefit from lessons from the one in progress. It is also important to consider whether the objectives of the learner and the company (in the case of professional training, for example) have been attained and also, in a much broader sense, whether the goals set are in line with local or national policy (to encourage or develop a particular sector or system, etc.). Assessment must be present all along the training and learning process, and concern the learner, the employer, the training course and the teacher.

Company needs should be established beforehand…

Projects, objectives and needs must be clearly defined. In the case of employment-related training, a precise study of company needs should be conducted beforehand, either internally by heads of departments and divisions, or by an external body in the form of an audit. The study should establish the nature of the training that would help the company meet those needs.

… as well as the needs of potential learners.

Naturally, early attention must also be paid to learners as well. Following internal consultation (with the director of human resources, heads of departments and other staff members concerned in the case of a company, for instance), the individuals expected to undergo training should be designated on the basis of several criteria: their desire to learn, their motivation, their real need for training, their expectations, their performance, and the relevance of the training to the work they do, if any. All these criteria must also be taken into account in determining the nature of the training.

Input from different actors and representatives will give organisers a clearer picture of those needs.

A company wishing to organise training for its staff – or a category of its staff – must do so in consultation with the different actors and representatives, because it is necessary to learn as much as possible about the individual. That way, the training proposed will correspond most closely to their expectations, and they will be less likely to drop out of the course before it is finished – always a costly eventuality.

The learner's own evaluation is essential, as is a non-judgemental assessment of the learner's results.

The individual must also be able to check whether their training is in line with their expectations, notably in terms of content, context, relationships formed, and monitoring. They must also have the benefit of an assessment of his/her results. Rather than being a (cardinal) measure used to judge them, this assessment should be educational and should help them make progress, or even improve their capacity for self-assessment.

Encouraging the spread of good practices

People must be encouraged to enter into broad partnerships – and observatories must be set up at all possible levels – for the purposes of detecting good practice in learning delivery, providing information, promoting the sharing of experiences and aiding co-ordination and assessment of the operations undertaken, as well as supporting the development of such operations. Problems in adult learning can then be better identified and the best advice can be given in the light of national cultures and circumstances.

Good practices should be detected, and shared.

To this end, the best way of introducing mechanisms to promote the widespread adoption of good practice would no doubt have to be determined for each country and culture. It should be noted that some major success stories have been dependent on one-off factors: sudden large-scale recruitment by a company or sector; a rarity of much sought-after qualifications, with the consequent guarantee of employment; strong political commitment on the part of a local official; the existence of a charismatic national figure, etc. At the same time it must be recognised that there have been fruitful experiments about which nothing is known. At the very least, an e-mail address could be provided ("good.idea@educ-labour.org"), to which individuals could send messages describing a particular experience and the reasons for its success or failure. Of course it would be possible to go further and provide an address to which anybody could send a question and be certain to receive a response, the same week for example. There are already numerous Internet sites devoted to adult learning; there is no question of adding more to them; rather, an interactive link could be established between all those working along the same lines who are unaware of each other's existence. It is also worth mentioning the recent effort at the European level with the European Commission Communication on "Making a European Area of Lifelong Learning a Reality".

It is not always possible to establish, let alone duplicate, the factors behind good practice.

Enterprise-based training

The company is no doubt the most relevant of all training providers. It is also clear that training within the company has a particular quality, being frequently geared toward professional goals or higher productivity on the part of the individual and the organisation as a whole. In any event it is an area of fundamental importance, which has been amply described in Section 5.2 of Chapter 5 and which also merits a section of its own in this chapter.

Promoting learning and training throughout professional life

Just as the state should have a strong political message and send out clear signals to citizens about the value of learning, the company should establish a system that adequately promotes training so that the individual willingly agrees to it – and on a regular basis – inside or outside the company. Company policy on this matter should be clear, consistent over time and unequivocal as to the value of lifelong learning. The more the staff knows about training opportunities and the more this knowledge is promoted, the greater will be the incentive to take advantage of them.

Companies should be the top training promoters.

Organising work in a way that facilitates the provision of training

The scheduling and conditions of training should not place constraints on the worker's private life.

Setting aside a specific number of working hours for training and establishing the particular conditions in which such training would be most effective would facilitate provision. The corresponding measures are generally taken under collective agreements negotiated between the different social partners. The idea is that employers have to create an environment that allows room for learning, so that the learner does not have to put up with too many constraints on private life and activities outside the workplace.

Providing for regular updating of knowledge

Training should not be seen as a one-off event.

A training session should not be regarded as an end in itself. The company must be able to ensure that the individual is not limited in their pursuit of training and is not obliged, for example, to wait a certain number of years before being able to proceed with further training. It is essential that a person who has embarked upon a training process is able to pursue and build upon it (if such a step is necessary, or felt to be necessary).

For the purpose of setting limits and safeguarding against unreasonable behaviour, it is always possible to devise systems in which each individual is allocated a certain number of working hours for training. The number of hours would be renewed regularly, in much the same way as paid holiday.

Enabling individuals to make progress in their job through training

Training related to work performed could advance the worker's situation in some way.

If the individual is to be aware of the value of training, they must be able to derive some advantage from it if they so wish. If the training followed is related to the work normally performed, it must enable the learner to make progress in their job. It should result in the company's giving them greater autonomy, perhaps more responsibility, a change in status, a promotion or a pay rise. The experience of training should ultimately increase their sense of self-worth.

Promoting personal development

Training should also advance the worker in personal or social ways.

The company should not see the purpose of training as being limited to improving the professional performance of its staff. Training should also enable the individual to acquire knowledge and skills, including behavioural skills, for purposes that are purely personal, in order to promote their general well-being; moreover, there may be social and professional repercussions, and indirect benefits for the operation of the company.

Establishing partnerships

Partnerships should be formed to further effective learning.

Partnerships should be established both within the company and with other companies, and also with bodies that are not companies (universities, schools, associations). They should be formed at local, regional, interregional, national and even international levels. They should be found at all professional levels, including the level at which attainments are validated. In the United Kingdom, a network of 101 Learning Partnerships has been in place since early 1999. These are non-statutory, voluntary groupings of local learning providers ranging from the voluntary sector to higher education institutions and others such as local government, Connections/Careers Service, trade unions, employers and faith groups. They were originally responsible for developing local targets linked to National Learning Targets and for co-ordinating local action in pursuit of them. Their objectives now involve working closely with local Learning and Skills Councils in order to:

- Deliver greater provider collaboration so that learning becomes more coherent, relevant and accessible to local people and employers.

- Help ensure that effective mechanisms are in place to provide feedback on the quality and accessibility of learning from both young people and adults.

- Encourage providers to work collectively with users to identify local learner, community and employer needs and to respond to them through their own actions and by influencing local LSCs.

The promotion of partnerships is also one of the strategic objectives identified by the Council of European Ministers of Education and Youth at their meeting in Brussels in February 2001. Their report emphasises the importance of "improving the teaching of foreign languages, promoting mobility and exchanges, and enhancing European co-operation on systems of accreditation and the recognition of qualifications and diplomas, in order to strengthen ties with the world of work and research" (CEDEFOP, 2001). It is necessary, for example, that knowledge and skills acquired in a company be recognised elsewhere.

These can range from intra-company to international.

The learner and the learning methods

Encouraging adults to follow courses and acquainting them with the idea of lifelong learning

Chapter 5 shows that the system of incentives that needs to be introduced is not simple. It involves other elements, such as extensive and exhaustive communication on the subject of the training options. It is also necessary to acquaint the learner with the idea of lifelong learning as soon as they embark upon education and initial training. This process often consists of proposing training with attractive content; encouraging the individual to regard learning as an opportunity to improve their personal, social and/or professional situation; and lastly, making them aware that any competency can be improved. This involves explaining that the opportunity to improve knowledge and skills is open to everybody at all times. The "adult learners' week" organised in many parts of the world seems to have made a positive contribution to the task of encouraging learning among the population.

Communication is all-important in winning workers over to the idea of lifelong learning.

Instilling or restoring confidence, whatever the initial level or the challenge

If future learners are to be made to feel confident or if their confidence is to be restored, it is vital that the training proposed takes account of their diversity and of their different experience. It is necessary to think in terms of a potential level of development which, given various forms of mediation, will make access to a higher level of development that much easier. The learning provider must therefore be in a position to propose the type of learning that will enable the individual to progress, and have a sufficient range of training programmes on offer to allow each individual to find a suitable course and to

Workers' existing and proposed levels of development should not be over- or underestimated.

173

select with perfect assurance the one that will enable them to flourish and to increase their knowledge and skills. The learner must be given maximum support and should not be under- or overestimated. Establishing a pedagogical relationship that respects the learner is of primary importance.

Taking account of the availability of learners, their motivation and expectations

Not all adults follow courses to gain knowledge. The cognitive dimension nearly always has priority, though not exclusively. Equally, not all adults follow courses in order to improve their professional situation. There are a great many reasons and arguments for embracing or rejecting a learning experience, and it is important to be able to define them in order to be able to deal with them properly. The individual should therefore have to the extent possible the benefit of a preliminary assessment of competencies or proper advice from specialised bodies.

Training should also prepare older workers for their coming retirement.

People preparing for or going into retirement feel the need to follow courses that help them to readapt to the new conditions of their lives and to examine their new role in society. For course planners who deal with this older population, adult learning must not be seen merely as a pleasant way of filling time but rather as something people take up at a special moment in life, intended to fill gaps (making up for lost time) and make them better prepared for the new phase they are entering.

It should in all cases take full account of what the learner wants and is able to achieve...

Learning, even if it is required by the company, should not be seen as a constraint by the individual. The training offered must therefore take full account of what the learner wants and is able to achieve. With respect to the motivation and personality of the individual, several variables must be considered, along with the possibility of their being modified in the course of time and the individual's social, psychological, financial and/or personal development.

"The motivation or the internal psychological motives behind learning evolve through the individual's unique life process in interaction with societal conditions and the individual's own interpretation of the process and of the interaction. [...] In the period of adulthood up to the life turn, learning is usually goal-directed on the basis of the individual's own aims and strategies, which are typically based on a weighted interaction between desire and necessity. Adults often have trouble stepping out of the accustomed pupil role, while at the same time they also expect to manage their own learning" (Illeris, 2000).

Taking account of the individual's personality and cognitive style

... as well as his/her personality...

The training provided and the method chosen must also take account of the personality of the individual. A shy, self-conscious person will be not at ease in a very competitive learning situation, for example. It is therefore necessary to begin – as we have seen – with training that will first restore their self-confidence and help them adopt a positive attitude towards the learning process.

... for s/he too brings input to the pedagogical process.

The teacher must take account of the motivation, the cognitive learning styles and the aptitudes of the learner when choosing the appropriate pedagogical method, bearing in mind that the individuals being taught will have a more or less elaborate contribution to make in any developed pedagogical process, and that they will find it more or less easy to contribute depending on their confidence in their abilities and on their personality.

In project-based pedagogy used for getting the individual back to work, for example, the learning activity is intense and a fairly high level of motivation and ambition is required if it is to be successfully concluded. Virtually all of the work on the project is done by the learner: researching it, developing it, testing it, acquiring the skills and competencies it calls for, making it relevant and modifying it. The activity of the teacher consists in raising the expectations of the learners, and encouraging them to draw upon the time and space allotted for training purposes.

The objectives of training should be clearly defined

It is necessary from the outset to ensure that training has a precise objective and that there is a goal to be reached. Training must therefore provide for and lead to a final result, on the basis of which it will be possible to assess what has been achieved. In the same way, the objectives of training must be explicit and shown to be in line with the expectations of the learners. Training must take account of the social realities of the learners and the environment, so that learners are able to satisfy the specific desires they had when embarking upon the course.

Training must lead to a result that is clearly established beforehand...

There is one type of training that might be put forward as a notable exception to this rule. As we have seen, and it must be re-emphasised here, the object of some types of training may simply be to bring the most sceptical individuals round to the idea of returning to learning. In that case the objective of learning may be less clearly defined and it may not be possible to describe the final purpose since it may represent a first step towards other forms of training whose objectives are better defined. In a sense the general rule still applies, since the final objective of the learning process has been tacitly defined. But it can only be spelled out at a subsequent stage if the individual is to retain the reassuring impression that the learning process presents no real challenge and is little more than a game (Section 5.1 of Chapter 5).

... except in cases where the goal is simply to encourage sceptics to return to learning.

This idea of developing mental suppleness is particularly relevant to individuals who gave up formal education a long time ago and/or gave it up with a sense of having failed. They must be encouraged to rediscover a spontaneous approach to learning, and should begin by following a method that develops their confidence and increases their desire to make progress.

Producing clear, tangible, recognised results

If a learning process is to meet its objectives, the individuals must have the sense of having made favourable progress and must be able to show that they have. At the end of the training process there should therefore be some special recognition of their achievement, whether in the form of a promotion, a diploma (a certificate), or at least a public acknowledgement. The recognition thus gained should be broadly valid, transferable, applicable and negotiable in other contexts. Since one of the objects of learning is to gain a qualification, the qualifications must be recognised outside the company if, for example, the corresponding training was given on the job. A specific

Training must lead to tangible results that are recognised outside the company.

nomenclature is therefore needed to establish levels of achievement recognised at national or even international level.

Learning to learn, emancipating

Its first objective must be to give the individual greater autonomy in achieving the goals defined.

Whatever the training followed, its first objective must be to give the individual greater autonomy in achieving the goals defined. Thus, a form of training that equips the individual for subsequent autonomous learning is to be preferred to one that simply imparts knowledge in the traditional way.

Adapting the methods to the participants: open, flexible and individualised

Several teaching methods should be employed in a flexible programme.

As far as possible, teaching should be planned in such a way that several teaching methods are used during the same course and the programme can be modified at any time according to the needs of the participants and their progress. It is therefore necessary to provide for diversified input and (particularly if the course is long or made up of several sessions) a process whereby lectures or work in large groups alternate with individual tutorials or work in small groups, for example.

Learners must feel comfortable with the process.

The methods chosen must make the learner, or the group, feel comfortable with the learning process: they must not be made to feel unsettled by a method that is too abrupt (lectures for an individual with a low level of academic attainment, or a situation that is too personal for one who is shy and lacking in initiative), or be left behind and excluded by a process that is too rapid.

The pedagogical method chosen must fit the learner.

Among the most important considerations in choosing a pedagogical method is its ability to be adapted to the participants. It must be compatible with the participants' level, their personality, their motivation, their aptitudes and their expectations. This simple list is in itself an indication of the complexity of the problem. The fullest possible consideration must be given to the advantages and disadvantages of each method; among those most often cited in the nine visited countries are:

- *The ICTs and learning via the Internet*, which are taken more and more seriously. The Internet certainly offers an interesting way of learning but it is not as democratic or effective as some would maintain, and learning is only possible under certain conditions: the individual must already be accustomed to using a computer and must already have learned how to learn. There is also some doubt as to whether the knowledge is adequately assimilated. The nature of the network and the speed with which information can be called up does not allow the time needed for the sound acquisition of new knowledge. On the other hand, a computer is infinitely patient and pinpoints all errors without making fun of the learner.

- *Distance learning*, which makes learning available at a time, place and pace that may suit the learners better in relation to their needs. The lack of "real" contact with the teacher and the autonomy of the individual in determining the pace of learning lead more often than one would wish to a certain lassitude on the part of the learner. Distance learning is abandoned more often than any other type of learning. Furthering the debate on the relative merits of traditional distance learning (paper and mail through the post) and the electronic kind (hypertext, word processing, and email), it should be pointed out that the Open University in the United Kingdom has expressly chosen not to use – or more precisely, not to require access to – a computer, since it is felt that this would tend to exclude the most socially disadvantaged or those most out of step with modern technological trends. It seems likely that this debate will disappear with the total democratisation of modern means of communication. It also seems likely that this will not happen tomorrow and that the question merits more detailed consideration.

- *On-the-job training*, which presents distinct advantages. Learning takes place *in situ* and the learner is able to acquire the precise skills needed. Investors in People, in England, does recognise on-the-job training to meet the skill needs of the business. However, this type of learning is often completely informal and is rarely recognised by the company as a means of obtaining the kind of additional knowledge and skills that might merit a special award in the form of promotion, a pay rise or greater responsibility. Moreover some forms of training on the job are simply intended to enhance performance (by developing working reflexes that lower the time needed to perform a task) and take no account of the individual or the personal advantage the individual might derive from such training. If the time spent on such training is regarded as genuine training time, the situation is particular worrying, since the individual might then be deprived of another form of training.

- *Cognitive methods*. The individuals must have the motivation to learn and the training must enable them to reach a precise goal and not be too long about it. If cognitive learning methods enable the individual to learn how to learn, it is better to offer them to people who have chosen to devote a relatively long time to their training. These methods generate very little in the way of practical skills and may produce a feeling of lassitude in the learner, who will therefore not feel inclined to persist.

- *Methods employing project-based pedagogy*, which should be used more discriminately with individuals who have chosen their training as part of a programme to get themselves back to work. The introspection and preliminary analysis of their personal career might discourage, disorientate and destabilise people who are already demoralised by a series of failures and do not have sufficient energy to embark upon a new path.

- *Methods involving group interaction* as the goal of training (role play, etc.) must be aimed more at individuals with a positive outlook on training (not those who view it with anxiety following previous failure – at school, for example).

Teacher training

Teacher training for adult education is undoubtedly the element in the overall structure that is least adequately provided for. It would seem that the specific character of adult education is denied or given insufficient prominence in the planning of teacher training. In any event, special training

Teacher training has been the most neglected aspect of adult learning...

for those who are to be responsible for teaching adults is rarely to be found. Adult education is not even identified as such in most cases. In Switzerland, the FSEA (*Fédération suisse pour l'éducation des adultes* – Swiss Adult Education Federation) has had to take responsibility for awarding adult education diplomas, and has adopted a very interesting approach (Box 6.1). In England, from September 2001, there is an objective that all new further education teachers will work towards a teaching qualification that includes literacy and numeracy among its key elements, to raise their awareness and allow them in turn to help people in their courses, who have literacy and numeracy skill needs. In Spain, many adult teachers hold special teacher certificates. These are available through the training networks established by the educational

---

Box 6.1. **Adult teacher training pathways in Switzerland**

There are four levels of teacher training for adult education: two FSEA diploma courses (Level 1 and Level 2); a continuing education university course for adult education, including a certification course; and a degree course in adult education (LMEA). All are based on a common strategy, namely to supplement teacher training with skills related to pedagogy or educational management. Teachers recruited as specialists in a particular field, for instance, may supplement their expertise with other skills more closely related to education.

FSEA diploma courses cover:

- The skills required to structure, analyse and evaluate teaching.
- Group management skills.
- Different forms of learning.
- Educational project-building skills.

The Level 1 certificate comprises a 130-hour course, combined with one year's practical work experience in adult education and a personal coursework project on teaching practice. Teachers can also enrol on another longer course for Level 2. Since 1995, 6 000 people have passed Level 1 and 1 200 Level 2. Furthermore, 44 teacher training institutions have obtained certification.

Since 1998, a working group has been engaged in an effort to modularise the Level 2 certificate as part of a general move to modularise vocational training. The ultimate goal is to provide an adult education training certificate corresponding to 1 200 hours' training. On the initiative of the FSEA, efforts are under way to set up a system that recognises and validates prior learning, leading to the award of a Level 1 certificate.

The University of Geneva runs a continuing education diploma course for teachers working in adult education, aimed at:

- Upgrading the skills specific to teachers in adult education: teaching, organisation/management, and context analysis.
- Building the capacity to analyse current practice in continuing education and training, in particular self-evaluation.
- Increasing the capacity for project research and development.
- Strengthening the unity, versatility and code of ethics of the education profession.

The University of Geneva also offers a degree course in adult education (LMEA), covering the three groups of skills required for work in adult education: teaching (teacher/student relations), organisation (educational engineering) and management, *i.e.* policies and policy implementation.

Source: OECD (2001b).

administrations themselves, or through the universities in courses of varying scope and duration. The one with the greatest scope is the postgraduate course in adult education, developed by the National Distance Education University (*Universidad Nacional de Educación a Distancia* – UNED) more than a decade ago.

The problem is clearly rooted in a failure to appreciate the issues related to adult education. However, the fact that this question does not rank sufficiently highly in the list of public priorities is not the only reason for the failure. The problem is further complicated by the extra costs that would have to be met by the training system. It would be necessary to establish new training cycles specifically catering to those who wish to go into adult education and to provide for corresponding qualifications. At present, such cycles would involve a very small number of candidates compared with the great many going into children's education.

... partly due to costs.

In addition to those already discussed relating to the respect of the learner and training adapted to the learner needs, certain principles or guidelines may be put forward if an effective system of teacher training for adult learning is to be established.

Certain guidelines could help remedy the situation.

The teachers must be in touch with the realities of the labour market and be able to give the learner effective counselling. They should also be able to suggest modifications to the training programme on the basis of the learner's expectations and demands. This too presupposes a modular, adaptable pedagogical method.

Teachers must themselves be in touch with the realities of the labour market.

A job that is clearly defined and properly recognised; regular review of practice and knowledge

Teachers need to be sufficiently well trained to be able to cope with the range of adult learning processes and the attendant difficulties, and they must be able to choose the andragogical method(s) most suited to particular learners. To this end it will no doubt be necessary to consider, not only teacher training *per se*, but also the regular review of teacher training and its recognition, at least at national level and preferably at international level.

They need to be aware of and able to choose from among the range of teaching methods.

At the present time, teacher training is very diversified, ranging from the absolute minimum necessary to highly specialised courses. Some adult education teacher training programmes attach particular importance to the delivery of teaching, others place more emphasis on the theoretical aspects of methods that have to be employed. For example, in Canada there is a form of training that combines theory and practice, in Switzerland there is a very practical training process and a corresponding federal teaching certificate.

If society is changing, so are jobs. Given the growing complexity of social systems and social intercourse, the interest in knowledge, and the developments in criteria for assessing competencies, it is also necessary to reassess teacher's jobs and skills, provide a clear definition of (new) responsibilities, and redefine priorities in terms of practice, approaches and the skills needed to fully develop their adult learning experiences.

Their skills and responsibilities also should be subject to ongoing reassessment.

The nature and content of teacher training courses clearly illustrate the trends of the past few years; much greater emphasis is placed on group learning, but there is also individual support based on the identification and development of individuals' projects, wishes, needs and expectations. The prospects are very promising.

The RAAPFA in Canada provides a concise description of what adult teaching should be.

Canada's RAAPFA (*Regroupement des associations d'andragogues et de professionnels de la formation des adultes*) no doubt gives the best formal account of the tasks to be assumed and the corresponding competencies required. It also gives a description and a definition of andragogy and of what the andragogue's work entails:

"The andragogue is a person who specialises in continuing education and whose role is to foster the development of skills in adults. His/her activity takes the form of providing support in learning, and such is the very basis of andragogy. Continuing education confers an additional asset which may serve both personal and organisational ends. The andragogue works in the workplace, in teaching establishments, in public and semi-public institutions and in the community. His/her functions include planning courses, analysing needs, drawing up training programmes, producing teaching materials, teaching, carrying out assessments, and managing or monitoring training. S/he might also work as a counsellor and take part in research and development in the field of andragogy." (*www.raapfa.qc.ca*)

Moreover, the Council of European Ministers for Education and Youth, meeting in Brussels in February 2001, agreed that "improving the education and training of teachers and trainers, developing and defining the competencies needed in the cognitive society" (CEDEFOP, 2001) was a priority strategic objective.

6.2. Delivery mechanisms to suit the learner

Meeting the learner's needs often means no more than accommodating scheduling and practical needs.

It may not come as much of a surprise, but in the countries participating in the thematic review, placing the learner at the centre of the learning process often meant no more than offering them training outside their normal working hours (weekday evenings and Saturday morning) and taking care of their most immediate practical needs: looking after children, providing a meal on the premises, providing transport, etc.

This is fairly positive in a sense, for it means that most training providers and players are conscious of the practical problems associated with organising training. It also means, on the more negative front, that the question of specific pedagogy has not yet been fully assimilated into their way of thinking – hence the importance of the findings in the previous section.

It also has to be said that there are still providers of training who remain impervious to the idea of offering adults services that go beyond what is strictly educational. This section includes good practices in this area.

Beyond setting, access and services, there is the question of context.

Most thought is given to scheduling, the location of training centres (in the suburbs, near to stations, etc.), access, and the nature of the buildings and classrooms, just to mention the most basic aspects. Some thought is also given to the services that might be offered to learners, as mentioned above. This section re-examines the context into which learning can and must be fitted, which is directly linked with the local level.

The general organisational framework

More in touch with social realities and demands

Organisers and planners must be adequately informed about social realities, innovative, and conscious of the needs and expectations of all parties (public authorities, companies, individuals). The training offered must be taken up by as many people as possible if the expected gain is to be achieved. It is therefore recommended that the environment and socioeconomic context be taken into account and that maximum benefit is obtained from the local neighbourhood. This should lead increasingly to the abandonment of "ready-made" courses in favour of more individualised training, taking full account of the circumstances and routine of the client company or the individuals that request it.

Organisers must be in touch with social realities and the needs of all parties involved.

Creating conditions favourable to learning

This idea is fairly general and applies in all areas. Every effort must be made to give the learner a setting that best suits them and the type of training they want. This point is relevant to everything associated with the course, whatever form the learning process may take, whether in the workplace, in another centre or at home. It also follows that any constraints on the learning process (in terms of free time) must be reduced to a minimum so that the individual is highly motivated to take up a course and to follow it through to the end.

Everything associated with the training must suit the learner and minimise their constraints.

By way of example, the Canadian study conducted by Dessaint and Boisvert (1991) considers what it is that motivates people aged 55 and over to follow a distance learning course rather than another kind. It would seem that physical restrictions, transport problems and financial considerations make distance learning a more practical proposition for this age-bracket; moreover, it does not tie them to a particular timetable or pace.

For instance, distance learning may best suit the older learners.

Organising training in such a way as to minimise obstacles that might cause the learner to give up

All the elements required to create a setting that encourages quality learning must be brought together. Whether learning takes place at work (in the case of courses held on company premises or organised by the company) or at a specific centre, it is necessary to consider all the constraints associated with the period the individual devotes to it. It is necessary to consider the cost, both in financial terms and in terms of the time spent (impact on time devoted to work, leisure, the family). This has as much to do with getting to the training centre (if the course is not given in the workplace) as with the timing and duration of the training sessions.

If impediments are to be limited, it is also necessary to consider the way in which the course itself is structured and the relations between the members of the group. Attention should be given to the size of the place where the training is to take place, the atmosphere, and any features that may make it a more pleasant place to work (heating, lighting). Lastly, it is necessary to find ways of dissuading people from abandoning the course before it is finished – by providing financial compensation, for example, or a genuine gain that makes the learner appreciate the benefits of completing the course.

Positive features will help dissuade workers from abandoning the course before it is finished.

Courses tailored to the level of the learners

Participants entering the course should have roughly the same level of attainment.

In addition to the discussion about the homogeneity of the group (to create or avoid some form of competition between learners) it is particularly important to consider the content of the courses drawn up by the planners in relation to the level of attainment of the participants. It seems more advisable here to plan a training programme for individuals with a comparable level. If weaker individuals find a training programme too difficult to come to grips with, they are likely to be unsettled and will tend to abandon it at an early stage. A training course should stretch the individual, but the difficulties should not appear to be insurmountable: any training envisaged should take the existing level of the participants as its starting point.

ANEFA's initiative in Portugal is an interesting example of a tailored programme.

In this connection, the initiative of the ANEFA (National Adult Education and Training Agency) in Portugal offers an interesting perspective. Those who follow these courses are able to study for a professional diploma and at the same time obtain qualifications corresponding to their 1st, 2nd and 3rd levels of initial education. Classes are very informal and flexible; they are especially aimed at unqualified adults and consist of individualised programmes that take account not only of each person's personal and professional experience, but also of their socioeconomic background.

Spain offers programmes and workshops that upgrade basic educational attainment.

In Spain's craft school workshop programmes, trade schools and employment workshops (Box 6.2), students who have not attained compulsory secondary education have the possibility of specific study arrangements to upgrade their basic educational attainment. This will later allow them to go into the labour market or pursue studies in the various upper secondary education programmes.

Box 6.2. **Craft school workshop programmes, trade schools and employment workshops in Spain**

The *craft school workshops, trade schools and employment workshops* integrate training, experience and information, together with techniques for employment and self-employment searches for people who are unemployed. In the first two, students receive hands-on training and learn through jobs at public works (rehabilitating public monuments, the environment, parks, etc.) or through community service of public or social usefulness (serving senior citizens, nursery schools, etc.). When they complete their programmes, the student-workers who have not found employment during the programme have already acquired qualifications and professional experience and know how to look for a job or become self-employed. Students also take vocational training and theoretical classroom courses.

The fundamental methodology and principles of the craft school workshops and trade schools' programmes have also been applied to adults with similar labour integration and reintegration difficulties through the *Employment Workshop Programme*, with specific focus on the concrete characteristics of adults.

For participants who have not attained compulsory secondary education, there are complementary specific programmes geared to offer them basic learning and vocational training that will allow them to integrate into active life or pursue studies in the various secondary education programmes.

Source: OECD (2002a).

Compliance with, and going beyond, quality standards

Complying with quality standards must not be neglected. Above all, the quality of the teaching must be recognised by the learner (and/or the instigator of the training, *i.e.* the company) and it must be experienced in practice as something that enhances personal and professional well-being. Quality standards should be improved whenever possible by proposing innovation and offering additional criteria, depending on a company's training requirements for example.

The quality of training must be recognised by the learner as well as the learning supplier.

The establishment of groups of teachers or course planners, or other associations accredited by Portugal's Institute for Innovation in Professional Training (INOFOR) is certainly to be encouraged. By way of example, it is worth mentioning one such Portuguese association, Talentus (the national association of teachers and teaching technicians). One of its main tasks is to induce training institutions to establish groups to improve the quality of teaching and thus become part of a strategic culture of continuing improvement in the quality of service. These groups encourage teachers, course planners and organisers to think about teaching and to perform practical work connected with course planning, methodological experimentation and good teaching practice.

Groups of teachers or course planners can have a positive influence.

Recognition of prior learning and certification of current learning

Recognition of previous learning (of any kind, whether it has been acquired through experience or in a formal learning situation, within the company or elsewhere) and certification come at the beginning and end respectively of the same learning process. Recognising an individual's previous achievement amounts to giving him/her the right of access to training at a higher level than they might be entitled to on the basis of formal diplomas.

Recognising previous learning may place the participant at a more accurate level than their diploma would have done.

Certification for a course successfully concluded marks the end of the learning cycle. It looks to the future, unlike the recognition of previous learning, though the principle is the same in both cases: certification of knowledge/skills acquired that can be used on a future occasion. But in this particular case certification serves a dual purpose. On the one hand the individual might wish to capitalise on his/her new competencies in the labour market and must therefore prove possession of them. On the other hand they will be able to make use of their achievement, formally recognised by a certificate, whenever they wish to return to learning.

Certification of the training offered paves the way for labour market entry and future training.

The principle

Course planners must take account of the learner's level in terms of whether their knowledge/skills were obtained in the educational system or by other means. A learner with an ISCED Level 2, for example, and twenty years of professional experience might, and in some cases should, be considered to have a general level higher than ISCED Level 2. Experience gained at work often goes beyond strict professional parameters and also gives the individual a level of maturity that enables him/her to aim higher than his/her school level would normally entitle him/her to.

The levels of entering participants should be based on professional experience as well as education.

Even acquired skills not related to the worker's normal activity should be taken into account.

When training is introduced for a precise purpose (to improve performance at work, for example), planners must take account of the skills workers have already acquired, *even if they are not essential to their normal activity.* In this way it is possible to avoid beginning a course with a long series of lessons on points already assimilated, which might cause the individual to drop out through boredom and the sense that the course is pointless.

At the outset, the individual who wishes to follow a course must be made to feel sure that it corresponds to his/her level and will take account of his/her previous experience. Professional acquirements and diplomas are not the only things to be considered. It should also be possible to take account of the personal experience of the individual applying for training, and of the social and economic circumstances. This is the point where problems arise and, in the interests of giving our discussion a coherent structure, we should address three forms of previous attainment: formal attainment, recognised by the award of a diploma or certificate; attainments derived from work; and attainments derived from experience.

Formal attainments are nearly always taken into account when individuals apply for courses

Formal attainments are on paper and generally recognised.

In the first place, there are the formal credentials in the form of diplomas or certificates obtained in the past. The value of these qualifications is fully recognised and they are easily taken into account in the countries participating in the thematic review, except in the notable case of a large number of migrant workers. For them, the problem tends to be one of identifying the real substance, in terms of competencies, that a certificate or diploma represents.

The problem of establishing equivalencies can discourage foreign workers from pursuing further learning.

This difficulty in establishing equivalencies is clearly prejudicial to lifelong learning, since it is recognised that the prospect of taking up a course beginning at the individual's true level is in itself a strong incentive to learn. On the other hand, the need to start again from scratch dooms the learner to failure in virtually all cases. To underscore the point further, it may be observed that even the European Union, though very eager to enhance its system of equivalencies and encourage the circulation of students and the assimilation of different EU languages, has made very little headway in the area of the equivalency of formal qualifications. Clearly, there is still a long way to go in the recognition of informal education and attainments derived from work and personal experience.

Professional experience is widely taken into account and many programmes exist

Professional experience is much tougher to quantify as previous attainment...

The second form of previous attainment is much more difficult to quantify, though the idea has been recognised for many years; the problem lies in the accreditation of what individuals have learnt and/or gained in the context of their work. In Finland, for example, the system of qualification based on competencies (*Näyttötutkintojärjestelmä*) provides for the accreditation of previous attainment and for the recognition of informal training. This practice is exemplary since it is fully geared to the system of qualifications based on competency, and this system is firmly rooted in practical attainments. The system gives real value to professional qualifications, both at upper secondary school level and at further education levels. In other words, Finnish experience shows that a system of certification of previous attainments that is fully incorporated into a system of national qualifications, just as it is in the United Kingdom, is more likely to win over individuals and workers. Norway's Competence Reform (*Kompetansereformen*) also explicitly allows previous attainments to be taken into account. Lagging slightly behind other countries involved in the thematic review in this respect, Sweden has just begun work on the development of a general system. There are however local initiatives, such as the SWIT (*Swedish Information Technology*) programme, which have gone so far as to evaluate the previous attainments of 80 000 individuals. The interesting point is that recognition of previous attainments is quite closely linked to the provision of counselling and information in Sweden. Experiments carried out show that the exercise is not an easy one, but this demonstrates that the evaluation of previous attainment is worthwhile: it is still a very useful source of information when a future training plan has to be devised.

This initiative is contemplated in Denmark, where special provision is to be made – as part of the adult education and training reform (VEU reform) – to give adults in the labour market the same opportunity to complete their education as young people. Moreover, this initiative needs to be seen in conjunction with the idea that adult education should be a continuation of initial education, as the initiative ties continuing training and further education programmes together into a coherent and more transparent adult learning system. Clearly, one of the main goals of the Danish reform is to establish a consistent system of accreditation for the training provided in the labour market. Tentative measures to achieve this goal have been adopted as part of the VEU reform but it would seem that here, as in other areas, the work comes up against the problem of evaluating time spent with the company: should it be inferred from the fact that somebody has worked for a company that they have acquired specific competencies? In Switzerland too, one of the priority goals of the FSEA is to develop a new co-ordinated continuing training system and to provide for the accreditation of individual attainment, whether professional or experiential. The recognition of experience gained outside educational institutions is also one of CIRFA's suggestions for adult education. More specifically, the idea is that the cantons should collaborate with the confederation in drawing up a system for the validation and accreditation of attainments derived from experience gained outside schools or colleges, whether professional or personal.

... although the Scandinavian countries and Switzerland, for example, have programmes or initiatives for evaluation and accreditation of attainment.

Portugal first introduced schemes as part of the National Action Plans in 2000 and 2001. The object is to identify both the knowledge and the skills of members of the workforce whose school attainment is weakest. For workers over 35, the national accreditation system is intended to give formal recognition of competencies actually gained through professional experience; it is also intended to facilitate the organisation of a training programme, providing a benchmark for the competencies needed in a certain type of job in a given sector. For unqualified young people aged between 16 and 18, the agreement between social partners in Portugal stipulates that 40% of working time must be devoted to education (Box 6.3).

Portugal has schemes to identify the knowledge and skills of workers whose school attainment is weakest.

In Spain, the new Vocational Training and Qualifications Bill is expected to establish a national system of professional qualifications, taking EU criteria as a reference in order to facilitate movement of workers. It will include the recognition of various means of acquiring professional qualifications, including work experience and informal apprenticeships.

Spain is planning a national system of professional qualifications.

Box 6.3. **A national system for the accreditation, ratification and certification of competencies in Portugal**

In addition to giving adults an incentive to take up courses, the Portuguese system is expected to provide an assessment of the teaching work that remains to be done to satisfy the benchmark standard of knowledge needed for future jobs. The system is aimed at adults aged 18 or older, who did not complete school, have no professional qualifications and are often unemployed. It is organised at local level by the ANEFA in partnership with CRVCCs (Centres for the Recognition, Validation and Certification of Competences). These centres are hosted by local public and private institutions accredited by the ANEFA, such as municipal and cultural associations, local development associations, business associations, municipalities, trades unions, schools and professional training centres. The national system defined by the ANEFA covers three central areas:

- The system of key competency benchmarks with directives on the process of recognising and validating four key competencies (language and communication; ICTs; everyday mathematics; employability and citizenship).
- The methodology of assessing competencies.
- A portfolio of personal competencies.

Six pilot CRVCCs were set up in December 2000; by 2006 there should be 84 of them, covering the whole of Portugal. The Seixal Centre is currently the only public CRVCC. The technical team comprises three people: a psychologist, a specialist in training from the ministry of employment and solidarity and a specialist in education from the ministry of education. The centre is open to anybody who wishes to have their competencies validated. The centre at the Minho industrial association in Braga, on the other hand, is mainly geared to meeting the needs of companies. Three people work there: a manager, who keeps in touch with the companies, and two psychologists who interview the workers, either in the workplace or on the association's premises. The idea is to encourage managers to join so that they will involve all of their staff in the project.

The most notable effort, pioneered by Portugal, involves two complementary measures. First, professional and school attainment is certified simultaneously in the context of continuing vocational training under the aegis of the *Instituto do Emprego e Formação Profissionnal* – IEFP (Institute of Accelerated Vocational Training). Second, certification of various levels of basic training can now be obtained from assessment centres established under the responsibility of the ANEFA. As to the first measure, based on a system of credits, the vocational training institutions not only certify technical competencies – their primary concern – but also the corresponding educational levels. There has been a call throughout the western countries for a closer link between vocational and general training, and in Portugal real progress on this long path can be observed. As to the second measure, a system for the recognition and validation of attainments has been established. The system is based on an original competency benchmark, devised in Portugal and implemented through the assessment centres. This benchmark identifies several groups of competencies, designated "key competencies", which are essential to civic responsibility and enable the individual to reach a suitable threshold of employability. Competencies acquired in various ways are validated as being equivalent to a corresponding school level. This bold system of equivalency represents an essential step forward in enabling adults with low school attainment to get back to the professional training system. It also serves to reveal hidden competencies for which no certification exists and thus to reduce the observed lack of competencies in Portugal among people over 35.

Source: OECD (2001a).

Attainment through experience is still at the experimental stage

Experience as a form of prior attainment is valuable but mostly ignored.

The third form of prior attainment is derived from experience, *i.e.* from simply having been involved in domains of activity in the past. The possibility of taking account of such experiential attainment is discussed in many countries participating in the thematic review but real, credible advances are rare. The idea is worth mentioning here even if little can be written on the subject, since experiential attainments are a valuable complement to professional attainments. Bearing in mind that the latter are an indispensable complement to formal attainments, in initial education for example, we begin to grasp the importance of recognising attainment in the overall learning sequence, not just in school and/or formal learning. At present, experiential attainments are quite often ignored since they are difficult to identify and even more difficult to quantify; or else they are mixed up with professional attainments in an approach that attempts to ascertain what the individual already knows (portfolio of competencies).

It must be acknowledged that it is difficult to evaluate the direct results of the consideration given to professional and experiential attainments in terms of number of participants. The results in terms of a higher level of participation in training arise mainly from the fact that adults do not start from scratch when they begin a training programme. They are able to begin at a higher level than they would if they had to show formal education certification. This system then is obviously more attractive and can be less expensive.

The results of recognition of attainment are difficult to gauge in terms of number of participants.

The difficulties are immense

Although the value of taking account of prior attainments no longer needs to be demonstrated, the difficulty of such judgements is nevertheless considerable. The idea that the real competencies of individuals were worth more than their most recent certificate or diploma was quite probably in the minds of teachers and employers long before it was formally enunciated by theoreticians of adult education. The economy nevertheless relied for a very long time on a market of diplomas rather than a market of competencies since diplomas could be observed and competencies could not, or not easily – and even if they could, they could still not be measured. The practicalities of recognising professional and experiential attainments therefore involve the enormous task of establishing benchmarks. If there is no yardstick by which to evaluate each person's individual experience, it will not be possible to advance to the stage where such consideration becomes standard practice. The problem no doubt lies in the fact that this benchmark is being developed very gradually, from observation of the experiences and competencies of the very individuals who come forward.

Diplomas are still preferred; benchmarks for individual experience are slow in coming.

A second major difficulty is deciding who should validate professional and/or experiential attainment. Many authorities are concerned here: the different ministries, the training providers, the professional sectors, etc. It is obvious that the body certifying a given attainment or a training process already under way will need to have sufficient authority in order for the qualification obtained by an individual to have any real value. This is important, as we have already seen, if the individual wishes to take a course in the future or wishes to capitalise on their attainments in the labour market (promotion or professional mobility). The key notions would therefore seem to be partnership and the definition of common objectives, so that professional sectors will be spared the need to establish their own certification system to make up for the lack of certificates with any recognisable worth. Nor would it be appropriate to establish any

Who should validate? Partnerships would seem the answer.

187|

form of competition between, for example, the ministry of education and the ministry of employment. Over and above the problem of prerogatives, concerted action is clearly necessary; competencies that the education specialists might be inclined to recognise would not necessarily be recognised by the actors in the labour market, and *vice versa*. Here, as in other fields, most of the countries participating in the thematic review normally adopted solutions that involved all of the social partners.

At the end of the learning process, new competencies should be certified, recognised and properly valued

Attainment should be validated...

Generally speaking, whenever a course is followed through to the end, it should be possible to validate that attainment. Recognition of what has been learned might take the form of a certificate, a diploma or a promotion in the workplace.

... and additional competencies recognised in the workplace...

Whether training is given at the request of the company or of the individual, whether it is strictly geared to professional ends or its scope is much broader, the extra competencies acquired must be recognised in the workplace. Moreover, to the extent possible, there should be a consequent readjustment of the worker's post, function, status or salary. Even if training is not initially associated with a specific project, the individuals should be able to profit from their attainments at a subsequent stage, if they so wish.

... for instance through a pay rise.

A costly though highly motivating solution might consist in giving a pay rise to people who followed a course that is relevant to any of the various jobs in the company. The use to be made of the newly trained worker would be up to the company, but the pay rise would be granted whatever happened, provided – it must be emphasised – that the training was relevant to the activity of the company. In other words, if training has been given, the salary will no longer depend on the post but on the worker. This obviously gives the company a stronger incentive to make better use of its workers and assign them to suitable posts once they have finished training. It also gives individuals an incentive, since the pay rise is guaranteed. A similar experience has been provided in Chapter 5, Box 5.5 on a pay incentive scheme in Norway. Two points do, however, qualify the argument. First, we know that financial argument is not always decisive in inciting individuals to learn, especially those who are not convinced of the value of learning. The second is related to the consequences for the company's salary policy: the difficulties associated with basing salaries on the qualifications rather than the function of an employee are well known. In short, the idea should only be seen as a possible avenue for investigation.

Detailed certification would basically solve the problem of recognising prior learning.

To conclude this section, it is well worth noting that if all learning were certified and reflected in a document sufficiently detailed and generally recognised within a given geographical area, the problem of recognising prior learning would eventually be limited to that of recognising experiential attainment.

But certification must have consensus.

As with the recognition of prior attainment, it is important that there be a consensus between all the actors if the training thus certified is to have any real value subsequently, when the employee wishes to return to learning or capitalise on his/her training in the labour market. Competencies acquired must be validated by the different players in the world of education and work. Finland's system of qualification based on competencies provides an example of an arrangement in which competencies are defined by employers and professionals in collaboration with educators. For the Finns, this guarantees that the certificate in question is recognised in the labour market. Moreover, because the competencies are certified on the basis of criteria that have been centrally defined, the certificate is recognised nationally.

Distance learning and e-learning

Distance learning and ITCs deserve a separate section in as much as the computer and communication networks, such as the Internet or Intranet, are often presented as a panacea for the problems of access to learning programmes, whether in terms of time or distance.

Mastery of IT is a basic competency like reading or writing

IT literacy seems to be a more important issue in some countries visited (Finland) than in others. However, mastery of the new information and communication technologies is a key issue in this comparative report on adult learning. This stage often has more to do with learning basic skills in the same way as reading, writing and arithmetic, at least in the nine countries visited. It does not necessarily come after the stages listed above. It needs to be conducted in conjunction with basic education, if only because one of the current ways of solving the shortage of training facilities in remote parts of the world or places where training is not adapted to the pace of modern life is to use electronic learning. It is worth noting that IT has brought writing back into fashion (Pont and Werquin, 2000) because it is necessary to be able to write to use e-mail or the Internet.

IT skills are basic, and should be taught in conjunction with basic education.

IT is a gateway both to the information economy and society and failure to master it can jeopardise the exercise of a citizen's fundamental rights and duties. The importance of widely available IT training for adults is thus underlined, though obviously the urgency and the problems are not the same as for the three basic skills (reading, writing, arithmetic).

Though often presented as a panacea, IT and e-learning[6] need to be placed in a broader framework that addresses the drawbacks as well as the benefits. Many of the nine countries visited are very large countries and/or countries with very low population densities. A very large proportion of Canadians live on a very small fraction of the country's territory along the border with the United States. A similar pattern is found in Finland, where virtually all the population is concentrated on the south coast. Sweden and Norway are also very thinly populated with populations tending to be concentrated in the south. The climatic factor also compounds the difficulties involved in setting up adult learning centres that are within reasonable reach of learners. Distance learning in general and e-learning in particular thus have a very useful role to play when local training facilities are lacking, especially in that employers who have relocated to remote areas for tax, economic or other

Distance learning and e-learning are indeed useful when local training facilities are lacking...

---

6. Self or distance learning by means of electronic tools like computers, the Internet and/or electronic mail.

reasons specific to their line of business (mineral deposits and forestry, for example) are often reluctant to support locally provided general education. However, it is necessary to look at the drawbacks of computer tools when used for general education purposes.

E-learning is still a very expensive solution for the individual

... but there are disadvantages...

First among the drawbacks is cost. This argument is twofold. First, contrary to much received opinion, the infrastructure is still not fully in place and is still fairly costly to develop. Second, in e-learning the marginal cost of an additional student is fairly close to the average cost. The first argument needs to be treated with caution given the glaring disparities between the countries concerned. While one can readily conceive that IT can be an effective way of providing advanced or vocational training of a specific type, it is difficult to see it being of use for basic education or general learning needs, at least in the near future. Even in those countries with the highest proportions of households equipped with computers, not only does a substantial proportion of the population not have access to a computer, but those that do are not necessarily connected to the Internet (Figure 6.2).[7]

... such as cost...

The second argument, which is never addressed head-on by the advocates of computer-based learning, is that in traditional teaching or training based on the idea that a group of people benefit from the knowledge of a teacher or instructor, it often costs very little to add an extra learner.[8] It is true that when training is very advanced or requires very expensive tools, the need for funds increases with the number of learners.[9] E-learning requires as many computers and/or hours of connection as there are users. The problem then becomes one of the number of instructors. It is clear from having visited numerous e-learning sites that contact between the learner and instructor is still considered necessary, even if it is only on a weekly or monthly basis rather than a daily basis. Increasing the number of learners immediately poses the problem of the number of computers and instructors, just to mention the most obvious material aspects. Cost may disqualify e-learning as a panacea for adult learning.[10]

The computer, both a tool for learning and the object of learning, must first be mastered

... and the parallel education needed, i.e. in using the computer...

There are further cultural impediments to the use of e-learning for general education. First, learners are often apprehensive about using a computer – the lower the level of education, the greater these barriers. Expressed differently, e-learning requires a minimum amount of computer

---

7. The cost of the connection, which is very often proportional to the connection time, also needs to be taken into account, and all the more so when the user is in a remote area. This can reduce the savings made possible by e-learning.
8. In discussions on this issue, the notions of average cost and marginal cost are frequently confused.
9. Here typically the average cost is close to the marginal cost.
10. The Wired up Communities initiative in the United Kingdom will be worth following in order to better grasp the size of the difficulties for disadvantaged groups: 14 000 households in seven pilot areas will receive the technology to have access to Internet.

Figure 6.2. **Households with access to a home computer and the Internet**
Percentage of households, 1999 and 2000

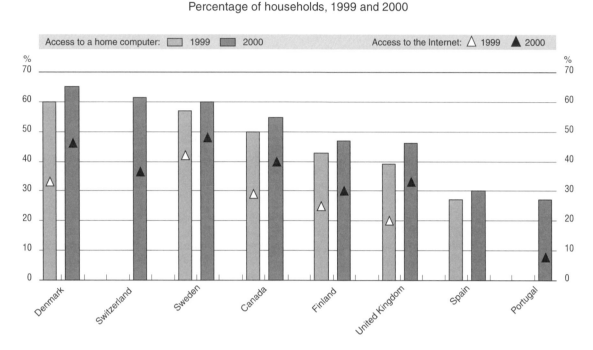

Note: Countries are ranked in descending order of access to a home computer in 2000.
Source: OECD (2001c, 2002b) and ICT database.

training. Otherwise, one can enter into vicious circles in which it is not possible to educate certain adults because they cannot use a computer or use it well enough, and it is not possible to teach them computer skills because they are undereducated. This applies to the hardware.

But it is also necessary to teach them how to use software and the Internet. While hypertext is undoubtedly an intuitive tool and the Internet is undoubtedly very convivial, it still poses barriers for a significant fraction of the population – those with the lowest level of education. A further problem, and not a minor one, is the amount of time that an individual can devote to learning. If learners have to cope with learning the use of a computer – both hardware and software – at the same time as the training itself, one can be fairly certain that the least motivated learners will be discouraged fairly quickly, so that the upshot is counter to the objective sought.[11] An interesting learning programme for adults to learn to use computers can be found in the Aulas Mentor in Spain (Box 6.4).

... its software, and the Internet.

_____
11. It should also be pointed out that the speed of the computer often exceeds that of the learning process. A fairly high minimum level of IT literacy is required in order to exploit the computer properly.

191

_____
© OECD 2003

Box 6.4.   **Aulas Mentor in Spain**

"Aula Mentor" (Mentor Classroom) is an open, free training system carried out over the Internet. Its purpose is to provide high-quality training using communication by computer, and so reach areas which, due to their distance from major towns, do not have any specialist courses. The main objective is that all citizens, regardless of their previous training, economic level or computing knowledge, have access to these training courses. A network of classrooms with public access to the Internet places at the disposal of adult students a "connected" computer, as well as a classroom monitor who advises and assists them. Other classrooms may be specifically for handicapped people or other groups. The training is in computer literacy, advanced computing, professional upkilling, and basic and advanced personal development.

As they have the advantage of high flexibility, the students take charge of their own learning and attend the classroom at a time agreed with the monitor according to their availability. The monitor's role as a facilitator of learning has emerged as one of the fundamental pillars of the project. There are several aspects to monitoring work. The classrooms have several work areas:

- Computer work stations (between five and 15) where each student can carry out course activities. These computers are connected in a network and to the Internet.

- An area for group tasks that encourage spontaneous collaboration between students on the same course.

- A general resources area where commonly used materials for consultation are available.

Source: OECD (2002a) and visit to Aula Mentor, Medina del Campo, Spain, November 2002.

Modularisation of courses

Modularisation would appear a sensible approach to devising training programmes…

At the outset, modularisation is a method of constructing training programmes. Each programme consists of a set of complementary modules associated with a job function; each module corresponds to a given skill. It identifies the knowledge and know-how needed to perform an occupational activity and sets the prerequisites for following this sequence – the learning targets, operational skills, skill levels, etc. Construction of the modules is hence based on an analysis of work functions, and continues according to set rules and requires validation from the occupational world.

… with distinct advantages in terms of educational and organisational objectives.

But the modularising of courses should not be regarded simply as a technical reform. A number of educational and organisational objectives should also be pursued. One is to make the continuing training market – or at least an important segment, the market for vocational training – more transparent. Participants would be able to identify the standard of training on offer by referring to the general framework (the modules associated with the various programmes). In addition, it would be easier for participants to have their skills recognised and to chart educational pathways to supplement their training. Modularisation explicitly seeks to ensure that the management of training programmes, and of individual learning paths, is flexible. Such flexibility combines with the following benefits and advantages:

- It sets the content of vocational and trade courses on a standard basis.

Box 6.5.   **The modularisation of courses in Switzerland**

The principle of modularising vocational courses under the responsibility of the federal government was accepted by Parliament in June 1993. An initial working party in OFIAMT (now OFFT) suggested that pilot experiments should be launched. They were co-ordinated by the Swiss Research Society in Vocational Training (*Société suisse de recherche appliquée en matière de formation professionnelle* – SRFP). Numerous people in training institution, and socioeconomic circles helped to construct programmes in this format.

Groups in various regions prepared the modules. Experiments were conducted in a number of areas: catch-up courses for basic training in commerce, computing and agriculture; training of human resource managers; training for trainers (modularisation of the FSEA, Certificate I course); and training in hotels and catering. The projects were evaluated, and it was decided that the process should be continued and broadened. The experimental phase was thus judged satisfactory and the process has been extended to all vocational courses.

Source: OECD (2001b).

- It assists transfers from one trade to another by comparing the modules and skills required for individual occupations; accordingly, it will be easier to identify shared skills.

- It should also assist vocational retraining without unduly lengthening the courses.

- It should enhance co-operation among all those involved.

- It will be easier to build bridges between general and vocational education.

The evaluation conducted in Switzerland (Box 6.5.) brought out a number of points worth noting:

The case of Switzerland revealed several important points.

- The advantage of a top-down approach (modules developed by the trade association and supplied to schools), which means that the content is validated without delay; the bottom-up approach, based on the schools and colleges, is not ruled out, but validation takes longer.

- Collective work by a number of training agencies took place on a co-operative footing, even though they are competitors in the training market. Other experiments showed there were difficulties in working together, as the cultures of the various agencies were too different. Importance was also attached to public events providing information about the modules, which is a key condition for the system's success.

- A wider range of people, in both quantity and level (new categories), have taken the courses; these groups include a larger number of women taking modular courses.

- In terms of standards, the experiments yielded differing results: in some cases the outcome is still unclear, while in others standards have risen.

- Modularisation means a greater workload on the administrative side, for example in running exams.

- The flexibility of the scheme appealed to participants, who considered the possibility of obtaining module credits as partial qualification a motivating factor.

- Modularisation is becoming an ongoing operation to change and develop education, which needs to alter its organisational practices.

- The evaluation also brings out the "transdisciplinary aspect of the modules and cross-recognition is still at the trial stage" (Gindros *et al.*, 1999).

- The results of the experiments indicate that a number of the hoped-for benefits are actually coming through. The question of standards was directly addressed: some experiments point to higher standards, while others seem to have highlighted steps needed to secure this. The scheme also brings further co-ordination. Rival training agencies work together to build modules, and other agencies have formed closer links with economic associations to validate the modules (bringing education and the economy closer together). Finally, the participants consider that modules will facilitate recognition of learning and the development of individual education projects.

Modularisation is gaining ground... Generally speaking, modularisation is gaining ground. It has its advantages and disadvantages (Box 6.6) and seems to have won over the institutional and other actors in countries such as Norway, Portugal, Spain and Switzerland, for example. In Spain, the system of Regulated and Vocational Training for the Unemployed is arranged in a modular format. The principal goal is not preparation for higher-level studies but receiving adequate qualifications for integration into the labour market. Validations for the professional modules corresponding to the intermediate level training cycles have been established, as well as access to predetermined first-cycle university courses, related to completed vocational training courses, for students who have obtained the higher technician qualification.

... but it will not cure a system already badly integrated. However, there seems to be a significant risk, in these countries and those that have made less progress towards modular courses, of modularisation becoming merely a justification *a posteriori* of the relative complexity of adult education provision. If the system already in place is complex and badly integrated, then to present the whole as a set of modules is not likely to help resolve the problem of complexity and lack of integration. In other words, and this is one of the major disadvantages of setting up a modular system (Box 6.6), modules must be planned as part of a whole. Indeed the whole idea of modularisation is to plan for complexity at the outset.

6.3. Outlook on delivery

Convincing adults of the value of learning is, as established earlier, an essential factor in encouraging them to take up courses. However, for any section of the population, whether or not they are persuaded of the merits of learning, it is possible to identify factors that will make it easier for them to take up courses and so facilitate the return to learning. Throughout Chapter 6 we have seen that they have to do with pedagogy itself as well as delivery. The important point is that certain elements are not necessarily more important than others. The hours, the practical conditions (buildings,

---

Box 6.6.   **Advantages and disadvantages of modularised adult education courses**

Disadvantages:

- High investment needed to overcome planning problems associated with drawing them up
- Cost of management and co-ordination of modules
- Presupposes co-operation between actors in the labour market and those in education
- The module does not necessarily provide a competency that is recognised in the market

Advantages:

- Possible gains in terms of scale and variety
- More rapid adjustment to changes in the labour market and in adults' needs
- Greater chance of return to the labour market if there is agreement between social partners
- Flexibility in the timetabling of training programmes; increased attractiveness to adult learners put off by a long, continuous course

---

Source: Chiousse (2001).

---

equipment, etc.), services such as care of children and/or invalid parents, the andragogical content and the flexibility of made-to-measure courses all help to increase the attractiveness of adult learning.

Certain ideas listed in this chapter came up repeatedly during the review: information and counselling, quality, assessment, transparency and consistency. Implementation of some ideas has already reached an advanced stage (recognition of prior learning, etc.). Some ideas are newer but a great stimulus to innovation: adapting supply to demand or introducing learning into the learners' social milieu or preferred activities. However, it is worth repeating a number of basic recommendations in the general context of adult learning policy. First of all, an initial education must give individuals the skills they need for access to further learning. The role of school is not simply to impart knowledge, but also to help learners continue to acquire new knowledge throughout life. The return to learning should never be perceived as the last resort, and initial education must not be seen as an end in itself. A second key issue is the adequate dissemination of information and anticipation of needs. All means should be used to circulate the available information: school, workplace, temping agencies, city hall, social services, media, public and private bodies, etc.[12] "Adult Learners' Week", launched in the United Kingdom in 1992 and now an annual event in about thirty countries, is intended to provide as much information as possible on the range of courses that are available. A third way of improving the system is to

---

12. The CRC (knowledge resource centre) established by the INOFOR in Portugal administers and responds to this need for information by working with agencies and professionals in the training sector.

195

provide individual counsellors to guide the individuals and assist them in embarking upon learning. Establishing partnerships is a fourth obvious recommendation. Finally, it is vital to hold routine and regular assessments of the measures implemented.

All these ideas about taking account of the specific nature of adult learning are directly linked to motivation and incentives (Chapter 5). That link would be even stronger if learners were to be monitored after their courses had finished. When all these conditions have been fulfilled, and all the fundamental practicalities (timetable, funding, and access) addressed and solved, and the specific quality of the pedagogy recognised, we will be able to make individuals masters of their own learning – and therefore, to a greater extent, their own lives.

BIBLIOGRAPHY

BERBAUM, J. (1996),
  "Apprendre à... apprendre", *Sciences humaines*, special issue, No. 12, February-March.

CEDEFOP (2000),
  CEDEFOP Info, *www.trainingvillage.gr/etv*

CEDEFOP (2001),
  CEDEFOP Info, *www.trainingvillage.gr/etv*

CHIOUSSE, S. (2001),
  Pédagogie et apprentissage des adultes, An 2001. État des lieux et recommandations, document prepared for the Thematic Review on Adult Learning (*www.oecd.org/edu/adultlearning*).

COMMISSARIAT GÉNÉRAL DU PLAN (2001),
  Jeunesse, le devoir d'avenir, report supervised by D. Charvet, La Documentation française.

COURTNEY, S. (1992),
  Why Adults Learn – Toward a Theory of Participation in Adult Education, Routledge, London and New York.

DESSAINT, M-P. and D. BOISVERT (1991),
  "Motivations des personnes âgées de 55 ans et plus à suivre des cours à distance", CADE, *Journal of Distance Education*, Vol. 6.2.

GINDROS, J.-P., R. JOST, E. KEMM, R. MARTY and J. WIDMER (1999),
  Formation professionnelle continue selon le système modulaire, final report, Société suisse pour la recherche appliquée en matière de formation professionnelle (SGAB-SRFP) and Office fédéral de la formation professionnelle et de la technologie (OFFT), Bern.

HOUSSAYE, J. (1994),
  Quinze pédagogues, leur influence aujourd'hui, Armand Colin, Paris.

ILLERIS, K. (2000),
  The Three Dimensions of Learning – Contemporary Learning Theory in the Tension Field Between Piaget, Freud and Marx, Roskilde University Press, Denmark.

National Action Plan (2000),
  "Portugal: National Implementation Report", April (*http://europa.eu.int/comm/employment_social*).

National Action Plan (2001),
  "Portugal, National Action Plan for Employment", April.

OECD (2001a),
  "Thematic Review on Adult Learning: Portugal Country Note", Paris (*www.oecd.org/edu/adultlearning*).

OECD (2001b),
  "Thematic Review on Adult Learning: Switzerland Country Note", Paris (*www.oecd.org/edu/adultlearning*).

OECD (2001c),
  STI scoreboard, July, Paris.

OECD (2002a),
  "Thematic Review on Adult Learning: Spain Background Report", Paris (*www.oecd.org/edu/adultlearning*).

OECD (2002b),
  Measuring the Information Economy, Paris.

OECD and US DEPARTMENT OF EDUCATION (1999),
  "How Adults Learn", proceedings of the conference held 6-8 April 1998, Georgetown University, Washington DC.

PARMENTIER, C. and F. ARFAOUI (2001),
  Tout savoir pour e-former – De la loi de 71 au e-learning, Éditions d'organisation, Paris.

PERRET-CLERMONT, A-N. and T. ZITTOUN (2002),
  "Esquisse d'une psychologie de la transition", *Éducation permanente*, 36, 2002/1, pp. 12-15.

PONT, B. and P. WERQUIN (2000),
"Literacy in a Thousand Words", OECD *Observer*, pp. 49-50, October, Paris.

REGROUPEMENT DES ASSOCIATIONS D'ANDRAGOGUES ET DE PROFESSIONNELS DE LA FORMATION DES ADULTES (RAAPFA),
www.raapfa.qc.ca

VIAU, R. (1996),
"La motivation, condition essentielle de la réussite", *Sciences humaines*, special issue No. 12, February/March.

VIMONT, C. (2001),
Le nouveau troisième âge – Une société active en devenir, Économica, Paris.

Chapter 7

PROMOTING BETTER INTEGRATION OF SUPPLY AND DEMAND

This chapter analyses policy options for addressing the problems of overly fragmented provision of training services and lack of support infrastructure. A number of improvements might be made to take fuller account of learners' needs and to enable more would-be learners to come forward and participate in learning programmes. Policy makers and training providers must face the challenge of responding better to the expectations of current and potential adult learners.

7.1. The diversity of provision of adult learning

Adult learning is provided by a complex set of institutions.

In Chapter 3 it was shown that the countries under review have a great diversity of institutions primarily devoted to providing adult education and training. The outside observers' initial impression in each country was that there is a complex set of institutions that are continually evolving to meet the specific needs of the time and to try to solve the problems that arise in implementing previous decisions and reforms. This impression is also found in the analysis of national observers. For example, the cantonal directors of public education in Switzerland speak of a "mixed bag" of adult training institutions [Conférence suisse des directeurs cantonaux de l'instruction publique (CDIP), 1999]. In light of this situation, it comes as no surprise that there are difficulties in co-ordinating the various institutions.

They have no standard classification, and different methods of counting participation.

If national administrative statistics in this field are examined, the situation appears to be even more confusing. The list of the various adult training bodies is different in each country and there is no standardised classification. The methods used to count participation by institutions and within each country may differ. Either the number of participants or the number of courses is counted, with a risk of double counting since individuals may participate in more than one course. It may also consist only of counting the hourly, weekly or monthly volume of training. The method of financing can also affect how participation is counted. For example, in Denmark the unit of measurement is the full-time equivalent participant, since financing is based on the "taximeter" principle.[1]

The enterprise is the most common learning venue.

Firms are very actively involved in the adult training process. They base their training initiatives on human resource policies that are often not transparent but differ depending on the sector, company size and specialisation. In Portugal, the expert team observed the following strategies among the various types of firms:

- Multinationals are highly selective in hiring and subsequently provide their employees with intensive training, negotiating specific training programmes and subsidies on a case-by-case basis.
- Some large companies develop strategies for internalising the direct and indirect benefits of training. For example, a large automobile assembly firm, the Salvador Caetano company, has developed specially organised and targeted group programmes for training young people and reskilling older workers that are not always tailored to the public subsidy system (Box 7.1).
- The SMEs that are the mainstay of Portugal's industrial base and account for nearly 80% of total employment are experiencing difficulties in developing and implementing a training strategy.

A more or less similar breakdown is found in many other countries, always with the same problem regarding training in SMEs.

Although a substantial share of training is provided directly at the workplace by private and public employers, the form, content and methods of training may

---

1. See Chapter 4. The Danish Government finances training institutions on the basis of specific rates and the number of full-time equivalent students.

Box 7.1. **An example of internalisation of education and training: the Salvador Caetano company in Portugal**

The visit to this firm enriched the analysis of the strategies aimed at raising skill levels in the Portuguese economy. The enterprise was established in 1945 by Salvador Caetano, who had not finished his initial education, but gradually went on to complete secondary school and earn an engineering degree, ultimately becoming the head of what is today a very large company. This group, which comprises some 50 firms, emphasises the training of young employees, including those with low qualifications and poor academic skills.

On the one hand, the firm's management model follows the typical pattern of a Japanese *Keiretsu* (a network of firms belonging to a single group) – on which it may be based, as it works with Toyota in the automobile sector.

1. Training targets a broad range of skills: technical (mastery of certain techniques), cognitive (analytical and organisational ability) and social (ability to listen, co-operate and communicate clearly).

2. To be profitable, this intensive training effort requires a degree of stability of employment, which is ensured by paying higher salaries than competitors and providing regular pay increases and various social benefits.

3. The constraints imposed by the public financing of training are sometimes seen as detrimental to adapting the training programme to the specific needs of the firm, for example when a minimum number of hours is required for each training session.

On the other hand, however, the training strategy is geared to the characteristics of the Portuguese economy, having been adapted through a process that could be described as hybridisation.

1. The certification process, which is beneficial to individuals and society as a whole, may to some extent undermine this type of training organisation, for it means that the skills acquired in the firm become largely, if not entirely transferable. This being the case, competitive wages and social benefits are an indispensable complement to the training strategy.

2. Since in some cases low levels of literacy or lack of basic mathematical skills prevent employees from acquiring job skills, the firm has developed special programmes such as that for 150 employees in its Gaia factory. As the firm is providing basic training and remedial education in such cases, these programmes qualify for public funding.

3. Lastly, the firm is opening up its training centres to outside companies that are either part of the group or act as subcontractors. In these cases, it works in co-operation with the Association of Portuguese Enterprises (AEP). This is another example of a firm internalising a segment of training throughout the industry in which it is involved.

Source: Visit to Salvador Caetano company and meetings with company managers (March 2001).

---

differ considerably. Training institutions that are independent of employers while working with them are a complementary component indispensable to the smooth running of the system as a whole. These institutions are in a better position than employers, for whom training is not the main activity, to accumulate training expertise by comparing experiences in the different sectors and types of firms in which they work and can therefore better meet expectations.

To support employee training, greater co-operation between training institutions and firms is important. The former provide general training and monitor learning, while the latter provide practical training courses. This type of co-operation is found in most of the countries visited. For example, one of

Greater co-operation between firms and training institutions is crucial.

the basic ideas behind the system of "integrated provision of continuing vocational training" developed in Denmark (Box 5.11), is that training is more effective if there is better contact between firms and organisers before, concurrently and afterward. The resource centres for competence in Norway (Box 5.12) and the local learning centres in Sweden (Box 7.2) also use this system.

In Quebec, firms and training institutions co-operate within the customised training programme introduced in 1986. In this programme, training for firms is provided by schools. Doray (2000) has studied the implementation of two customised long training activities provided to the employees of two firms. In both cases, the average age of participants was 47. The first programme was designed to enable office employees to advance to higher level jobs, and the second targeted the professional development of foremen. In both cases, this training enabled employees with relatively low levels of prior training to advance in their careers. Doray explains that the success of this programme is due to a combination of two factors: first, firms' proactive policies in reorganising work and professionalising certain occupational categories, and, second, the flexible provision of training programmes, which has made it possible to match the content of training closely with job content.

Universities should forge closer ties with outside partners. Universities also have a role to play, as was argued in Norway's green paper on higher education issued in May 2000. It recommends that closer ties are developed between universities and outside partners, especially private firms. The recognition of non-formal competencies is a means of enabling those without formal diplomas to be admitted to universities.

Box 7.2. **The local learning centre in Sweden**

Masugnen (the Blast Furnace) is a learning centre established in the municipality of Lindesberg to serve local and regional education, training and learning needs. The municipality, with a current population of 23 000, has traditionally been dependent on mining and metalworking. These industries have gradually been replaced with a broad variety of small and medium-sized industry and service enterprises as well as by a substantial amount of public sector institutions. This new situation has created a need for flexible and varied provision of adult education and training, frequently targeting specific needs in the local economy. The centre has been designed according to the objective of flexible learning: individuals and enterprises should be able to combine the services of the centre with their daily activities. An individual employee wanting to study a certain subject should be able to do so without having to leave his or her job. An enterprise should, in the same manner, be able to pursue staff updating and training without major disruptions in ordinary activities. The centre underlines the importance of IT-supported learning for achieving these flexibility gains. Another important aim of the centre is to mobilise local knowledge and competence resources. While on the one hand saving costs, using local resources is also a way of establishing and strengthening local learning networks. So far, *Masugnen* is one of the few centres of this kind established in Sweden. The model is interesting as it illustrates the potential of local learning centres, as well as the problems facing them.

Source: Meeting with managers, Lindesberg, May 2000.

Public education and training institutions do not play as central a role in adult learning as in initial education, although their role in this regard varies across countries. In the Nordic countries, non-subsidised private adult learning activities are negligible and nearly all training programmes can qualify for full or partial public funding. For example, in Denmark, even the folk high schools, which are representative of private education, depend on financing by the state according to rules laid down in legislation. In Portugal, the state is also the main actor in training provision. It takes the lead in organising most adult education and training systems, if only because public financing from the national budget and EU funds (ESF) plays a key role in the operation and development of the system. A very different situation prevails in Switzerland since adult education and training institutions are mostly private, and subsidies are only granted to certain vocational training programmes intended primarily for the unemployed. Institutions that organise recreational and general courses do not receive subsidies. However, there are exemplary private initiatives in this field, such as that of the Migros supermarket chain, which runs a large network of training centres offering a wide array of courses (Box 7.3).

Public institutions must play a leading role...

Box 7.3. **Migros "club schools" in Switzerland: an exemplary private initiative**

The Migros "club schools" (*écoles-clubs*) constitute a large network of training centres offering a broad range of courses sponsored by a supermarket chain. Gottlieb Duttweiler, the founder of the Migros food retailing chain, had a humanitarian vision derived from the protestant social movement of the 1920s and 1930s. In 1944, he set up language courses for adults and in the 1950s he expanded the clubs' range of courses to include handicrafts, art and sports. Since then, the clubs have broadened their activities even further by adding courses of a more vocational nature. For example, they introduced courses in computer science and award Microsoft training certificates. Language courses account for 40% of offerings, recreational and leisure courses 34%, and business and work-related courses 20%. They are open both to individuals and to firms. The courses are financed partly by participants and partly by the Migros' 1% corporate cultural contribution, which makes up the difference between income derived from the courses and the centres' operating costs, and amounts to 150 million Swiss francs per year.

The network has 48 training centres and employs 8 000 trainers and 1 500 other employees (responsible for planning, advertising, management of centres and preparation of educational materials). Each centre is responsible for its own programme, but for the past few years there has been a central co-ordinating body, the Co-ordination Office, which is responsible for advertising, production of educational material and the awarding of certificates for officially recognised courses.

The Migros club school of Saint-Gall is an excellent example of one of its centres. It opened in 1999 in the town centre, occupying a former railway station, which has been fully renovated, and offers a variety of activities. The list below is not complete, but shows just how wide a variety there is:

- Lessons in music, visual arts, dance and crafts for "amateurs".
- Business computer courses for firms and private individuals.
- Foreign language classes.
- Jewellery-making classes for "amateurs" and "semi-professionals".
- Music classes (jazz) for professional musicians.
- Fitness classes.

Source: Meetings with managers, Saint-Gall, December 1999.

203

... otherwise governments may lose their capacity to sustain collective, public concerns.

The acquisition of skills has become a major public need and a fundamental issue for governments. As this field is gradually privatised and governments defer to the private sector's priorities, there is a danger they may lose their capacity to sustain collective, public concerns (Crouch, Finegold and Sako, 2001). Private institutions will take over the training of the more advantaged participants and the role of government will be to act as the provider of last resort for disadvantaged participants. If government action is restricted to this group, that will limit its capacity to contribute at the leading edge of an advanced skills policy.

New providers emerged in the 1990s.

In many countries (mainly the Nordic countries), most adult education and training institutions have had deep roots for over fifty years. The 1990s have been a period of relative opening up of the adult education and training market with the emergence of new providers. The Polytechnics (AMK) of Finland are a good example of this new type of provider that offers adults who already have diplomas vocational training at the border between initial and adult education. They are managed on a commercial basis, but receive public subsidies while competing in the market. Their main competitors are the universities, which showed reluctance toward these generously subsidised new providers at the beginning of the 1990s, especially in the initial phase. The case of Häme Polytechnic clearly illustrates the dynamism of this type of institution (Box 7.4).

Box 7.4. **Häme Polytechnic in Finland**

Häme Polytechnic, situated in Hämeenlinna, is an integral part of the regional development fabric. Most of its services are educational, but they also engage in other activities, *e.g.* quality control or production line improvements in local companies. The region does not have a university to compete with it, although Tampere University in the neighbouring region is geographically close by.

Häme Polytechnic has a large number of projects. Their clients are chiefly looking for development of expertise and research and product development. The main areas of expertise are IT, biosciences, the environment, and health and welfare. Project contracts deal with IT and media technology, workplace learning, and environmental projects such as Santa's road with the National Tourism Network.

Of the 6 000 students at Häme, 2 633 are under 25. The average student in the over-25 age group has about eight years of work experience. The majority of students are doing an initial degree combined with work, and attending evening, week-end, and summer courses. Adult groups have less classroom hours and more individual tuition than junior students do, and some of the classes are mixed. Course work and projects exploit their experience and the opportunities offered by their workplaces. The standards and exams are the same for all students. The remaining adults attend continuing professional development courses. They are concentrating on upgrading to initial degree level the education of adults who spent two or three years in the former post-secondary institutes. But when this is complete the profile of students will change, and they will compete with universities. Their aim is to concentrate on the level of expert in companies (considering there are three levels of employees – workers, experts and bosses). Many people work with ICT and there is a shortage of these skills in the area. Some participants come to do specific courses in ICT for one year. They also try to anticipate needs and are providing targeted courses in hardware and ICT courses in graphics for artists and people with artistic talent.

Adult student motivation comes from wanting to have a degree in case they decide to change jobs. Formal qualifications are becoming a requirement in many jobs and they would like to have the security of a degree. There is also competition from the better-educated young people, so they want to upgrade their skills.

Source: Meeting with managers, Häme, February 2001.

It must be observed that there are virtually no private for-profit organisations providing training at low educational levels. It is possible that the low demand for private training on the part of these groups makes private provision unprofitable in this segment, and private providers therefore focus on more lucrative training for better-educated groups. In many countries, local associations, non-governmental organisations and other non-profit groups play an important role in the training of adults with low skills, for their community service mission brings them into contact with these groups. In fact, these organisations form a network that can attract people who are outside or on the fringes of the labour market, such as those on welfare, retired persons, mothers, minorities and immigrants. Although their primary objective is to enable these groups to read, write and count, the acquisition of those basic skills is a necessary prerequisite for developing vocational training. In Norway, this is the specific role assigned to the initiatives of trade unions, such as the Reading and Spelling Shop of the Workers' Education Association (AOF) of the Norwegian Trade Union Confederation (LO) (Box 7.5).

No training at low educational levels is provided by for-profit organisations.

7.2. The functioning of the adult education and training market

This section will deal with the functioning of the adult education and training market in the various participating countries. It will examine some mechanisms of

---

Box 7.5.   **The AOF Reading and Spelling Shop in Norway**

Along a main street in Sarpsborg, a small storefront has been turned into a friendly and comfortable place for adults with substantial reading disabilities. The average age of the mostly Norwegian students is 33, and there are three times as many men as women. About one-third are unemployed. The third that are working earn about 80% of the average wage. Some are in a day school supported by social services. The classes are small (five to seven) and based on five modules that take about 102 hours each to complete. Assessments are used at least three times in each module with a variety of instructional methods, including enhancing students' motivation and self-esteem. The Reading and Spelling Shop staff stays on top of the research related to the needs of the labour market and adult learning. They estimate that approximately 15% of the total population have learning disabilities but believe that in the northern part of Norway the number is closer to 25%. They feel that their programme specifically addresses the needs of this group.

The curricula have been adapted from several sources, including primary school materials made appropriate for adults. The Reading and Spelling Shop has now developed a compendium of materials, including instructions for starting a programme, and is planning to sell it to others.

Staff believe that the programme's low dropout rate, which they report is virtually nil, is due to the emphasis on building a strong social network among students and the attention to the individualised needs of each. Their first goal is to help people confront their reading problems and the second is to help people deal with them. An example of success is that about 150 of their "graduates" are on their way to becoming apprentices – about one-third of this group could not read at the sixth-grade level upon entering the programme.

AOF Sarpsborg launched this project with support from the Ministry of Education (KUF). As of 2000 it is "self-financed" in that it no longer receives funds from KUF. It does receive support from social services, the participants cover some costs, and the union and some employers have also contributed. A similar programme launched in Denmark served as the model. AOF is planning to expand the project in at least six other communities in the near future.

Source: Meeting with managers, Sarpsborg, March 2000.

this market's functioning, such as whether it is integrated or fragmented, whether it is supply- or demand-driven, and its degree of transparency.

There is indeed an adult education and training "market".

The existence of a "market" is one of the characteristics of the adult education and training system. On the supply side, training is implemented by firms themselves, trade associations, the public education system and private (profit and non-profit) institutions. On the demand side, training is sought by firms for their employees, by employees themselves, by jobseekers and private individuals. The relations between the main actors are of a contractual nature. Although the training supply needs to be varied to meet all the diverse demands of adult learners, certain ways of organisation of the market through partnerships are more promising for fostering an integrated approach. The challenge is how to balance partnership and some measure of competition, at least in terms of quality, between providers. Government plays a central role in this regard. It should intervene directly as a major provider, but also indirectly by defining standards and conditions for access to training and its organisation.

The current market structure is not sufficiently transparent.

In most countries, the adult education and training market is fragmented and highly segmented, and often dominated by a few large public institutions. The prices on the market largely depend on the possibilities of financing, which are often linked to a certain type of group such as jobseekers, employees or private individuals. The prices of public training are low, while those of private training bodies cover a very broad range but with a higher floor price. These substantial differentials have led many institutions to combine their sources of financing (employers and public funds) so as to be able to propose training at a moderate price sufficient to ensure high quality. Attempts are being made to develop ISO-type approaches that award recognised quality of service labels. For example, in Switzerland, the new federal legislation on vocational training requires training institutions to use quality management systems (Spichiger-Carlsson and Martinovits Wiesendanger, 2001). Within ten years nearly all training institutions will have a quality management system, not because it is required by the Confederation but because of growing pressure to introduce increasingly integrated quality systems. Institutions that fail to do so will compromise their future.

Competition can be a source of resentment.

There is some measure of competition between the various providers. This competition is sometimes a source of resentment, for government-financed private institutions can in principle compete unfairly with unsubsidised private institutions. In most countries, given the decentralisation and privatisation that have occurred over the past three decades, greater numbers of educational institutions tend to compete at the local level to supply the same type of courses. Concern has been expressed about the discrepancies in costs for the same services at different educational establishments and about the lack of transparency for the participants.

More consistent pricing and a measure of transparency are needed.

More consistent pricing and a measure of transparency are prerequisites to a better organisation of the education and training market, so that the quality and price of the services provided by training providers can be evaluated. It would be desirable for the market to be regulated somewhat differently from the current system, in which management is increasingly administered and in which supply and funding providers, rather than demand, play the predominant role. The mechanisms implemented might be based on using tendering procedures for the training of jobseekers, including job placement requirements in training services, emphasising specific learning approaches for the disadvantaged, and providing incentives to ensure that training better meets the expectations of more socially marginal learners.

What is important to note is that in most of the countries under review the adult education and training market has been traditionally supply driven. Today a certain shift towards a more demand-driven market can be observed, coinciding with the emergence of lifelong learning strategies. However, there are often long waiting lists for training courses, which shows that supply does not adequately meet demand. This is particularly the case for adults lacking basic education in Canada or for long-term unemployed adults in Finland.

The market is supply-driven, but is shifting towards the demand side...

This refocusing of public financing towards the demand side and the needs of learners is often recommended to broaden adults' participation in education and training, for existing training institutions may not be able to cover all needs. A government supply policy, by standardising procedures, can have a major impact by involving a large number of adults in training programmes, but cannot easily take into account the variety and differences of the demand for training. Furthermore, when unemployment rises rapidly, the labour market authorities tend to launch large-scale training programmes. These strategies were applied on an emergency basis in Switzerland at the beginning of the 1990s. The major difficulty is to increase the size of training programmes rapidly when adequate infrastructure has not been established. In Denmark, public financing has created an incentive for providers to broaden the type of training offered to meet the needs of demand. However, structural problems (inadequate infrastructure) have led to an over-diversification of supply. The reform of adult education and training (VEU-Reform) introduced in January 2001 sought to re-establish greater coherence and more efficient allocation of resources within the framework of the taximeter system.

... which could well broaden adults' participation in education and training.

This predominance of supply strategies can explain why some groups of learners, in particular adults with low qualifications, lack training opportunities, since their demand does not reach the market and therefore cannot be taken into account. This being the case, the problem is how to find a way of enabling this group to express its needs and to stimulate an appropriate provision of training. This means finding mechanisms that will make it possible to better understand supply and demand for training. One possibility is to move towards greater decentralisation regarding the choices made by the co-investors constituted by firms and employees, such as giving employees more leeway in choosing how they use their training entitlements – in particular in the form of training "vouchers" or "accounts" – and by asking training institutions not only to provide a catalogue of classes but also customised courses. If the services provided by training institutions are to be better adapted to the needs of SMEs, it is important that they be less standardised and be integrated into the plans of SMEs (Guiraudie and Terrenoire, 2000).

The best practices for the most difficult to reach groups must be identified and disseminated. For example, local development associations have long played a key role by proposing original ways of attracting and training disadvantaged adults. Greater attention must be given to the often highly interesting examples provided by the experience of non-governmental associations that use a community-based approach to promote access to training. There is a need to ensure a more balanced interaction between a top-down approach to training – in which government defines organisation and financing procedures – and a bottom-up approach that would enable local actors in the field to provide feedback on the problems they face and the innovative solutions that they have found to try to solve them.

7.3. New directions for guidance, counselling and support services

Guidance, counselling and support services are necessary if access to adult learning is to be broadened.

For adults to continue or to resume learning, they must have ample access to adequate guidance, counselling and support services. These are designed to help them make educational and occupational choices and make them a reality by providing the expertise of counsellors. Problems of child care and of travel to the training site during a busy schedule must also be addressed. Unless these services are made available to all, the right to education and training will remain the privilege of the few.

Adult education and training systems are generally far from simple and are rarely based on standardised courses such as basic literacy or primary- or secondary-level courses. Instead, adults face complex systems that offer a wide range of choices of courses and options. In the case of simple systems, there is a need for well-developed guidance services, but in complex systems, information, guidance and counselling services are even more essential to help adults to find their way among all the possible options. The ideal solution would be to have a widespread guidance and counselling network. For example, the Province of Saskatchewan has an extensive network with 20 Career and Employment Centres (Box 7.6).

These services are generally underdeveloped in relation to needs.

The thematic review on adult learning has observed that information, guidance and counselling services for adults are generally underdeveloped in relation to needs. The adults most in need of these services may be reluctant to use them, except for procedures necessary to maintain their unemployment or welfare benefits. In fact, there is no market or quasi-market for adult guidance services. In a comparative study of Germany, France and the United Kingdom, Rees, Bartlett and Watts (1999) reach the conclusion that there is little sign of a genuine market in which individuals pay the market price for the services sought. Outplacement is an exception, with employers paying a high price to promote the external mobility of their high-level employees. In many countries, government is the main producer of information that can be used for educational and vocational guidance and counselling, and some services remain free of charge, such as access to actual information and contact sessions. There is however a trend, particularly in the United Kingdom, towards charging to cover some of the costs of extensive or customised counselling services, although provision of free in-depth guidance is currently being trialled for those in the hardest-to-help groups. These costs may be jointly financed by stakeholders, individuals, employers or government.

The groups in need of counselling are very diverse.

One of the effects of broadening adult participation in education and training is that guidance and counselling services are faced with an increasingly diverse range of participants. Counsellors must propose

---

Box 7.6. **The Saskatchewan Career and Employment Centres in Canada**

Twenty Centres throughout Saskatchewan provide various kinds of information related to finding or changing jobs and careers. Individuals who come for employment advice are first introduced to computer-based sources of information about career planning, resumé preparation, and interviewing methods; the Centres have information about the courses and programmes operated by the various universities, technical institutes, and regional colleges in the province. They give a series of 3 to 6 hour workshops on topics like methods of looking for work, interview techniques, electronic job searches, and exploring career options. There's a good deal of informal one-on-one advice, and individuals can also talk with employment counsellors; there are special options for those with income support. In these services the philosophy of the Centres are that "we provide advice and guidance", with the client taking the necessary initiative. In addition, Centres create partnerships with community-based organisations including those representing the disabled, immigrants, aboriginal people, and the francophone community; and the Centres post jobs from employers through the public employment agency Saskatchewan Jobs – though there are relatively few of these job postings, and they are probably for low-quality jobs.

The Centres combine provincial and federal funds, with perhaps 25% coming from the federal level. The federal funds are the result of the 1996 federal offer to provinces and territories for the design and delivery of programmes under Labor Market Development Agreements. In this case, however, the province wanted to locate Career and Employment Centres in the regional colleges, which were already providing some counselling and information. As the federal offer to transfer programme and administration funds to all provinces and territories included the commitment that former federal employees become provincial employees, colleges were not chosen as sites.

Source: Meeting with managers, Regina, January 2001.

---

customised pathways to take into account each adult's specific needs and goals. Skill assessments and individual action plans are increasingly used tools. However they are organised, information, guidance and counselling services are often provided in many different frameworks and by a broad range of actors: communities, public and private employment services, social services, tertiary education, schools, private consultants and online services.

Institutions differ vastly in how they operate and in the nature and quality of the services that they provide. For example, it has been observed that there is some difficulty in obtaining updated information and a regular updating of training programmes from training institutions. Furthermore, services are often overly compartmentalised, which prevents certain continuity when an adult's status changes from that of an employee to an unemployed person or vocational trainee. Networking the different high-quality services would help learners enormously.

Networking different high-quality services would ensure continuity for learners.

Creation of a "one-stop shop" where adults can find information and advice on a whole range of questions related to education and employment and social aspects is one possibility. This one-stop shop is often developed online, but the possibility of direct personal contact should be maintained. Face-to-face meetings should not be eliminated, especially for groups that cannot use computers, sometimes because they cannot read.

"One-stop shops" are one answer...

... and other online guidance systems have been developing rapidly.

Online information and guidance systems have been developing rapidly in recent years. Many sites now offer "job search systems" that provide information on jobs and occupations and help with job-related decisions, and sometimes allow access to counsellors and experts, self-evaluation services and links with databases on available training. The United Kingdom's University for Industry/learndirect service is an example of a strategic use of this type of method. Learndirect provides information, advice and basic guidance on learning and careers, as well as related issues such as child care and funding. Information is provided through a free and impartial helpline and the learndirect website. Callers who require more intensive face-to-face guidance will be referred to their local provider of these services. The learndirect website also provides access to learndirect futures, an online careers and diagnostics package.

It is a problem of organisation more than of financing.

According to adult education and training experts and practitioners, the lack of adult participation in learning is largely due to problems in the organisation of training. Given the fragmentation and diversity of adult training, there is a need for brokerage services that can act as intermediaries that help individuals to find their way within a system that has become increasingly complex over time. The goal is to place those seeking training at the centre of a locally based system. It is only by building this local base in co-operation with all local partners that vocational training can be made less complex and accessible to everyone, and that each individual will be empowered to determine his/her own training.

Partnerships are particularly necessary here.

Partnerships at the local level for information, counselling and guidance services are particularly necessary to provide services adapted to the adults most in need of further education, to encourage more of them to take advantage of training possibilities and thereby raise local skill levels. England has resolutely opted for this partnership approach to information, advice and guidance (IAG) at the local level (Box 7.7).

There is an outreach problem to solve.

Even when training supply attempts to meet the learners' demand, these policies can only meet explicit demands and are not able to reach the would-be learner who is invisible because he or she does not show up or is not motivated. It is not enough to distribute brochures, for according to service providers, information circulates by word of mouth and many adults who genuinely need training do not come forward. This is particularly a problem for disadvantaged adults. Consequently, there is an outreach problem to solve. Even in the Nordic countries, which have a long tradition of adult education, it is recognised that some adults remain marginal to the learning process and new ways of motivating them must be found. This group can also include adults living in outlying rural areas and older adults. Often this requires using tools that are not directly related to the learning process and involving other actors than those working in education. The objective is to encourage and enable adults with low motivation to participate in the process of upgrading their skills through an integrated approach that takes into account all the economic and material factors that affect access to training (transport, work schedules, child care, grants, and especially the realisation that higher skills lead to higher wages).

Box 7.7. **Advice and guidance services for adult learners in the United Kingdom (England)**

Information, Advice and Guidance (IAG) partnerships are set up specifically for adults at the local level under the co-ordination and supervision of local Learning and Skills Councils (LSCs). The partner institutions include Employment Service, public and private employment and career management agencies, further education institutions, trade unions, employers, associations, non-governmental organisations (NGOs) and higher education career management services. This partnership will make it possible in the future to move towards a systemic approach to advice and guidance for adult learners.

For example, the Kent and Medway IAG partnership includes a large number of associations and NGOs with experience in assisting and counselling disadvantaged categories of adults (people on welfare, ethnic minorities, refugees, gypsies, etc.). These adults are particularly difficult to reach and do not come forward on their own. The outreach and support work is carried out by community learning advisors who help disadvantaged adults in a number of ways: establishing personal contacts; helping to overcome various barriers to participation in learning (transport and child care problems, costs, lack of confidence); contacting other local associations so that needs can be met locally; acting as a go-between between learners and training institutions; setting up tutoring; continuing to advise and encourage individuals throughout the learning period and helping them to progress through each stage of the system (first steps and courses on a trial basis in local associations, followed by enrolment in more general training programmes).

Information and advice services are provided free of charge, although in-depth guidance services may be on a fee-paying basis. The Department for Education and Skills (DfES) is financing pilot projects to assess the effectiveness of an in-depth guidance service provided free of charge to disadvantaged groups. DfES has also established the National Information Advice and Guidance Board to supervise the co-ordination of advice and guidance services provided by its varioUS departments.

Although there are separate institutions for adults and young people, greater attention is being given to co-ordinating the work of the IAG partnerships and the Connexions partnerships for young people between the ages of 13 and 19, particularly within LSCs.

Working in partnership requires meeting a specific quality standard (matrix quality standard for Information, Advice and Guidance services) which has been developed by the DfES and is accredited by the Guidance Accreditation Board.

The Department for Work and Pensions manages the Jobcentre Plus agencies that provide a growing range of support and advice services aimed at assisting the unemployed and adult jobseekers to find jobs, in particular through the Worktrain programme and the nationwide ICT databank.

The main problems faced in the services provided to adults are:

- Recruiting, selecting and retaining competent and qualified guidance and orientation staff.
- Co-ordinating services for adults and young people.
- Finding resources for the development of individualised services, such as skills diagnoses and assessments that make it possible to better identify clients' competencies.
- Providing more viable long-term services for adults and that are less dependent on short-term financing.

Source: NICEC/CRAC (2001); NICEC Briefing (2000, 2001).

More effective work in the field may be necessary, including a more active effort to reach out to adults in the workplace, associations, churches, trade unions and in other public or community-based institutions, and to provide them with more personal contact in sifting through alternatives and potential learning pathways. Community-based organisations are well suited to pursue outreach to these groups by making available information and guidance and providing transitional programmes (*e.g.* reading and writing

Community-based organisations are well suited to pursue outreach.

courses) and support (such as tutoring). The Reading and Spelling Shop run by the Workers' Education Association (AOF) in Norway is a good example in this regard (Box 7.5). Mention should be made of the extensive network of support, guidance and information centres that has been established in Portugal [Saber Mas (Learn More) Centres], which are themselves located in cultural and educational centres and institutions. As is well known, the difficulty of training adults who have previously failed in school and are convinced of their own incompetence stems not only from the problem of selecting a suitable learning programme, but also from the fact that it is necessary to persuade them that they can successfully participate in such a programme. Consequently, the Saber Mas Centres will be able to act as facilitators that can inform and encourage these adults and refer them to assessment centres, which will in turn help place them in the education and training system.

The implementation of an enabling strategy for adult learning also requires that current providers offer the collateral support services to reduce barriers to participation such as transport and child care services. In general, adults with family responsibilities are confronted with fewer difficulties in participating in learning in countries where there are public measures and family-friendly arrangements by firms encouraging a higher participation by parents in paid employment (OECD, 2001). The lack of support services was often quoted as a barrier to participating in learning in Switzerland and Portugal. Family responsibilities widen the gap between men and women, but also between women according to their skill level; women office and manual workers, unlike women in management or in intermediate professions, find it more difficult to organise their personal life so that they can take training courses. For normal career development, it is now assumed that workers between the ages of 25 and 40 will be available to continue to learn and to improve their job skills. The polarisation of continuing training during a period of life when family responsibilities are particularly heavy penalises women with the lowest skills. To reduce inequalities of access, continuing training must be viewed in the perspective of all time commitments, *i.e.* actual time worked, travel time, time at home and free time.

7.4. Key aspects for promoting better integration

- Firms are very actively involved in the adult training process and training institutions have an important role to play in accumulating training expertise by comparing experiences in the different sectors and types of firms in which they work so as to better meet expectations.

- Public institutions must be more than the providers of last resort for disadvantaged adults, and must play a leading role in an advanced skills policy.

- It would be desirable for the market to be regulated somewhat differently from the current system in which management is increasingly administered and in which supply and funding providers, rather than demand, play the predominant role.

- A refocusing of public financing towards the demand side and the needs of learners is necessary to broaden adults' participation in education and training, for existing training institutions may not be able to cover all needs.

- The best practices for the most difficult to reach groups must be identified and disseminated – in particular those of local development associations, which have long played a key role by proposing original ways of attracting and training disadvantaged adults.

- There is a need to ensure a more balanced interaction between a top-down approach to training – in which government defines organisation and financing procedures – and a bottom-up approach that would enable local actors in the field to provide feedback on the problems they face and the innovative solutions that they have found to try to solve them.

- Adult education and training systems are complex, and information, guidance and counselling services are necessary. Networking these services would make it possible to ensure continuity for learners. The creation of "one-stop shops" where adults can find information and advice on a broad range of social, education and employment issues is a step in the right direction.

- Unless access to support, information and guidance is ensured for all, the right to education and training will remain the privilege of the few.

- There must be a strong policy to implement a transparent and efficient organisation of information and guidance services at the national, regional and local levels.

- One of the effects of broadening adult participation in education and training is that guidance and counselling services are faced with an increasingly diverse range of participants. Counsellors must therefore propose customised pathways to take into account each adult's specific needs and goals.

- It is necessary to place those seeking training at the centre of a locally based system. It is only by building this local base in co-operation with all local partners that vocational training can be made less complex and accessible to everyone, and that each individual will be empowered to determine his/her own training.

- Partnerships at the local level for information, counselling and guidance services are particularly necessary to provide services adapted to the adults most in need of further education, to encourage more of them to take advantage of training possibilities and thereby raise local skill levels.

- The polarisation of continuing training during a period of life when family responsibilities are particularly heavy penalises women with the lowest skills. To reduce inequalities of access, continuing training must be viewed in the perspective of all time commitments, *i.e.* actual time worked, travel time, time at home and free time.

- Guidance and advice services are necessary to reach those with little motivation to learn. This often requires using tools that are not directly related to the learning process and involving other actors than those working in education. The objective is to encourage and enable adults with low motivation to participate in the process of upgrading their skills through an integrated approach that takes into account all the economic and material factors that affect access to training (transport, work schedules, child care, grants, and especially the realisation that higher skills lead to higher wages).

213

BIBLIOGRAPHY

CONFÉRENCE SUISSE DES DIRECTEURS CANTONAUX DE L'INSTRUCTION PUBLIQUE (CDIP) (1999),
"La formation des adultes dans les cantons", Dossier 56b, Bern.

CROUCH, C., D. FINEGOLD and M. SAKO (2001),
Are Skills the Anwer? The Political Economy of Skill Creation in Advanced Industrial Countries, first published in 1999,
Oxford University Press.

DORAY, P. (2000),
"Enjeux de la professionalisation de la formation continue au Québec : le cas de la formation sur mesure", in
V. Vandenberghe (ed.), *La formation professionnelle continue. Transformations, contraintes et enjeux*, Bruylant-Academia,
Louvain-la-Neuve.

GUIRAUDIE, I. and J. TERRENOIRE (2000),
"L'avenir des emplois peu qualifiés : que peut la formation ?", *Cahiers du Groupe Bernard Bruhnes*, No. 5, June.

NICEC/CRAC (NATIONAL INSTITUTE FOR CAREERS EDUCATION AND COUNSELLING/CARREERS RESEARCH AND
ADVISORY CENTRE) (2001),
"Home Internationals 2: Lifelong Guidance for Economic and Social Success: Report on a policy consultation",
12-13 June, Belfast.

NICEC (2000),
"Growing Guidance in the Community", NICEC Briefing, September, Cambridge.

NICEC (2001),
"Guidance for Adults: Harnessing Partnership Potential", NICEC Briefing, June, Cambridge.

OECD (2001),
Employment Outlook, Paris.

REES, T., W. BARTLETT and A.G. WATTS (1999),
"The Marketisation of Guidance Services in Germany, France and Britain", *Journal of Education and Work*, Vol. 12,
No. 1, pp. 5-21.

SPICHIGER-CARLSSON, P. and A. MARTINOVITS WIESENDANGER (2001),
"La certification ISO des instituts de formation : évaluation des processus de certification liés aux systèmes de
gestion de la qualité", *La Vie économique*, No. 11, pp. 65-70.

Chapter 8

DESIRABLE FEATURES OF ADULT LEARNING SYSTEMS

8.1. The increasing policy-relevance of adult learning

Over the past decade or so, the issue of adult learning has attracted considerable interest among policy makers and society at large. Of course, the issue is not new. Many OECD countries have long traditions of formal structures for adult learning. For example, in Scandinavian countries the folk high school has been an established institution for 150 years. In the United Kingdom, workers' education associations developed in the 19th century. In Canada, agricultural extension programmes started at the end of the 19th century. In Switzerland, Migros "club schools" sprang from the current of social idealism of the 1920s. In some cases the state has assumed responsibility for both organising and funding such services. In other cases they have been organised by non-government associations with individuals meeting at least part of the costs of tuition. Adult learning services such as these have often been propounded on two grounds: to provide a means for individual, cultural and social improvement; and to address inequities in access to initial education.

Personal development, cultural development and equity are traditionally used to argue for a public role in adult learning.

These arguments continue to be used to support adult learning as a focus of public policy, and they have helped to develop much of the culture and traditions of the adult education movement in many OECD countries. The Adult Education Initiative in Sweden is a good example of public support to provide upper secondary education to adults who lacked basic educational attainment. Alongside these traditions, public intervention in adult learning has also been propounded on the basis of a need to address labour market problems. The need to adapt workers' skills and competencies to changing labour market requirements and to meet specific skill shortages has led to training programmes for adults becoming an important component of employment policies in many OECD countries. The adult vocational training system (AMU system) in Denmark is a good example of a public provider meeting these challenges. In some countries, public policy has attempted to stimulate the amount of training provided by and within enterprises because the enterprise is the most common learning venue. In addition, training programmes have focused upon developing the skills and the long-term employability of the unemployed as a key component of active labour market policies (ALMPs). The vocational training programme for the unemployed organised by the National Employment Institute in Spain is an example of these ALMPs.

Changing labour market requirements and the need to respond to unemployment and to the challenges of the knowledge-based society are major new justifications.

Moreover, recent studies have found a strong link between investment in human capital (of which adult learning is a part) and economic growth. Altogether, the emerging reconsideration of the place of adult learning in public policy, of which this thematic review is a sign, has come from a number of sources:

A reconsideration of adult learning policy is being driven by a number of forces.

215

- A growing body of evidence helps to highlight the role that the overall education level of the inhabitants of a country plays in economic growth (OECD, 2000; OECD, 2001a; OECD, 2001b).

- Many OECD governments have become aware that they must find ways to maintain labour market dynamism and flexibility in the face of ageing populations, and that addressing the adult skills base is one key to this. Indeed, training throughout the entire working life may help workers stay longer in the labour market.

- As OECD economies increasingly become knowledge-based, individuals' capacity for continual renewal of their knowledge and qualifications, in the face of constant technological innovation and structural changes, becomes one key to national economic growth and competitiveness.

- There now seems to be a clear agreement among OECD policy makers that a lack of basic skills of the sort revealed by the International Adult Literacy Survey (OECD and Statistics Canada, 2000) may impinge on the well-being of the population and the issues related to democracy and citizenship. This view emerged clearly in the national consultations undertaken during the thematic review.

8.2. The challenges ahead: improving equity and efficiency in provision

Yet, participation remains uneven...

Though the importance of the issue is increasingly acknowledged, the fact is that participation in adult learning remains markedly unequal across groups. Those with higher levels of initial educational attainment benefit the most from further education and training. Those who work in large firms or the service sector and have a white-collar, high-skilled occupation are more likely to be involved in learning activities. Younger adults and those living in an urban area are more likely to enter learning programmes.

... delivery is highly fragmented, and multiple actors are involved.

In most of the countries that have taken part in the thematic review, adult learning is provided by many different suppliers. Moreover, the adoption of lifelong learning policies has resulted in the emergence of new providers, shifting towards a more demand-driven market. There is a tendency for private providers to take over the training of high-skilled adults and for community-based providers to deal with leisure and recreational programmes, leaving government to act as a provider of adult basic education and training for disadvantaged groups. There are exceptions. In Sweden, for example, adult education is provided free of charge to individuals who want to undertake any type of learning activity, from basic adult education to advanced education and training.

As a result, programme visibility is poor and there are few evaluation studies of what works and does not in adult learning policies.

Such highly segmented provision results in poor visibility: for learners, for employers and for other customers. Associated with poor visibility, delivery of adult learning is often notable for the absence of appropriate support services such as day care, advice and guidance. A related problem is the fact that the knowledge base for adult learning systems is not always sufficient to support policy development and programme implementation. Data on key issues such as participation, financing and outcomes are weak. More generally, there are few evaluation studies on what works and what does not in adult learning policies. Most available evaluations are dogmatic, rather than outcome-based. Evaluation should be based on a wider variety of approaches and measurement of results, including a closer examination of the programmes' initial objectives and results achieved. Finally, evaluation should be conducted over a longer period of time, so as to assess the total economic and social impact of training courses, and should be systematically embedded in policy design.

In short, governments are faced with three challenges:

- Improving learning opportunities for all adults, including through rectifying past educational deficiencies and making full use of the capacities of adults.

- Raising the efficiency and quality of adult learning provision, public and private, including through appropriate financial mechanisms.

- Ensuring better coherence in the mechanisms for knowledge renewal and higher efficiency in the delivery of learning.

8.3. Addressing the challenges: key features of an integrated approach to adult learning policies

In the face of these challenges, this review offers a comprehensive policy strategy that addresses a number of issues: government policies and approaches to the provision of adult learning; the individual's incentive to engage in adult learning; financial and other arrangements that may encourage firms to invest in the human capital of their workers; pedagogical issues and issues of quality control in the delivery of training courses and effective evaluation of outcomes.

A coherent adult learning strategy is therefore needed.

Making adult learning more attractive to adults, including the low-skilled

One of the most interesting findings of this review is that a majority of low-skilled individuals lack the motivation to engage in adult learning programmes. As shown in Chapter 5, almost half of the people with low skills (literacy Level I) believe that their skills are good or excellent, and a similar proportion of people with low skills (literacy Levels I and 2) do not believe their skills are limiting to their work. If adults are to return to learning, therefore, it is important that learning be made valuable and attractive to them.

First, motivation issues have to be addressed.

An examination of good practices carried out for the purposes of this review shows that the way training courses are organised can help improve individuals' motivation:

This means that learning should be made more accessible, e.g. by organising modular courses,...

- This can be done by providing courses that meet a wide range of adults' learning needs: basic and remedial education; upper secondary qualifications or their equivalent; specific vocational preparation in skill upgrading; leisure and recreational courses; and courses that lead to formal qualifications as well as those that do not.

- One of the key elements of an attractive adult learning system is the use of a pedagogy suited to adults rather than to the young. Contextualising learning to make it relevant to adults' experience and using project-based methods are among the ways in which this can be done. The craft school workshops, trade schools and employment workshops in Spain are a good example of integration of training, experience and information, together with techniques for employment and self-employment searches for people who are unemployed.

- Another way of making learning attractive is by allowing adults to study at their own pace. As highlighted in Chapter 6, one of the most promising ways is the creation of a modular system (as has been done in countries like Denmark, and Switzerland, and initiated in Portugal). A modular system is an interesting way of bringing flexibility and transparency to adult learning, provided that the modules are built as parts of a coherent system and not seen as a justification for a piecemeal system.

- ICT and distance education can be part of national policies to ensure wider access. However, they should not be seen as universal solutions, for a number of reasons. Many adults lack the skills needed to handle the necessary software and hardware; ICT can be difficult to access and expensive to purchase; and access via the Internet can be costly. Where distance education is built into access policies, a face-to-face component is still often important for adults.

- Good information, advice and guidance, suited to the individual needs of adults, are among the key factors that make learning more accessible. National policies can improve the information and advice available to adults by funding national education information call centres; funding community groups to develop guidance services; funding educational institutions to develop information and advisory services; developing high-quality career information products that can be accessed both in print and electronically; and ensuring that public employment staff are trained and qualified to advise adults on education and training for career development.

- Outreach policies to provide information to the general public can help to widen access. Publicising adult learning activities and the benefits of following them through campaigns in the mass media – as in the example of Adult Learners' Week (initiated in the United Kingdom in 1992 and replicated in almost all reviewed countries) – is a way of reaching adults who otherwise might not consider formal learning. Learnfestival in Switzerland is another example of efforts to promote access and participation of adults in learning. Outreach is also important to reach those with little motivation to learn. Good practices in this area can focus on outreach through the web of public social services or through children's schools to parents.

... that a well-functioning system of recognition and certification of learning has to be established...

Recognition of prior learning is also a key to making learning more attractive for adults, and one of the key policy initiatives that governments can take as part of an integrated approach to adult learning. Low-skilled employees are often put off by traditional theoretical educational methods. Recognition of skills as they are put to use can create a process that will facilitate subsequent access to certificates by avoiding the discouraging effect of a "ladder" that is already too high. Portugal is in the process of implementing 84 centres of recognition, validation and certification of competencies (CRVCC), covering the whole country. In British Columbia, Canada, there are guidelines that cover prior learning recognition of both the K-12 system and of adult education and the Centre for Curriculum Transfer and Technology carries out training modules, enhancement projects, publications and conferences about best practices, and other activities intended to promote PLAR. Assessing and giving credit for knowledge and skills acquired in work, home or community settings are two of the main ways to attract adults by making sure they do not waste time learning again what they already know.

Certification of the skills and competencies acquired through learning is another important way in which it can be made attractive. This can be done in the form of an official and recognised document given to all learners who have complied with the requirements of a course. Certification will generally be more valuable if it is recognised by the labour market.

The physical design of institutions matters too. This means that, to be effective, programmes need to take into account day care facilities, parking, canteens that serve meals after normal working hours, and accommodation assistance where relevant. In particular, in most of the countries participating in the thematic review, the distance to the next adult learning centre is an issue. Locating learning institutions in an equitable way across geographic regions seems an appropriate way of solving some of the access problem. Providing an adequate public transport service is also a concern in some areas.

Finally, scheduling learning so that it suits adults' circumstances is a key issue in all countries participating in the thematic review. Policies targeting wider adult access need to ensure that institutions and learning centres are open when adults are able to participate – not only within normal working hours but also on evenings, weekends, and during summer holiday periods for example – and secure the arrangements with teachers that this entails.

... and that appropriate learning facilities have to be created.

Enhancing the financial incentives to invest in the human capital of adults

The financing of the adult learning systems is a key but complex issue. As Chapter 4 shows, adult learning is funded by both public and private sources in all the countries under review. And indeed it seems agreed that responsibility for financing should be shared among all partners. Governments can provide the right incentives to create a conducive environment for adults to participate. Enterprises should be involved too, through the provision of on-the-job or other training activities and, according to the context, with co-operative financing mechanisms. In some cases, making individuals participate in the financing, if they can afford it, can also be applicable as a return on the benefits that they receive from participation. Sweden's stand on this is different, as they believe adult learning, like mandatory education, is a public good that should be provided by the state, and so study support should be given to those who need it.

Second, shared financing is important.

There is also a need for governments to provide equitable access to learning opportunities and to cater to the needs of the disadvantaged. Indeed, when considering financing systems and incentives structures, it is essential to take into account one major challenge: the limited learning opportunities available to unskilled workers and other groups at risk. For instance, some countries are considering the possibility of providing greater government support to those groups and correspondingly lower direct public support to skilled workers.

Financial arrangements should take into account learning needs of vulnerable groups...

... so that both individuals and firms have an incentive to invest in human capital.

In general, it is acknowledged that financing arrangements should improve incentives to participate in learning programmes (in particular for low-educated workers) while at the same time remaining affordable. There are several possible policy avenues to achieve this: giving entitlements to learning leave during working hours; study leave (as recently introduced in Norway); or finance for study in the form of loans, grants or tax incentives. Alternation leave in Finland has a twofold purpose: employees can have leave from work and unemployed job seekers can obtain work experience. New financing mechanisms such as learning credits, subsidised tuition fees, individual learning accounts and low-interest loans are policy initiatives that can address affordability.

But financing arrangements have to be consistent with those of the broader set of education and labour market institutions. In particular, working time practices have to allow for learning leave. And wage-setting mechanisms should be such that certified learning leads to higher pay. This is also one reason why the role of social partners is so important when discussing adult learning policies.

Financial incentives can also be increased by allowing training to be treated as an investment for taxation purposes rather than an expenditure (as in Norway, where there is tax exemption for employer financed education); by establishing enterprise training levies (as in the Canadian province of Quebec, the Swiss canton of Geneva, or Spain); or by setting up a national or sectoral training fund.

Improving the quality of learning programmes

Third, a number of steps can be taken to improve quality control.

This volume stresses the importance of mechanisms that improve the quality of learning programmes. Improvement can be achieved, for example, through better monitoring and evaluation; through improving statistical systems; through better accreditation systems; through better performance evaluation at the institution level; and through better monitoring of student outcomes and graduate destinations. The programmes *EduQua* in Switzerland and QUALFOR in Portugal are interesting examples of how closer monitoring forms part of the quality assurance system. Many countries have also created institutes in charge of evaluating the quality of education and training, devoted exclusively to adult learning (such as VOX in Norway) or more broadly to all kinds of learning (such as the National Board of Education in Finland and EVA in Denmark).

Setting standards for service delivery and publicly certifying the achievement of these standards constitute another approach to quality improvement that can be incorporated in an integrated policy. The Investors in People (IiP) programme in the United Kingdom is an example.

Learning can be made attractive to adults by making sure that the curriculum is relevant and useful to their needs. This could be achieved, for example, by regularly monitoring students' views on their courses and by updating the curriculum accordingly. Such assessments should not be carried out only after a course but throughout the entire learning activity, so that timely feedback can be given to curriculum designers.

Adopting a holistic approach to adult learning

Forth, an integrated policy framework is needed.

The above policies provide a rationale for a holistic adult learning policy. Such a holistic rationale places adult learning policies at the centre of national labour market policies, not just as one part of policies to deal with unemployment or a tool for addressing short-term and limited skill shortages. It includes a strong preventive element, by enhancing workers' employability and thus reducing the risk of long-term unemployment – which often entails more expensive interventions *vis-à-vis* the preventive approach. It also makes adult learning, alongside initial education and training, a tool for achieving national goals of economic development and social cohesion. This explains the recent emphasis on national policies for adult learning that has been observed in the countries participating in the thematic review.[1] Indeed, countries are grappling with ways to develop comprehensive and integrated policy frameworks for adult learning.

In contrast to the fragmented approach that can be observed in many countries, a holistic approach – encompassing both formal and informal learning as well as general education, vocational education and enterprise training – requires co-ordination:

This means better policy co-ordination within government and between social partners…

- This needs to occur within government, as well as between government and a wide range of non-government actors such as employers, trade unions, private and public educational institutions, and community groups. Examples of specific institutions to help co-ordinate adult learning policies include ANEFA in Portugal and the Learning and Skills Council in the United Kingdom.

- A co-ordinated approach involves the need to ensure balanced interaction between a top-down approach – in which governments define structures and financing procedures – and a bottom-up approach that enables local actors to provide feedback on the problems they face and the innovative solutions that they have found to try to solve them. Monitoring the implementation process of reforms is also essential.

- A holistic approach can also be considered through a comprehensive approach to national qualification systems, as in Finland and the United Kingdom and work in this direction in Spain.

- Partnerships can also contribute to a holistic approach, and have appeared in a number of countries as a means of co-operation and co-ordination. Examples are those developed in Canada and in the Autonomous Community of La Rioja in Spain. Partnerships allow potential learners to be reached and use regional synergies in terms of funding, physical space and the optimisation of public and private resources.

- Policy processes that co-ordinate well across the sectors and among the many actors involved, that incorporate rational funding mechanisms, and that build monitoring and evaluation into policy development all make systems more effective. These are the aims of the recent adult education and training reform (VEU-Reform) in Denmark.

- In the face of present gaps in the knowledge base, providing better support of policy choices requires research and analysis.

---

1. Examples include: Canada's Skills and Learning Agenda; Denmark's Adult Education Reform; Finland's Joy of Learning report; Norway's Competence Reform; Portugal's Strategy for the development of adult education and the agreement on employment, labour and education and training policy between the government and the social partners; Spain's National Vocational Training Programme; Sweden's Adult Learning Initiative; Switzerland's Law on Vocational Training; and the United Kingdom's New Skills and Learning Act.

... as well as greater coherence between individuals' and firms' incentives to invest in human capital...

Such integrated policy frameworks also need to place the individual and the enterprise at the centre – in shaping incentives to participate; in funding mechanisms; in the design of adult learning programmes; and in determining outcomes. They need to make explicit the relative responsibilities of individuals, enterprises and governments within an overall framework. As in initial education, they need to balance goals of economic development with equity goals and social and personal development. They need to recognise the reality that many adults in OECD countries have at best completed lower secondary education; they often have low levels of basic skills; and many have been away from formal learning for some years.

... and stronger complementarities between market signals and public provision.

The efficiency of adult learning systems will be improved by strengthening the market signals that can allow supply and demand to match one another, *e.g.*: by decentralising to the local or regional levels decisions on which course to allocate resources to; by providing funds to individuals rather than to institutions; by improving occupational and educational information systems; by involving enterprises in the governance of education and training institutions; and by stimulating local partnerships that can initiate programmes and assist in their management.

A balance between efficiency and equity must be found.

Finally, efforts must be made to strike a reasonable balance between efficiency and equity. Public institutions must be more than the providers of last resort for disadvantaged adults; they must play a leading role in an advanced skill policy. A refocusing of public financing towards the demand side and the needs of learners is necessary to broaden adults' participation in education and training, since existing training institutions may not be able to cover all needs.

8.4. In conclusion

Governments have many tools to stimulate adult learning markets and to make them more effective.

The thematic review has revealed both the existence of an active market for adult learning in many countries, and the range of interventions that are open to governments in order to stimulate that market, to make it more effective, and to address market failure.

Machinery for the recognition of adult learning is normally in the hands of government, and there is much that governments can do centrally – through stimulating better certification systems, through encouraging the recognition of prior learning, and through introducing credit transfer mechanisms – to improve adult learning policies. The involvement of social partners is crucial in this process. Governments must be involved in some of the key decisions having to do with quality assurance through establishing systems for the accreditation of both public and private learning providers.

Recognition systems and incentive policies are among them.

Another key role for the government lies in its capacity to influence the incentive system for all actors involved in adult learning: the learners, the employers, and educational institutions in particular. This can be done through tax incentives or by an appropriate loans and grants system. Government can also stimulate demand for learning activities by encouraging the creation or extension of a right to study leave. More flexibility in work schedules helps to reconcile learning with the other obligations adults have.

Governments have to take the lead in addressing market failures. This includes addressing deficiencies in adults' basic skills, especially among people living in deprived areas or at risk of being socially excluded, and preventing the risk of firms investing too little or too unevenly in training, especially among low-skilled workers, older workers and workers in SMEs. With such deficiencies addressed, there is strong evidence that policies to support adult learning activities that are embedded in the community are successful, as is less formal learning provided on the job. Governments can play a role through the provision of information, through shifting resources, through helping to create a conducive environment to support such initiatives, and through better recognition and validation of less formal learning. Best practices of training for disadvantaged groups must be identified and disseminated; best practices would in particular include those of local development associations, which have long played a key role by proposing innovative approaches for the groups in question. Governments' influence over national legislation and public resourcing policies is perhaps the most important way it can express clear commitment to supporting integrated policies for adult learning.

Governments should intervene to address market failures.

BIBLIOGRAPHY

OECD (2000),
> OECD *Economic Outlook*, No. 68, Paris.

OECD (2001a),
> *The Well-being of Nations. The Role of Human and Social Capital*, Paris.

OECD (2001b),
> *The New Economy: Beyond the Hype*, Paris.

OECD and STATISTICS CANADA (2000),
> *Literacy in the Information Age. Final Report of the International Adult Literacy Survey*, Paris and Ottawa.

Annex 1

COMPARABLE SOURCES OF DATA ON ADULT LEARNING

There is a broad array of data sources rich in information on adult education and training. It is true that there are comparability limitations across countries – and thus to providing a homogeneous picture. Nonetheless, the data used in this publication offer a basis for comparing, contrasting, and conveying the different realities across the participating OECD Member countries. This annex provides an overview of the sources available, and explains the main areas of comparability difficulty.

It is important to note that there are a number of efforts under way to provide harmonised information on education and training statistics. At the OECD, the working party on employment and unemployment statistics already furnished an overview of the data variations and set up a framework for harmonisation of training statistics (OECD, 1998). The INES network launched a project to develop an International Continuing Education and Training Module (OECD-Module) in April 2001, and to try to achieve comparable data across OECD countries on adult learning and training statistics.

1. Available data sources

- TRAL: Thematic Review on Adult Learning country data request. Data requested specifically from countries participating in this activity. Countries responded to a common questionnaire, but sources vary according to country and are not homogeneous. Results are presented whenever comparison permits.

- IALS: The International Adult Literacy Survey, co-ordinated by the OECD and Statistics Canada, collected data on the basis of a common questionnaire for 20 participating countries or regions of the world at different periods from 1994 to 1998. These countries are Australia, Belgium, Canada, Germany, Ireland, the Netherlands, New Zealand, Poland, Sweden, Switzerland (German-speaking), the United Kingdom and the United States for the first cycle, and Chile, the Czech Republic, Denmark, Finland, Hungary, Norway, Portugal and Slovenia for the second cycle. The survey measured adult literacy levels in prose, documentation and quantitative skills. It had a special module on adult education and training. The question asked was: "During the past 12 months, *that is 19xx*, did you receive any training or education including courses, workshops, on-the-job training, apprenticeship training, arts, crafts, recreations courses or any other training or education?" Adults in their initial formal education processes have not been counted. Results of the IALS can be found in OECD and Statistics Canada (2000).

- ELFS: The European Labour Force Survey (EUROSTAT) is a household survey based on national labour force surveys. EUROSTAT has mapped European national LFS data items into a common file structure but there are some differences in the way the questions are asked. Questions refer to all education and training, whether or not relevant to the respondent's current or possible job. They comprise initial education, further education, continuing or further training, or training within the company, and can also include courses followed for general interest. The data provided in the ELFS refer to participation in education and training during the four weeks prior to the survey, except for Switzerland which has a one-year training period (EUROSTAT, 2000). Data for Portugal and Sweden refer to current participation in education and training activities.

- ESWC: The Third European Survey on Working Conditions (European Foundation for the Improvement of Living and Working Conditions, Dublin), based on the total active population, was carried out simultaneously in each of the 15 member states of the European Union in March 2000. It contains information on work organisation and working conditions. Regarding adult education and training, this survey contains information about employer-sponsored training (self-financed if the worker is self-employed) taken over the 12 months prior to the survey. The question asked to individuals from the age of 15 upward was: "Over the 12 months, have you undergone training paid for or provided by your employer or yourself if you are self-employed, to improve your skills or not? If YES, how many days?"

- CVTS: The Continuing Vocational Training Survey, on continuing vocational training in enterprises, is carried out on the EU level in a co-ordinated manner (outline questionnaire, common definitions, common recommendations with respect to the fieldwork). Launched by the European Commission in 1994 (12 member states) and in 2000/2001 (all EU member states and nine candidate countries), it is an employer survey of enterprises with more than 10 employees. Its reference period is 12 months.

2. Overview of differences

The differences across surveys make comparing data challenging. A comparison of existing adult learning statistics and of national survey questionnaires confirms that, despite existing harmonisation efforts and progress in data collection and conceptual and analytic work, important discrepancies across countries remain. The main areas where there are difficulties for comparability are: *a*) the reference period, *b*) the population coverage, and *c*) the coverage of the types of learning.

The differences appear not only at policy and administrative level – depending on the concept of adult learning adopted – but also statistically, depending on the questions asked in surveys; these might vary significantly from the country concept. There are two main challenges: *i*) the concept of adult learning might include formal learning, informal learning, or learning related to employment, and *ii*) the reference period for training can vary from one week to the past four weeks to the past six months to last year, etc.:

- *Reference period*. Some surveys use a 12-month reference period (IALS, Canada's Adult Education and Training Survey, Finland's Adult Education and Training Survey, Switzerland's Education and Training Supplement), while others, such as the ELFS and national labour force surveys, are based on 4-week reference periods.

- *Population coverage*. A specific problem concerning the population covered is whether surveys include adults who are in their initial formal education processes or not. This can change results, especially for those between 25 and 30 years old who are in the initial education system but who can be included in training surveys as adult learners. The TRAL questionnaire asked for data on those who were outside of the initial education system and had returned to education afterwards so as to cover adult learners appropriately. Furthermore, some surveys may cover only enterprise-based training, while others cover individuals.

- *Types of learning covered*. Different types of training might be surveyed, such as on-the-job training, employment-related training, personal interest learning, or informal or formal learning activities. Furthermore, there is the difficulty of people recognising the differences between learning for personal reasons and for professional reasons. For example, people might undertake language learning for leisure but use it professionally at a different period in their careers.

BIBLIOGRAPHY

EUROPEAN FOUNDATION FOR THE IMPROVEMENT OF LIVING AND WORKING CONDITIONS (2000),
Third European Survey on Working Conditions, Dublin.

EUROSTAT (2000),
European Labour Force Survey, Brussels.

EUROSTAT (2001),
New Chronos Database, CVTS2, Brussels.

OECD (1998),
"Harmonisation of training statistics" (*www.oecd.org/edu/adultlearning*).

OECD and STATISTICS CANADA (2000),
Literacy in the Information Age, Paris and Ottawa.

DATA FOR FIGURES

Data for Figure 2.1. **Literacy levels in selected countries**

Percentage of population aged 25-64 at each prose literacy level, 1994-98

	Level 1	Level 2	Level 3	Level 4/5
Canada	17.8	26.0	33.1	23.1
Denmark	10.6	36.7	46.8	5.9
Finland	12.1	28.9	39.6	19.4
Norway	9.4	26.4	48.6	15.6
Portugal	55.1	26.5	15.6	2.8
Sweden	8.5	21.5	39.6	30.5
Switzerland	21.0	35.4	35.4	8.2
United Kingdom	22.6	30.4	31.1	15.9

Source: International Adult Literacy Survey (1994-98).

Data for Figure 2.2. **Ageing of the population**

Evolution of the 45-64 year-olds as proportion of total population, 1950-2020

	Canada	Denmark	Finland	Norway	Portugal	Spain	Sweden	Switzerland	United Kingdom
1950	17.9	21.6	18.9	22.0	17.5	18.7	23.2	23.2	23.5
1951	17.8	21.9	19.2	22.2	17.5	19.0	23.4	23.6	23.8
1952	17.6	22.1	19.4	22.3	17.6	19.2	23.6	23.9	24.0
1953	17.5	22.3	19.7	22.5	17.8	19.3	23.9	24.0	24.3
1954	17.4	22.5	19.9	22.7	18.0	19.5	24.1	24.1	24.5
1955	17.3	22.7	20.1	22.9	18.2	19.6	24.4	24.1	24.7
1956	17.3	22.9	20.4	23.1	18.5	19.8	24.7	24.1	25.0
1957	17.3	23.1	20.6	23.3	18.8	19.9	24.9	24.0	25.2
1958	17.3	23.3	20.8	23.5	19.1	20.0	25.2	23.9	25.3
1959	17.3	23.5	21.0	23.6	19.3	20.1	25.4	23.7	25.4
1960	17.4	23.6	21.1	23.8	19.5	20.1	25.5	23.5	25.4
1961	17.4	23.6	21.1	23.9	19.6	20.1	25.6	23.2	25.3
1962	17.4	23.6	21.1	24.0	19.6	20.1	25.7	22.8	25.2
1963	17.5	23.6	21.0	24.0	19.6	20.1	25.7	22.4	24.9
1964	17.6	23.5	20.9	24.1	19.5	20.1	25.6	22.1	24.7
1965	17.7	23.5	20.9	24.1	19.5	20.1	25.6	21.8	24.5
1966	17.8	23.4	21.0	24.2	19.6	20.2	25.6	21.6	24.4
1967	18.0	23.4	21.2	24.2	19.8	20.3	25.6	21.5	24.3
1968	18.1	23.4	21.4	24.2	19.9	20.4	25.5	21.5	24.2
1969	18.3	23.3	21.5	24.2	20.1	20.5	25.4	21.5	24.0
1970	18.4	23.2	21.6	24.1	20.2	20.6	25.3	21.4	23.9
1971	18.6	23.1	21.7	24.0	20.3	20.7	25.1	21.4	23.8
1972	18.7	22.9	21.7	23.8	20.4	20.7	24.9	21.4	23.7
1973	18.8	22.7	21.6	23.6	20.5	20.8	24.7	21.3	23.5
1974	18.8	22.5	21.6	23.3	20.5	20.8	24.4	21.3	23.4
1975	18.9	22.2	21.5	23.1	20.5	20.9	24.1	21.3	23.3
1976	18.9	22.0	21.5	22.8	20.5	21.0	23.8	21.4	23.1
1977	18.9	21.8	21.4	22.5	20.4	21.1	23.4	21.5	22.9
1978	18.9	21.6	21.3	22.1	20.4	21.3	23.1	21.6	22.7
1979	18.9	21.4	21.3	21.8	20.4	21.4	22.8	21.7	22.6
1980	18.9	21.3	21.3	21.5	20.5	21.5	22.6	21.8	22.4
1981	18.9	21.2	21.3	21.1	20.7	21.6	22.3	22.0	22.3
1982	18.9	21.2	21.4	20.8	21.0	21.7	22.1	22.2	22.2
1983	18.9	21.2	21.4	20.5	21.3	21.8	22.0	22.3	22.1
1984	19.0	21.2	21.5	20.3	21.5	21.9	21.9	22.5	22.0
1985	19.0	21.3	21.6	20.0	21.8	21.9	21.8	22.5	22.0
1986	19.0	21.4	21.6	19.8	22.0	22.0	21.8	22.6	21.9
1987	19.0	21.6	21.6	19.6	22.2	22.0	21.8	22.6	21.8
1988	19.0	21.8	21.6	19.5	22.3	21.9	21.9	22.5	21.8
1989	19.1	22.1	21.7	19.5	22.4	21.9	22.0	22.6	21.8
1990	19.2	22.4	22.0	19.6	22.5	21.9	22.2	22.7	21.8
1991	19.4	22.7	22.3	19.8	22.6	21.9	22.4	23.0	21.9
1992	19.8	23.2	22.8	20.1	22.7	21.9	22.7	23.4	22.0
1993	20.1	23.6	23.4	20.5	22.7	22.0	23.1	23.8	22.2
1994	20.5	24.0	24.0	20.9	22.7	22.0	23.4	24.3	22.4
1995	21.0	24.4	24.5	21.3	22.8	22.0	23.8	24.7	22.6
1996	21.4	24.8	25.0	21.7	22.8	22.1	24.1	25.0	22.8
1997	21.9	25.1	25.5	22.1	22.9	22.1	24.5	25.3	22.9
1998	22.3	25.4	25.9	22.5	23.0	22.1	24.8	25.6	23.1
1999	22.9	25.7	26.4	23.0	23.1	22.2	25.2	25.9	23.3
2000	23.4	26.0	26.8	23.4	23.2	22.4	25.5	26.3	23.6
2001	24.0	26.3	27.2	23.9	23.4	22.6	25.8	26.7	23.8
2002	24.6	26.5	27.5	24.3	23.5	23.0	26.2	27.2	24.1
2003	25.3	26.8	27.9	24.8	23.7	23.4	26.5	27.6	24.4
2004	25.9	27.1	28.2	25.3	23.9	23.8	26.8	28.1	24.7
2005	26.5	27.3	28.5	25.7	24.2	24.3	27.0	28.6	25.1
2006	27.1	27.5	28.9	26.1	24.4	24.8	27.2	29.0	25.6
2007	27.7	27.7	29.2	26.4	24.7	25.2	27.4	29.5	26.0
2008	28.2	27.8	29.5	26.7	25.1	25.7	27.5	29.9	26.5
2009	28.7	28.0	29.7	27.0	25.4	26.2	27.6	30.3	27.0
2010	29.0	28.1	29.7	27.2	25.7	26.7	27.6	30.6	27.4
2011	29.1	28.2	29.6	27.3	26.0	27.2	27.7	30.9	27.7
2012	29.2	28.2	29.4	27.5	26.2	27.7	27.7	31.1	27.9
2013	29.2	28.2	29.1	27.6	26.5	28.2	27.7	31.2	28.0
2014	29.1	28.3	28.7	27.7	26.7	28.7	27.7	31.3	28.2
2015	28.9	28.3	28.3	27.8	27.1	29.2	27.7	31.3	28.3
2016	28.8	28.4	27.9	27.8	27.5	29.7	27.7	31.3	28.4
2017	28.7	28.5	27.5	27.9	27.9	30.3	27.8	31.2	28.5
2018	28.5	28.6	27.2	28.0	28.3	30.8	27.9	31.0	28.6
2019	28.3	28.7	26.8	28.0	28.7	31.4	27.9	30.8	28.6
2020	28.0	28.7	26.5	27.9	29.1	31.9	27.9	30.5	28.6

Source: United Nations (2001).

Data for Figure 2.3. **Younger generations are more educated**

Percentage of adults with at least upper secondary education[1] by age group, 1999

	Ages 25-34	Ages 55-64
Canada	87	62
Denmark	87	70
Finland	86	46
Norway[2]	94	68
Portugal	30	11
Spain	55	13
Sweden	87	61
Switzerland	89	72
United Kingdom[3]	66	53

1. Excluding 3C short programmes.
2. Year of reference 1998.
3. Not all ISCED 3 programmes meet minimum requirements for ISCED 3C long programmes.
Source: OECD (2001), *Education at a Glance – OECD Indicators*, Paris.

Data for Figure 3.1. **Participation in adult learning by gender**

Percentage of population 25-64 years old in adult learning by gender according to different reference periods

	Participation in past year (IALS)			Participation in past 4 weeks (ELFS)		
	Women	Men	Total	Women	Men	Total
Canada	36.0	37.0	36.5	. .	. .	. .
Denmark	58.8	53.7	56.2	23.8	17.9	20.8
Finland	62.0	54.4	58.2	21.6	17.7	19.6
Norway	47.7	49.1	48.4	13.8	12.8	13.3
Portugal	12.0	14.0	13.0	3.4	3.2	3.3
Spain	. .	. .	. .	5.4	4.4	4.9
Sweden	56.0	52.6	54.3	24.1	19.2	21.6
Switzerland	39.6	43.6	41.5	29.4	40.0	34.7
United Kingdom	44.2	45.7	44.9	24.4	17.9	21.0

Note: Period of reference is one year for Switzerland in both surveys.
Source: International Adult Literacy Survey (1994-98); Eurostat, European Union Labour Force Survey (2001).

Data for Figure 3.2. **Participation and average days of training**

Percentage of people in training and average days of training, 2000

	Participation rate	Average days of training
Denmark	12.9	13.3
Finland	46.0	9.1
Portugal	56.5	20.4
Spain	19.6	29.9
Sweden	54.2	13.7
United Kingdom	53.0	10.9
6-country average	42.9	14.9

Source: European Foundation for the Improvement of Living and Working Conditions, Third European Survey on Working Conditions, 2000.

Data for Figure 3.3. **Participation in adult learning by age groups**

Percentage of population 25-64 years old in adult learning by age according to different reference periods

	Participation in past year (IALS)					Participation in past 4 weeks (ELFS)				
	25-29	30-39	40-49	50-59	60-64	25-29	30-39	40-49	50-59	60-64
Canada	48.7	40.5	37.0	31.3	10.4	37.2	34.0	30.8	23.7	10.8
Denmark	66.9	60.3	65.3	47.6	24.0	36.3	22.9	21.8	14.6	6.9
Finland	71.1	69.0	62.2	48.7	20.2	30.7	23.1	21.2	15.7	4.5
Norway	55.5	53.8	53.0	39.8	19.9	15.4	15.9	13.9	11.2	3.9
Portugal	28.4	17.3	10.0	7.6	5.0	11.9	3.5	1.7	0.5	0.0
Spain	..	..	..	..	..	18.1	5.0	2.6	1.0	0.7
Sweden	56.1	57.5	60.1	53.8	26.6	32.2	23.8	20.9	17.0	10.8
Switzerland	55.7	45.0	44.3	33.0	22.0	44.0	37.4	38.0	32.1	10.7
United Kingdom	55.8	51.5	51.9	32.5	17.9	27.1	24.0	22.8	16.6	10.5

1. Period of reference is one year for Canada and Switzerland in both surveys.
Source: International Adult Literacy Survey (1994-98); Eurostat, European Union Labour Force Survey (2001) except for Canada (1997 AETS data).

Data for Figure 3.4. **Adult learning by educational attainment**

Ratio of participation rates at each educational level to the total participation rates for population 25-64 years old, 2000

	Educational attainment		
	Low	Medium	High
Canada	0.4	0.8	1.3
Denmark	0.5	0.9	1.5
Finland	0.4	1.0	1.5
Norway	0.3	0.8	1.6
Portugal	0.3	4.0	2.9
Spain	0.2	1.8	2.6
Sweden	0.7	0.9	1.4
Switzerland	0.3	1.0	1.5
United Kingdom	0.3	0.9	1.6

Note: Period of reference is four weeks except for Canada and Switzerland, where it is one year.
Source: Eurostat, European Union Labour Force Survey (2001) data except for Canada (1997 AETS data).

Data for Figure 3.5. **Participation in adult learning by literacy levels**

Percentage of population 25-64 years old in adult learning by document literacy levels, 1994-98

	Literacy levels				
	Total participation rate	Level 1	Level 2	Level 3	Level 4/5
Canada	35.9	15.1	28.0	37.5	58.9
Denmark	54.6	25.4	43.0	59.2	69.5
Finland	56.9	20.9	44.3	67.6	77.7
Norway	47.7	16.1	36.9	50.6	62.0
Portugal	12.4	4.4	17.6	30.9	51.0
Sweden	54.4	29.4	41.4	57.8	62.4
Switzerland	41.1	19.0	35.4	47.3	63.3
United Kingdom	44.7	21.8	34.3	56.2	70.9

Source: International Adult Literacy Survey (1994-98).

Data for Figure 3.6. **Adult learning by residence situation**

Ratio of participation rates by residence situation to the total participation rates for population 25-64 years old, 2000

	National	Foreigner
Canada[1]	1.03	0.89
Finland	1.00	0.88
Spain[2]	1.00	0.71
Switzerland	1.10	0.62
United Kingdom[2]	0.86	0.96

1. 1997.
2. "Citizen" and "not citizen" instead of "national" and "foreigner".
Source: OECD Secretariat questionnaire on Adult Learning. See Annex 1 for details.

Data for Figure 3.7. **Reasons for adult learning**

Percentage distribution of adult learners 25-64 years old by reason, 1994-98

	Career- or job-related purposes	Personal interest	Other
Canada	79.1	19.2	1.7
Denmark	83.7	12.4	3.9
Finland	61.6	30.1	8.3
Norway	90.8	5.8	3.4
Sweden	39.6	48.0	12.5
Switzerland	60.1	37.7	2.3
United Kingdom	85.3	13.5	1.2

Source: International Adult Literacy Survey (1994-98).

Data for Figure 3.8. **Adult learning by labour force status**

Ratio of participation rates by labour force status to the total participation rates for population 25-64 years old, 2000

	Participation in past year (IALS)			Participation in past 4 weeks (ELFS)		
	Employed	Unemployed	Not in labour force	Employed	Unemployed	Not in labour force
Canada	1.15	0.82	0.63	. .	. .	. .
Denmark	1.08	0.91	0.69	0.99	1.23	1.01
Finland	1.20	0.51	0.55	1.15	0.83	0.53
Norway	1.12	0.69	0.45	1.10	1.07	0.50
Portugal	1.28	0.76	0.36	0.86	1.82	1.39
Spain	. .	. .	. .	0.80	2.10	1.10
Sweden	1.11	0.84	0.53	0.85	1.19	2.09
Switzerland	1.10	0.78	0.66	1.75	0.31	0.20
United Kingdom	1.25	0.74	0.32	1.09	0.94	0.66

Note: Period of reference is one year for Switzerland in both surveys.
Source: International Adult Literacy Survey (1994-98); Eurostat, European Union Labour Force Survey (2001).

Data for Figure 3.9.   **Adult learning by occupation**

Ratio of participation rates by occupation to the total participation rates for population 25-64 years old, 2000

	White-collar high-skill	White-collar low-skill	Blue-collar high-skill	Blue-collar low-skill	Total training rate
Denmark	1.33	1.02	0.49	0.41	20.80
Finland	1.55	1.07	0.63	0.53	19.60
Norway	1.49	0.89	0.75	0.48	13.30
Portugal	1.99	1.15	0.19	0.31	3.30
Spain	1.37	1.00	0.22	0.37	4.90
Sweden	1.12	0.81	0.52	0.45	21.60
Switzerland	1.63	1.06	0.74	0.46	23.80
United Kingdom	1.44	1.06	0.59	0.50	21.00

Note: Period of reference is four weeks except for Switzerland, where it is one year.
Source: Eurostat, European Union Labour Force Survey (2001).

Data for Figure 3.10.   **Training enterprises and type of training**

Percentage of enterprises that train by type of training, 2000

	Training enterprises		
	as a percentage of all enterprises	that provide CVT courses	that provide other forms of CVT
Denmark	96	88	87
Finland	82	75	72
Norway	86	81	75
Portugal	22	11	20
Spain	36	28	27
Sweden	91	83	78
United Kingdom	87	76	83

Source: Eurostat, New Chronos Database, CVTS.

Data for Figure 3.11.   **Adult learning by firm size**

Ratio of participation rates by firm size to the total participation rates for population 25-64 years old, 2000

	Canada	Denmark	Finland	Norway[1]	Switzerland[2]	United Kingdom[3]
Less than 20	0.65	0.48	0.77	0.59	0.96	0.80
20 to 99	0.88	1.30	0.99	0.78	1.08	1.10
100 to 199	1.02	1.43	1.00	0.76	1.23	
200 to 499	1.19	1.28	1.14	0.85		
500 or more	1.30	3.43	1.17			

1.   200 or more employees instead of 200 to 499.
2.   100 or more employees instead of 100 to 199.
3.   Less than 25 instead of less than 20; more than 25 instead of 20 to 99.
Source: OECD Secretariat questionnaire on Adult Learning. See Annex 1 for details.

Data for Figure 4.1. **Sources of adult learning financing by labour force status**

Percentage distribution of financing by labour force status for population 25-64 years old, 1994-98

		Training or education financially supported by:			
		Individual	An employer	The government	Others
Canada	Employed	38.5	51.3	4.2	6.1
	Unemployed	37.4	11.6	49.1	1.9
	Not in labour force	55.5	6.1	5.9	32.5
Denmark	Employed	17.5	67.4	4.6	10.4
	Unemployed	49.6	12.9	37.5	0.0
	Not in labour force	52.2	8.0	32.1	7.8
Finland	Employed	15.5	72.6	3.9	8.1
	Unemployed	42.7	36.5	20.8	0.0
	Not in labour force	41.1	18.2	25.7	15.1
Norway	Employed	22.3	71.2	1.8	4.7
	Unemployed	12.7	79.0	8.3	0.0
	Not in labour force	31.4	13.6	49.6	5.4
Switzerland	Employed	46.7	39.5	7.6	6.2
	Unemployed	31.6	47.4	21.0	0.0
	Not in labour force	89.0	0.0	9.3	1.7
United Kingdom	Employed	10.5	79.0	3.4	7.1
	Unemployed	22.7	28.2	49.1	0.0
	Not in labour force	16.5	53.7	20.4	9.3

Source: International Adult Literacy Survey (1994-98).

Data for Figure 5.1. **Self-assessment of reading skills by prose literacy level**

Percentage of population 25-64 years old at each self-assessment level by prose literacy level, 1994-98

	Respondents' self-assessment levels					
	Excellent	Good	Moderate	Poor	No response	Total
Prose literacy levels						
Level 1	13.4	32.2	34.6	9.5	10.2	17.2
Level 2	32.5	48.1	16.7	0.9	1.7	28.6
Level 3	52.2	39.8	6.7	0.2	1.2	35.7
Level 4/5	70.2	27.1	2.2	0.0	0.5	18.5

Note: For example, 13.4% of the respondents ranked at Level 1 on the prose scale consider their reading skills to be excellent.
Source: International Adult Literacy Survey (1994-98).

Data for Figures 5.2 and 5.4. **Prose literacy level by self-assessment of reading skills in selected countries**
Percentage of population 25-64 years old at each prose literacy level, 1994-98

	Respondents' self-assessment levels	Prose literacy levels			
		Level 1	Level 2	Level 3	Level 4/5
Canada	Excellent or good	6.9	24.6	38.0	30.6
	Moderate or poor	46.6	29.8	21.8	1.8
Denmark	Excellent or good	6.7	34.9	51.5	6.9
	Moderate or poor	32.7	45.0	22.4	0.0
Finland	Excellent or good	4.1	23.1	45.5	27.3
	Moderate or poor	17.0	42.7	36.1	4.2
Norway	Excellent or good	3.9	22.6	54.5	19.0
	Moderate or poor	24.5	38.1	33.0	4.4
Portugal	Excellent or good	26.9	34.8	31.1	7.2
	Moderate or poor	70.8	22.0	7.2	0.1
Switzerland	Excellent or good	11.0	37.1	42.1	9.8
	Moderate or poor	66.1	22.4	10.5	1.1
United Kingdom	Excellent or good	10.6	28.4	38.6	22.4
	Moderate or poor	42.6	37.8	15.5	4.1
All countries	Excellent	5.4	21.5	43.0	30.1
	Good	14.4	35.7	36.9	13.0
	Moderate	44.1	35.2	17.7	3.0
	Poor	83.6	13.0	3.4	0.0

Note: For example, in Canada, 6.9% of those who consider their reading skills to be excellent or good are at prose Level 1.
Source: International Adult Literacy Survey (1994-98).

Data for Figure 5.3. **Prose literacy level by response to whether reading skills limit opportunities at work**
Percentage distribution of literacy levels within each response for population 25-64 years old, 1994-98

	Prose literacy levels				
	Level 1	Level 2	Level 3	Level 4/5	Total
Greatly limiting opportunities at work	57.1	17.6	22.2	3.1	2.2
Moderately limiting opportunities at work	41.6	38.2	17.9	2.4	8.9
Not at all limiting opportunities at work	13.4	27.9	38.0	20.7	88.2

Note: For example, 57.1% of respondents who consider that their reading abilities greatly limit their opportunities at work are at prose Level 1.
Source: International Adult Literacy Survey (1994-98).

Data for Figure 5.5. **Learners and non-learners by educational attainment**
Percentage of population 25-64 years old by educational attainment who is learning or not, 1994-98

Educational attainment	Learners	Non-learners	Total
Primary	10.8	89.1	13.1
Lower secondary	33.1	66.8	34.3
Upper secondary	46.4	53.6	27.3
Non-university tertiary	59.9	40.1	10.8
University tertiary	68.4	31.6	13.4

Note: For example, among all individuals at primary educational level, 10.8% had had some learning activity during the 12 months preceding the survey.
Source: International Adult Literacy Survey (1994-98).

Data for Figure 5.7. **Unsatisfied demand for learning**

Percentage of population 25-64 years old who could not participate in at least one learning session, by type of training, whether it finally took place or not, 1994-98

| Learning finally took place | Unsatisfied demand for training | | | | |
| | For vocational reasons | | For personal reasons | | Total |
	At least one failed attempt to train	Never had a failed attempt to train	At least one failed attempt to train	Never had a failed attempt to train	
Yes	32.1	67.7	29.2	70.6	43.2
No	18.9	81.0	19.7	80.2	56.6
Total	24.6	75.1	23.8	75.8	About 100*

Note: For example, of all those who received vocational training, 32.1% had at least one failed attempt to train another time (see Figure 5.9 for the reasons).

* A few people refused to answer one or the other of the two questions.

Source: International Adult Literacy Survey (1994-98).

Data for Figure 5.8. **Unsatisfied demand for training by educational attainment**

Percentage of population 25-64 years old who could not participate in at least one learning session, by type of training and educational attainment, whether training finally took place or not, 1994-98

| Educational attainment | Unsatisfied demand for training | | | | |
| | For vocational reasons | | For personal reasons | | Total |
	At least one failed attempt to train	Never had a failed attempt to train	At least one failed attempt to train	Never had a failed attempt to train	
Primary	9.1	90.8	12.1	87.7	7.5
Lower secondary	17.3	82.6	17.4	82.5	38.0
Upper secondary	29.1	70.7	27.6	72.2	28.1
Non-university tertiary	36.9	63.1	29.8	70.2	11.2
University tertiary	33.6	66.3	34.8	65.0	14.1
Total	24.6	75.1	23.8	75.8	About 100*

Note: For example, among all individuals at primary educational level, 9.1% had had at least one of their attempts at vocational learning frustrated (see Figure 5.9 for the reasons).

* A few people refused to answer one or the other of the two questions.

Source: International Adult Literacy Survey (1994-98).

235

Data for Figure 5.9. **Reasons for not participating in adult learning activities**

Percentage of population 25-64 years old, by reasons for not participating and type of training, 1994-98

	Vocational training[1]	Other learning
Unsatisfied demand for training	24.6	23.8
Reasons explaining non-participation		
Time management		
Lack of time	36.1	55.1
Too much work	17.4	16.4
Family matters	15.4	17.1
Nature of training		
Courses not available	12.8	5.5
Cost of training	23.3	16.7
Course timetable	12.2	10.2
Language of course	0.5	0.3
Personal situation		
Lack of employer support	10.2	0.6
Health issues	3.7	5.2
Lack of qualifications	1.9	0.3
Other	13.3	9.2

Note: The totals do not come to 100% because several replies were possible.

1. Data on vocational training are not available for Portugal and Sweden.

Source: International Adult Literacy Survey (1994-98).

Data for Figure 5.10. **Return to training by initial educational attainment**

Proportional mean wage differences[1] for workers trained by initial educational attainment, 1990s

	Less than upper secondary	Upper secondary	Non-university tertiary	Tertiary
Australia	6.9	8.6	4.2	1.8
France	30.2	16.1	2.3	−1.3
Germany	16.0	9.5	−7.6	17.9
Italy	15.7	23.8	. .	6.8
Netherlands	17.6	0.7	0.0	−15.9
United Kingdom	20.2	4.3	19.8	3.0

1. Mean earnings of workers trained minus mean earnings of workers not trained, divided by mean earnings of workers not trained.

Source: OECD (1999).

Data for Figure 5.11. **New participants in public training programmes**

Percentage of the labour force, 1998-2001

	Total	Unemployed	Employed
Canada (1997-98)	1.6	1.6	. .
Denmark (2000)	15.9	5.8	10.2
Finland (2001)	2.8	2.6	0.2
Norway (2001)	0.9	0.9	. .
Portugal (1998)	9.9	0.6	9.3
Spain (2001)	14.6	1.5	13.0
Sweden (2001)	2.3	2.3	. .
Switzerland (2001)	1.3	1.3	. .
United Kingdom (1999-2000)	0.5	0.5	0.1
Unweighted average (9 countries)	5.5	1.9	6.5

Source: OECD database on labour market programmes.

Data for Figure 6.2. **Households with access to a home computer and the Internet**

Percentage of households, 1999 and 2000

	Acces to a home computer		Acces to the Internet	
	1999	2000	1999	2000
Canada	50	55	29	40
Denmark	60	65	33	46
Finland	43	47	25	30
Spain	27	30	..	..
Sweden	57	60	42	48
Switzerland	..	61	..	37
United Kingdom[1]	39	46	20	33

1. Last quarter of 2000.
Source: OECD (2001c, 2002b) and ICT database.

Annex 3

NATIONAL CO-ORDINATORS AND REVIEW TEAM MEMBERS

Canada

National Co-ordinators

Mr. Robert Patry
Council of Ministers of Education, Canada
Ontario, Canada

Ms. Wendy Salmon
Skills and Learning Policy Directorate
Human Resources Development Canada (HRDC)
Ottawa, Canada

OECD Review Team for the visit 8-19 January, 2001

Mr. Norton Grubb (*Rapporteur*)
Professor
School of Education
University of California
Berkeley, California, the United States

Mr. Idès Nicaise
Professor
Hoger Instituut voor de Arbeid (HIVA)
Katholieke Universiteit Leuven (KUL)
Leuven, Belgium

Ms. Beatriz Pont
Administrator
Education and Training Division
Directorate for Education, Employment, Labour and Social Affairs
OECD
Paris, France

Mr. Albert Tuijnman
Director
Institute of International Education
Stockholm University
Stockholm, Sweden

Mr. Patrick Werquin
Principal Administrator
Education and Training Division
Directorate for Education, Employment, Labour and Social Affairs
OECD
Paris, France

Denmark

National Co-ordinator

Ms. Annelise Hauch
Head of Section
Department of Adult Education
Ministry of Education
Copenhagen, Denmark

OECD Review Team for the visit 7-14 November, 2000

Ms. Danielle Colardyn (*Rapporteur*)
Professor
College of Europe
Bruges, Belgium
Education Consultant
Paris, France

Mr. Helmut Höpflinger
Senior Administrator (Ministerialrat)
Federal Ministry of Economic Affairs and Labour (Bundesministerium für Wirtschaft und Arbeit)
Vienna, Austria (Wien, Österreich)

Mr. Gregor Ramsey
Director
Tertiary Education Consulting Services
Education Consultants
Mosman, NSW, Australia

Ms. Anne Sonnet
Administrator
Employment Analysis and Policy Division
Directorate for Education, Employment, Labour and Social Affairs
OECD
Paris, France

Mr. Patrick Werquin
Principal Administrator
Education and Training Division
Directorate for Education, Employment, Labour and Social Affairs
OECD
Paris, France

Finland

National Co-ordinators

Mr. Jorma Ahola
Mr. Ville Heinonen
Division of Adult Education and Training
Department for Education and Science Policy, Ministry of Education
Helsinki, Finland

OECD Review Team for the visit 1-9 February, 2001

Ms. Martina Ni Cheallaigh (Rapporteur)
Project Manager – Lifelong learning
European Centre for the Development of Vocational Training (CEDEFOP)
Thessaloniki, Greece

Mr. Richard P. Phelps
Senior Study Director
WESTAT
Rockville, Maryland, United States

Ms. Anne Sonnet
Administrator
Employment Analysis and Policy Division
Directorate for Education, Employment, Labour and Social Affairs
OECD
Paris, France

Mr. Vincent Vandenberghe
Professor
GIRSEF – Université Catholique de Louvain (UCL)
Louvain-La-Neuve, Belgium

Mr. Patrick Werquin
Principal Administrator
Education and Training Division
Directorate for Education, Employment, Labour and Social Affairs
OECD
Paris, France

Norway

National Co-ordinator

Ms. Marit Viggen
Advisor
Department of Adult Education
Ministry of Education, Research and Church Affairs (KUF)
Oslo, Norway

OECD Review Team for the visit 15-24 March, 2000

Ms. Mia Douterlungne
Professor
Hoger Instituut voor de Arbeid (HIVA)
Katholieke Universiteit Leuven (KUL)
Leuven, Belgium

Mr. Jean-Louis Kirsch
Senior Researcher
Centre d'études et de recherches sur les qualifications (Céreq)
Katholiefe Universiteit Leuven (KUL)
Marseilles, France

Ms. Anne Sonnet
Administrator
Employment Analysis and Policy Division
Directorate for Education, Employment, Labour and Social Affairs
OECD
Paris, France

Mr. Patrick Werquin
Principal Administrator
Education and Training Division
Directorate for Education, Employment, Labour and Social Affairs
OECD
Paris, France

Ms. Joan Wills (Rapporteur)
Director
Center for Workforce Development
Education for Educational Leadership
Washington DC, United States

Portugal

National Co-ordinators

Ms. *Lisete Matos*
Ms. *Maria Teresa Braz Gonçalves*
National Agency for Adult Education and Training (ANEFA)
Lisbon, Portugal

OECD Review Team for the visit 12-19 March, 2001

Mr. *Robert Boyer* (*Rapporteur*)
Professor
Centre national de la recherche scientifique (CNRS)
Centre d'études prospectives d'économie mathématique appliquées à la planification (CEPREMAP)
École des hautes études en science sociale (EHESS)
Paris, France

Mr. *Ross Finnie*
Research Fellow and Adjunct Professor
School of Policy Studies
Queen's University
Kingston, Ontario, Canada

Ms. *Anne Sonnet*
Administrator
Employment Analysis and Policy Division
Directorate for Education, Employment, Labour and Social Affairs
OECD
Paris, France

Mr. *Johnny Stroumza*
Professor
Faculté de psychologie et des sciences de l'éducation (FDEP)
University of Geneva
Geneva, Switzerland

Mr. *Patrick Werquin*
Principal Administrator
Education and Training Division
Directorate for Education, Employment, Labour and Social Affairs
OECD
Paris, France

Spain

National Co-ordinators

Mr. Manuel Corredoira López
Deputy Director General of Vocational Training
Ministry of Education, Culture and Sport
Madrid, Spain

Ms. M. Amparo Azorín-Albiñana López
Adult Education Service Manager
Vocational Training Division
Ministry of Education, Culture and Sport
Madrid, Spain

Ms. Rita Osorio Guijarro
Documentation and International Projects Service Manager
Occupational Training Management Division
National Employment Institute

OECD Review Team for the visit 13-23 November, 2001

Mr. Paolo Federighi
Professor of Adult Education
University of Florence
Florence, Italy

Mr. Juan Enrique Froemel-Andrade (Rapporteur)
UNESCO-OREALC (UNESCO Regional Office for Education in Latin America and Carribbean)
Partner
Evaluarte, Froemel and Asociados
Santiago del Chile, Chile

Mr. Antonio Morfín Maciel
Professor
University of Anahuac
Mexico City, Mexico

Ms. Beatriz Pont
Administrator
Education and Training Division
Directorate for Education, Employment, Labour and Social Affairs
OECD
Paris, France

Sweden

National Co-ordinator

Ms. Viveka Wetterberg
Division of Adult Education
Ministry of Education and Science
Stockholm, Sweden

OECD Review Team for the visit 3-12 May, 2000

Mr. Jens Bjørnåvold (Rapporteur)
Expert
Division of Education and Culture
European Commission
Brussels, Belgium
(Previously at: CEDEFOP, Thessaloniki, Greece)

Ms. Marie Lavoie
Professor
Department of Economics
York University
Toronto, Canada
(Previously at: Human Resources Development Canada,
Ontario, Canada)

Mr. Gerald Makepeace
Professor
Cardiff Business School, Cardiff University
Cardiff, United Kingdom

Ms. Beatriz Pont
Administrator
Education and Training Division
Directorate for Education, Employment, Labour and Social Affairs
OECD
Paris, France

Mr. Patrick Werquin
Principal Administrator
Education and Training Division
Directorate for Education, Employment, Labour and Social Affairs
OECD
Paris, France

Switzerland

National Co-ordinator

Mr. André Schläfli
Director
Swiss Federation for Adult Education (FSEA/SVEB)
Zurich, Switzerland

OECD Review Team for the visit 13-17 December, 1999

Mr. Arne Carlsen
Expert
Danish National Institute of Educational Research
Copenhagen, Denmark

Mr. Pierre Doray (Rapporteur)
Professor
Centre interuniversitaire de recherche sur la science et la technologie (CIRST)
University of Québec (UGAM)
Montréal, Canada

Mr. Klaus Schömann
Senior Research Fellow
Social Science Research Centre (WZB)
Berlin, Germany

Ms. Anne Sonnet
Administrator
Employment Analysis and Policy Division
Directorate for Education, Employment, Labour and Social Affairs
OECD
Paris, France

Mr. Patrick Werquin
Principal Administrator
Education and Training Division
Directorate for Education, Employment, Labour and Social Affairs
OECD
Paris, France

United Kingdom

National Co-ordinators

Ms. *Katherine Costello*
Ms. *Wendy Humphreys*
Ms. *Jayne Lievesley*
Mr. *Andrew Milton*
Department for Education and Employment (DfEE)
Sheffield, United Kingdom

OECD Review Team for the visit 10-18 February, 2001

Mr. *Lex Borghans* (*Rapporteur*)
Principal Researcher
Research Centre for Education and the Labour Market (ROA)
University of Maastricht
Maastricht, Netherlands

Mr. *Norman Bowers*
Head of Division
Employment Analysis and Policy Division
Directorate for Education, Employment, Labour and Social Affairs
OECD
Paris, France

Ms. *Maria Jesús San Segundo*
Professor
University Carlos III de Madrid
Madrid, Spain

Mr. *André Schläfli*
Director
Swiss Federation for Adult Education (FSEA/ SVEB)
Zurich, Switzerland

Mr. *Patrick Werquin*
Principal Administrator
Education and Training Division
Directorate for Education, Employment, Labour and Social Affairs
OECD
Paris, France

Annex 4
COUNTRY CODES USED IN TABLES AND CHARTS

Thematic review countries	Code
Canada	CAN
Denmark	DNK
Finland	FIN
Norway	NOR
Portugal	PRT
Spain	ESP
Sweden	SWE
Switzerland	CHE
United Kingdom	UKM

Other countries	Code
Australia	AUS
Austria	AUT
Belgium	BEL
Czech Republic	CZE
France	FRA
Greece	GRC
Hungary	HUN
Ireland	IRL
Italy	ITA
Japan	JPN
Korea	KOR
Netherlands	NLD
New Zealand	NZL
Poland	POL
Turkey	TUR
United States	USA

Annex 5

ACRONYMS

AAD	Ministry of Labour and Government Administration, Norway
ACL	Adult and Community Learning, United Kingdom
AEC	Adult Education Centre, Finland
AEI	Adult Education Initiative, Sweden
AER	Arbejdsgivernes Elevrefusion – Employers' trainee reimbursement, Denmark
AETS	Adult Education and Training Survey, Canada
AF	Public Employment Service, Denmark
ALI	Adult Learning Inspectorate, United Kingdom
ALL	Adult Literacy and Lifeskills (Survey)
ALMP	Active Labour Market Policies
AMK	Ammattikorkeakoulu – Polytechnic institute, Finland
AMS	Labour Market Authority, Denmark
AMU	Continuing Vocational Training, Denmark
ANEFA	Agência Nacional de Educação e Formação de Adultos – National Agency for Adult Education and Training, Portugal (merged with the Department for Vocational Training in 2002)
AOF	Workers' Educational Association of Norway
APL	Accreditation of Prior Learning
AVU	General Adult Education, Denmark
AUF	Arbejdsmarkedets Uddannelsesfinansiering – Labour Market Institution for Financing of Education and Training, Denmark
BSA	Basic Skills Agency, United Kingdom
CAE	Conseil d'analyse économique – Council for Analysis in Economics, France
CAL	Computer-aided learning
CDIP	Conférence suisse des directeurs cantonaux de l'instruction publique – Swiss conference of cantonal directors of public education
CDL	Career Development Loans, United Kingdom
CEDEFOP	Centre européen pour le développement de la formation professionnelle – European Centre for the Development of Vocational Training
CERUK	Current Educational Research, United Kingdom
CHST	Canada Health and Social Transfer
CIRFA	Conférence intercantonale des responsables de la formation des adultes – Intercantonal conference of adult education officials, Switzerland
CITB	Construction Industry Training Board, United Kingdom
CMEC	Council of Ministers of Education, Canada
CPMT	Commission des partenaires du marché du travail – Committee of Labour Market Partners, Switzerland
CRCefa	Centro de Recursos em Conhecimento de Educação e Formação de Adultos – Resource knowledge centres in adult learning, Portugal
CRIF	Centre régional intégré de formation – Regional Integrated Training Centre, Canada
CRVCC	Centro de Reconhecimento, Validaçao e Certificaçao de Competências – Centre of recognition, validation and certification of competencies, Portugal
CVTS	Continuous Vocational Training Survey
DfEE	Department for Education and Employment, United Kingdom (previous name – now: DfES)
DfES	Department for Education and Skills, United Kingdom
DTI	Danish Technological Institute
DWP	Department for Work and Pensions, United Kingdom

EC	European Commission
ECITB	Engineering Construction Industry Training Board, United Kingdom
ECHP	European Commission Household Panel
ECTS	European Credit Transfer System
EduQua	Swiss Certificate for Quality Insurance for adult learning providers, Switzerland
EFA	Educação e Formação de Adultos – Adult Education and Training, Portugal
ELFS	European Labour Force Survey
ERDF	European Regional Development Fund
ESF	European Social Fund
ESPA	Enquête suisse sur la population active – Swiss labour force survey
EU	European Union
EUROSTAT	Statistical Office of the European Commission
EVA	Danish Evaluation Institute
FE	Further Education
FEFC	Further Education Funding Council, United Kingdom
FFPP	Fonds en faveur de la formation et du perfectionnement professionnels – Funds for Training and Vocational Improvement, Switzerland
FHS	Folk High School
FNFMO	Fonds national de formation de la main-d'œuvre – Labour Force Training National Fund, Switzerland
FORCEM	Fundación para la formación continua – Foundation for continuous training, Spain
FSEA	Fédération suisse de l'éducation des adultes – Swiss federation for adult education
FVU	Preparatory Adult Education, Denmark
GNVQ	General National Vocational Qualification, United Kingdom
GVU	Basic Adult Education, Denmark
IALS	International Adult Literacy Survey
IAG	Information, Advice and Guidance
ICL	Income Contingent Loans
ICT	Information and Communication Technology
IEFP	Instituto do Emprego e Formação Profissional – Institute for Employment and Vocational Training, Portugal
IFPA	Instituto de Formação Profissional Acelerada – Institute for Accelerated Vocational Training, Portugal
IiP	Investors in People, United Kingdom
ILA	Individual Learning Accounts
ILO	International Labour Organisation
INCUAL	Instituto Nacional de las Cualificaciones – National Qualifications Institute, Spain
INEM	Instituto Nacional para el Empleo – Public Employment Service, Spain
INOFOR	Instituto para a Inovação na Formação – Institute for Innovation in Training, Portugal
ISCED	International Standard Classification for Education
ISO	International Organisation for Standardisation
IT	Information Technology
K-12	Kindergarten through 12th grade
Komvux	Kommunal vuxenutbildning – Municipal Adult Education, Sweden
KUF	Ministry of Education, Research and Church Affairs, Norway (previous name – now: UFD)
KY	Advanced vocational training, Sweden
LFS	Labour Force Survey
LMEA	Licence mention éducation des adultes – Academic degree in adult education, Switzerland
LO	Norwegian Confederation of Trade Unions
LOGSE	Ley orgánica de ordenación general del sistema educativo – Basic law on the education system, Spain
LSC	Learning and Skills Council, United Kingdom
MRK	Mosjøen Skills Resource Centre, Norway
NACETT	National Advisory Council for Education and Training Targets, United Kingdom
NBE	National Board of Education, Finland
NCVQ	National Council for Vocational Qualifications, United Kingdom
NFU	Norwegian State Institution for Distance Education
NGO	Non Governmental Organisation

NHD	Ministry of Trade and Industry, Norway
NHO	Confederation of Norwegian Business and Industry
NIACE	National Institute of Adult Continuing Education, United Kingdom
NICT	New Information and Communication Technology
NITOL	Norway net with IT for Open Learning (previous name, now: NVU)
NKI	NKI Distance Education, Norway
NTO	National Training Organisation, United Kingdom
NVI	Norwegian Institute of Adult Education
NVQ/SVQ	National Vocational Qualification (United Kingdom)/Scottish Vocational Qualification
NVU	Network University, Norway
OEFP	Observatório do Emprego e Formação Profissional – Observatory for Employment and Vocational Training, Portugal
OFFT	Office fédéral de formation professionnelle et de technologie – Federal Office for Vocational Training and Technology, Switzerland
OFS	Office fédéral de la statistique – Federal Office for Statistics, Switzerland
OFSTED	Office for Standards in Education, United Kingdom
Opintoluotsi	Open search service in educational information, Finland
PES	Public Employment Service
PLAR	Prior Learning Assessment and Recognition
PPP	Purchase Power Parity
QCA	Qualifications and Curriculum Authority, United Kingdom
QUALFOR	Programa para a Certificação de Organismos de Formação – Programme for Certification of Training Institutions, Portugal
RAAPFA	Regroupement des associations d'andragogues et de professionnels de la formation des adultes – Association of andragogues and professionnals for adult learning, Canada
Saber+	Know more centres, Portugal
Sarvux	Adult education for those with disabilities, Sweden
SBS	Small Business Service, United Kingdom
seco	Secrétariat d'État à l'Économie – State Secretariat for Economic Affairs, Switzerland
Sfi	Swedish Tuition for immigrants
SFIA	Sea Fish Authority, United Kingdom
SIALS	Second International Adult Literacy Survey
SRFP	Société suisse pour la recherche appliquée en matière de formation professionnelle – Swiss society for applied research into vocational training
SRV	Norwegian Centre for Adult Education
SSC	Sector Skills Council, United Kingdom
SVU	State educational support for adult, Denmark
SWIT	Swedish Information Technology
T&E Centre	Employment and Business Development Centre, Finland
TIQ	Total Involvement in Quality
TRAL	Thematic Review on Adult Learning
UFD	Ministry of Education and Research, Norway
UfI	University for Industry, United Kingdom
ULF	Union Learning Fund, United Kingdom
UNED	Universidad Nacional a Distancia – National Distance University, Spain
UOC	Universidad Oberta de Cataluna – Catalunia Open University
VET	Vocational Education and Training
VEUD	Vocationally-Oriented Education and Training for Adults, Denmark
VEU-Reform	Adult Education and Training Reform, Denmark
VOX	Norwegian Institute for Adult Education (established 1 January 2001 following the merger of NVI, NFU and SRV)
VUC	General Adult Education Centres, Denmark
YLE	Finnish Broadcasting Company, Finland

OECD PUBLICATIONS, 2, rue André-Pascal, 75775 PARIS CEDEX 16
PRINTED IN FRANCE
(91 2003 04 1 P) ISBN 92-64-19943-8 – No. 52721 2003